The Festivals of Nepal

First Published in 1971, *The Festivals of Nepal* describes the most important festivals from the country, which have been arranged according to the ancient Nepalese calendar, beginning with the New Year in mid-April. The author provides, moreover, a brief introductory sketch of Nepalese geography, history, and religion, to give background to what follows.

When Mary Anderson began her five-year residence in Kathmandu as the wife of a diplomat, she attended the frequent Nepalese festivals up and down the Valley because they were mysterious, colourful and great fun. But soon she became more deeply absorbed in the meaning of these ancient activities as she grew quickly aware that to the Nepalese themselves the ancient processions and rituals were of great importance. Somewhere, almost every day, there seems to be in Nepal a festival of some kind, but now that this hitherto secret land has been opened up to tourists and foreign influences, much of this historic pageantry may well be lost. The modernization of Nepalese society is certain to have its effects, but when these artless celebrations become the goal of spectators from outside, they will also lose its spontaneity. Mary Anderson was determined to record as many of them as she could, explaining their mythological, religious and historical backgrounds and relating some of the wealth of legends and folk tales that surround them. This is an interesting read for students of sociology of culture, South Asian studies, South Asian religion and culture and Hindu religion.

The Festivals of Nepal

Mary M. Anderson

Routledge
Taylor & Francis Group

First published in 1971
by George Allen & Unwin Ltd.

This edition first published in 2024 by Routledge
4 Park Square, Milton Park, Abingdon, Oxon, OX14 4RN

and by Routledge
605 Third Avenue, New York, NY 10017

Routledge is an imprint of the Taylor & Francis Group, an informa business

© George Allen & Unwin Ltd, 1971

Publisher's Note
The publisher has gone to great lengths to ensure the quality of this reprint but points out that some imperfections in the original copies may be apparent.

Disclaimer
The publisher has made every effort to trace copyright holders and welcomes correspondence from those they have been unable to contact.

A Library of Congress record exists under ISBN: 0043940013

ISBN: 978-1-032-88880-4 (hbk)
ISBN: 978-1-003-54013-7 (ebk)
ISBN: 978-1-032-88881-1 (pbk)

Book DOI 10.4324/9781003540137

1. Kumari, the Living Goddess, rides in her chariot procession during Indra Jatra in Kathmandu   (Shridhar Manandhar)

THE FESTIVALS OF NEPAL

by Mary M. Anderson

First published in 1971

ISBN 0 04 394001 3

Printed in Great Britain
in 12 point Barbou type
by W & J Mackay Ltd,
Chatham

Dedicated to my grandson
Park Anderson Howell

Contents

Illustrations

ILLUSTRATIONS

Author's Note

For a work of this type, in which many of the legends
have been handed down orally from generation to
generation, I have not burdened the reader with foot-
notes and references within the text. A bibliography
may be found at the end, listing books to which I
referred for religious and historical background.

Foreword

At the beginning of my five-year residence in Nepal I attended Nepalese festivals because they are mysterious, colourful and fun. Soon I became absorbed in the meaning of the ancient processions and rituals, the mythological, religious and historical backgrounds of the ceremonies, and the wealth of delightful legends and folk-tales surrounding them.

I came to see that, for the Nepalese, the continuous flow of interrelated festivals throughout the year is literally a way of life, reflecting their joys and fears, dreams and sorrows. The festivals become a calendar, marking the changing seasons, the revolving of the years and ages, giving continuity and meaning to their lives. They cement the strong and vital bonds between individual members in each family, as well as the ties within established social groupings of caste and clan and class. And to a degree the festivals are instrumental in welding together the citizens of a recently democratized nation.

Fearing that much of this pageantry may eventually be lost with the gradual encroachment of modernization and increasing exposure to foreign ways, I determined to record the festivals in detail.

Unlike we Westerners, with our compulsive need for careful documentation and our unbending addiction to proven fact, the majority of Nepalese unquestioningly accept and enjoy their festivals as 'something they have always done'. They love the widely varying folk-tales and earthy scriptural stories. The fact that many are contradictory bothers them not at all. The average Nepali worries little which may be the One True Version, and I suspect is amused and intrigued by the foreigner's attempt to find it.

Most of the festival celebrations originated centuries ago and have carried down through the ages from some mythological or perhaps actual event, still re-enacted for reasons blurred by the passage of time. The ancient Hindu and Buddhist texts on which most of the festivals are based are interpreted in several different versions. Much of Nepal's scantily recorded ancient history has been destroyed with the years, and many of the remaining documents are incomprehensible, possibly more myth than fact. And there are charming inconsistencies in the folklore and legends, with embellishments and omissions of each narrator down through the generations.

Thus I learned, as do all who delve into Nepalese culture, that the possibility of error cannot be avoided, and have come to believe that anyone who devotes himself to recording only substantiated facts in this field will record very little indeed. One comes to understand the Chinese historian, Tai T'ung, who wrote in ancient times, 'Were I to await perfection, my books would never be written.'

In Nepal, as in all countries, festivals are celebrated in slightly different ways and with varying degrees of intensity, depending upon locality, economic and social status, education, religious and family background, and personal inclination. I am presenting the festivals as I saw them, with religious and legendary interpretations to which the majority of Nepalese seem to adhere.

For time-oriented Westerners an explanation should be given of the hour and dates of the festivals. Actually, as the Nepalese say, 'the time is not fixed' for the beginning hour of different ceremonies. I have seen crowds milling patiently for three or four hours, waiting for the astrologer-priests to announce the 'auspicious' moment when the planets and stars are lying just right in the heavens. Only then can festivities begin, and this may well be the middle of the night.

The annual dates for the festivals were fixed long ago on specific days of the ancient lunar calendar. Obviously these do not coincide with the solar calendar currently used in Nepal, nor with our Gregorian calendar. Calendars are printed each spring at the beginning of the Nepalese year which show all three dates – the lunar, the Nepalese and our Gregorian. The Nepalis skip nimbly from one to the next while Westerners flounder in confusion.

The old lunar month was divided into two fortnights: the light or bright fifteen days building up to full moon; and the dark fortnight or half-month of the waning moon. Nepalese know each year that a specific festival will occur, for instance, on 'the third day of the light fortnight' of a certain month. Even this may vary slightly, for in the old lunar calendar a day is often 'lost', omitted entirely, while another day must be duplicated, giving as an example *two* 'fifth days' of the 'dark half' of a certain month. This is further complicated by the necessity of adding an extra month to the lunar calendar every three or four years, making a total of thirteen months for that year.

Thus, unless one is a learned astrologer, possessed of mathematical genius, there is no way to foretell the exact date for next year's festivals. We know for certain that they will occur at the same time each year on the lunar calendar – for example, on the ninth day of the bright fortnight of late July or early August. For this reason I am recording the holidays in the chronology of their occurrence showing the fixed day of the light or dark lunar fortnight of the closest month on our calendar.

Within this work I am unable to cover all of the minor festivals of Kathmandu Valley, nor the festivals of distant, outlying regions of Nepal. Although many of the latter are duplications of those celebrated in and around Kathmandu Valley, there are others which are peculiar only to certain villages and regions. It is my earnest hope that some day some brave soul will record them all.

The following pages will present a brief sketch of Nepalese geography, history, religion and culture, with emphasis on the Kathmandu Valley, to paint a background for the festivals. But it is in the ensuing festival stories themselves wherein I hope will be found the real picture of Nepal and her people.

M.A.

Introduction

The Kingdom of Nepal

The Nepalese people say that somewhere every day in the little Asiatic Kingdom of Nepal there is a festival, and the gods have provided them with a perfect setting.

To the north, all along the border of Chinese-occupied Tibet, stretch the giant Himalayas, their snowpeaks and glaciers towering to heights of 26,000 to 29,000 feet, where Mt Everest is the highest point on earth. Their melting ice-fields have cut deep gorges and treacherous ravines down through bleak and rugged mountains, with rivers rushing southward through hills and lush valleys to the heavily wooded jungle belt. There the waters are slowed by torrid flatlands extending the length of the 500-mile southern border, before flowing over the plains of India and into the sacred Ganges.

Thus the water from the 'roof of the world' travels a long and circuitous route, dropping to an elevation of just a few hundred feet above sea-level at the Indian frontier, while actually covering a distance of only 100 to 150 miles as the crow flies north to south.

Nepal is one of a chain of small Shangri-La countries which stretches from west to east along the Himalayan range, starting with Kashmir, crossing a narrow strip of upper India, through Nepal, and on to Sikkim, Bhutan and Assam in the east.

In a general way Nepal might be divided into three areas – the northland of gigantic peaks and perpetual snow; the broad central belt of rugged mountain ravines, terraced hills and gentle valleys; with the jungles and flat grasslands along the south. These are not clearly cut demarcations, for one area pushes both deep and shallow inroads into the next, resulting in a flowing and blending of terrain and climate from north to south. Somewhat in the same way, the races and cultures of one region have blended with or become absorbed into the next, with those of the south heavily influenced by India, those of the north by Tibet, China and the plateaus of Central Asia, with a decided mingling of both in the middle regions.

Since the dawn of history the huge Himalayan snowpeaks have struck men's hearts and imaginations with awe and wonder. To the Nepalese each peak is a goddess who protects the people and surrounding lands, where mythical treasures lie buried beneath massive white depths. To mountaineers, who come from all over the globe, these stupendous heights present a challenge to the will, the strength and the intellect. This is the land of the fabled Abominable Snowman, who is a reality to the mountain people, and not easily dismissed by Westerners who have seen snow tracks of some strange creature which walks upright like a man. This is Sherpa country – those pleasant, sturdy little men who back-pack tremendous loads through precipitous snowbound passes – and the home of the hardy highlanders who migrate annually with their shaggy yak herds to lower climes, following the seasonal changes.

The Nepalese of these high elevations, with their slanted narrow eyes, yellow skin, black braided hair, dark red cheeks and often flat, merry faces, bear out the supposition that their ancestors descended from the Mongolian races of the Central Asian plateaus. Their culture and dialects reveal a close affinity to Tibetans, and theirs is the Buddhist religion of Tibetan Lamaism.

For centuries Nepalese porters have trod the ancient trade routes, carrying on their backs heavy loads of salt, wool and grain from Tibet through high Himalayan passes over the hill trails to India, returning with rice, spices and cloth. With the Chinese occupation of Tibet in the late 1950s, when the political and spiritual leader of Tibet, the Dalai Lama, fled to India, hundreds of Tibetan monks and lamas have settled into the monasteries of northern Nepal, and thousands of refugees are still ensconced in the middle hills.

Throughout the ages waves of immigrants and conquerors from India, often themselves fleeing from invaders, have come to the central hills and valleys of Nepal, where their blood, culture and religions were absorbed by the Nepalese, who retained all their own ancient ways and gods and festivals and continued to cultivate their valleys and hillsides in the manner of their forefathers.

Thus can be seen in the laughing, almond-shaped eyes of the Nepalese in the central hill regions the age-old, and still continuing, blending of the races and cultures – Mongolian and Tibetan from the north, Indo-Aryan from the south. Most of these people are cultivators of the soil, their clustered villages and terraced fields clinging to the hill slopes, perching on mountain-tops and dotting the narrow valleys.

From this middle region come the brave little Gurkha soldiers, long famous as mercenaries in the British and Indian armies. Their pensions have for many years been a mainstay of the economy of Nepal. These returning soldiers, intensely proud of their military training and discipline, are the leading citizens of their villages, highly honoured and respected for their knowledge of far-away lands.

All along the low hills of the southern belt of Nepal tigers, leopards, rhinos and wild elephants roam magnificent forests and jungles, a land remembered as the hunting grounds of fabulous Maharajas with their court followers and caparisoned elephants of a few decades ago. Here, and through the flatlands at the border, the Nepalese people are in general indistinguishable from their dark Indian neighbours in appearance, dress, mode of living and Hindu religion.

Thus while landlocked Nepal has long been remote and isolated from influences of the Western world, and within her own borders the rugged terrain often precludes communication between one secluded valley people and the next, the races and tribes from India and from north of the Himalayan barrier have been assimilated by the Nepalese people, and this assimilation makes them what they are today.

Who are the Gods and Goddesses?

To understand why the Nepalese so adore their deities and why they have continued to celebrate their numerous festivals down through the centuries, one must trace the religion which permeates every aspect of Nepalese life, culture and history. And to understand religion in Nepal one must look both inside and outside her borders.

Since remotest time the people of Nepal, as well as those of the surrounding lands, have clung to the animistic belief that all things have souls, that a multitude of good and bad spirits dwells everywhere – in stones, snakes, animals, trees, streams and mountains. A great deal of skill in the arts of magic and spells is required to avoid and cure disease, to make one's body fertile, to protect against calamity, prolong life, destroy and harass enemies, and to avoid being possessed by evil spirits. Coupled with this animism, though perhaps not so ancient, is the practice of mother-worship and father-worship. Honour is paid to ancestors, and prayers are offered up for the welfare and propitiation of the souls of the recently dead.

These beliefs are still very much a part of religion in Nepal, absorbed and blended with the gods, rituals, ceremonies and festivals introduced by invaders, immigrants and pilgrims from neighbouring cultures, especially from the south. For there is no natural barrier between Nepal and India, and whatever happens in India has always been reflected in Nepal.

About 1,600 years before the birth of Christ, Aryan tribes from the north-west, probably from around the Caspian Sea, came into northern India as invaders and permanent settlers. These same tribes overran Europe and Persia. To the indigenous, subjugated people of India the Aryan conquerors brought their nature gods of sky, earth, wind, water, sex, sun and fire. All these Vedic gods the people embraced in time, placed them side by side with their old native spirits and demons, worshipping and propitiating all together in rites and rituals still seen today in Nepalese ceremonies and festivals.

The Aryans, outnumbered by their subjects, whom they con-

sidered inferior, attempted to protect their racial identity by for-
bidding marriage outside their group, or inside, within a near
degree of kinship. Thereby came the distant beginning of the
Hindu caste system of religious and social barriers.

Gradually, as religion grew in importance and ritual complexity,
expert intermediaries between men and the ever-increasing pantheon of gods and goddesses were required, which resulted in a
hierarchy of Brahman priests organized to form the highest caste.
For a time there was a struggle for ascendancy between the
Brahmans and the noble warrior caste, but the latter finished in
second place, leaving the Brahmans to increase in number and
power until they held complete sway over the lives and religion
of the multitudes.

Hinduism or Brahmanism lived on through waves of terrible
persecution from overpowering conquerors, through the intro-
duction of opposing faiths, heretics and dissenters, due largely to
the patience, tenacity and foresightedness of the Brahman priest-
hood. Always tolerant of new thought and ready to make adjust-
ments to suit the masses and the passing ages, but jealously
reluctant to accept new custom, new forms of expression or
changes in ritual, the Brahmans guided the Hindu religion down
through the eras, still practising the same rites and ceremonies and
festivals of the early believers.

An ancient Hindu text boasts that Hinduism has 300 million
deities, an incredible figure only partially explained by the fact
that each god is known in countless forms and under many names,
each with different attributes and abilities. One god may appear in
male, female or neuter form; human, animal or inanimate; and in
aspects benevolent, kind and generous, or again as bloodthirsty
and ferocious. Hindus propitiate, worship and make offerings to
this great array of gods in the hope of avoiding their displeasure,
seeking their protection against misfortune and evil, imploring
their beneficence in bestowing prosperity and happiness, and
assistance in easing the way into life hereafter.

Essentially, however, learned Hindus are monotheistic, praying to and through the deities to reach the One Universal Spirit,

the One Absolute Reality. They do not confuse God with the gods. The One Supreme Being has manifested himself in the creation of three emanations – Brahma, Vishnu and Shiva – usually thought of as the Hindu triad.

Brahma is the Great Creator who formed the world and everything in it, including, it seems, the caste system wherein the highest caste of Brahman priests issued from Brahma's head. The noble ruler-warrior caste came from his arm, while the merchants, traders and landowners came from his leg, and servants, menials and labourers came from his feet. In Nepal Brahma is rarely depicted in idols or images, a deity so mighty and lofty as to be little understood or revered by the multitudes.

Vishnu the Preserver, protector of all that Brahma created, is greatly adored and widely worshipped by millions of devotees called Vishnavites, in all his many forms and incarnations, and by all his countless names. Through the long epochs of time Vishnu has presented himself nine times on earth on behalf of the gods and mankind, the last manifestation, some say, in the form of Lord Buddha himself. To the Nepalese, Vishnu is especially beloved in his manifestations as Krishna, Rama and Narayan

Third in the Hindu triad is the Great Destroyer, Shiva, who represents Time, which eventually destroys and overcomes all things. To non-Hindus Shiva is a most complex divinity in that he also represents the force of procreation as the god of reproduction. All things male spring from Shiva, but he further embodies the female element, depicted as his various wives and female consorts. Shiva and his wives are further multiplied in both kindly and terrifying aspects, their idols carved as serene and devoted lovers, or again as the most terrifying monsters, who can only be propitiated with the blood of sacrificed animals and intoxicating liquors.

One of the idols most commonly seen in Nepal is Shiva symbolized as the Shiva lingam, a vertical stone-carved pillar or simple oblong rock representing the male genital organ. His female aspect is portrayed in various motifs of the yoni, a flat disc with a lip opening to one side, resembling the female uterus, often seen in conjunction with the phallic Shiva lingam.

From the followers of the Shiva cult, Shivaites as they are called, has emanated the Shakti-Tantric school, where Shakti is the female Supreme Energy embodied in the Great Mother Goddesses, all of whom are deeply and widely revered in Nepal. In the Shakti sect female sexual energy is worshipped as Goddess Durga or Kali, usually in various ceremonies involving Tantric rites of mysticism, magic incantations and the casting of spells as written in the Tantra texts, rituals which the Brahman priests are said to look upon – or overlook – with tacit disapproval. For the appeasement of these goddesses, under all their various names, requires blood sacrifices, often the offering and consumption of liquor, and sometimes strange, secret sexual rites.

Westerners have long been amazed and baffled by these rituals, unable to comprehend sex as a part of religion. Mahatma Gandhi said, 'It has remained for our Western visitors to acquaint us with the obscenity of many practices which we have hitherto innocently indulged in. It was in a missionary book that I first learned that the Shiva lingam had any obscene significance at all.' Here is the age-old worship of fertility, the desire to beget many offspring, especially male children, for the holy books declare that a Hindu can neither attain Heaven after death, nor can his ancestors remain there, unless he has begotten a son.

Both Hindus and Buddhists believe in transmigration of the soul when it leaves the earthly body. If during his lifetime a man has committed sin, his soul may be reincarnated as a stone, a weasel or an untouchable person, to be born and reborn again and again through long ages of time at a level higher or lower, commensurate with the balancing of his good deeds against bad. If through his deeds he has gained sufficient merit, his soul may be reincarnated at a level as high as a Brahman. If he has lived the life of a saint, which is very unlikely, entirely without sin, his soul may be taken directly to the highest level of spiritual life where he will remain for ever at rest in the presence of the Universal Spirit, in a state of heavenly bliss, never to be born on earth again. Thus he has gained Eternal Release, the ultimate goal.

Vital for all good Hindus and Buddhists is the accrual of

religious merit during one's time on earth to assure that life in the next world will be better. Toward this end offerings are made to the gods, especially on feast and festival days; alms are given to Brahmans, cripples and religious mendicants; ritual holy baths are taken, for one can become defiled through eating forbidden foods, coming in contact with offal, a corpse, an outcaste person or a menstruating woman; holy fasting and meditations are undergone; and the sacred cow is worshipped as representative of divinity.

Thus innumerable *pujas* are performed which may be small private ceremonies in the home before an idol in a wall niche, before a picture of the deity in the *puja khota* or prayer room, with or without a priest in attendance, or again before a sacred rock which represents a deity enshrined at the base of a great peepul tree. There are many ritual family *pujas*, as well as great community gatherings at the temples which we call festivals. In all, the deity is honoured, worshipped, appeased or beseeched for some blessing with offerings of flowers, lighted wicks, holy water, rice, coloured sacred powders and pastes, coins, often fruits and vegetables, and sometimes liquor and blood sacrifices. In return the devotee receives *prasad*, a gift or blessing, back from the god. This may be a coloured *tika* mark placed on his forehead by the temple priest or by his own hand, bits of the flower petals he has just offered placed atop his head, or the headless body of the animal or fowl he has just sacrificed.

At certain festivals *jatras* are performed, when the idol is decorated and carried about in gala religious procession for a variety of reasons – to honour him, give him a pleasurable outing, present him to other gods and goddesses, take him for his annual bathing ceremony, or simply to allow him the opportunity of watching some festival or ceremony with the celebrating populace.

Possibly it was the Greeks and Persians who introduced sculpture and architectural styles into India in ages past. Idols and statues and images of the gods and goddesses, religious saints and heroes, and of benign or evil spirits became popular, and as increasing numbers of devotees pilgrimaged to see and worship these sacred objects, temples were built to house them. Festivals were inaugurated to celebrate annually some event in the scriptures, to pacify the gods, to thank them for the harvest, to honour their birth dates or to celebrate some miraculous performance attributed to them. Often kings or wealthy men built temples, installed idols therein and made sure that both would be revered for ever by instituting annual festivals in honour of the deity.

Thus Hinduism has survived through the ages, even though it waned for five or six hundred years while Buddhism came and passed quietly on to other lands.

Gautama Buddha was born a Hindu in southern Nepal five centuries before Christ, an event which made Nepal for ever sanctified ground for Buddhists round the world. Most of Buddha's manhood was spent walking from town to town in north India, and probably into Nepal, teaching a new concept – The Middle Way – a gentle religion with the simple doctrine of tolerance between humans, kindness to animals and peace on earth. Buddhism retained much of the Hindu philosophy, the idea of reincarnation and many of the deities, but Buddha himself rejected all forms of excess and fanaticism. He taught the value of ridding oneself of desire for meaningless earthly pleasures through learning, meditation, and a benevolent regard for the welfare of others, thereby attaining Nirvana – a state of superior spiritual peace.

Buddha did not teach men that he was a god. He was a superior human being – a Buddha – who had received illumination and enlightenment, became all-knowing and free from sin. Adherents believe that six different Buddhas lived on earth before Gautama. However, by the beginning of the Christian era the Scythian invaders of north-western India adopted Buddhism, elevated Buddha himself to a superior god and transformed 'aspiring Buddhas', or Bhodisatvas, into deities. This sect of Buddhism accepted the Hindu gods, rites and legends and spread to foreign lands.

We are not certain when Buddhism entered and pervaded Nepal. Very probably it was introduced during Buddha's lifetime, and grew when the great Indian Emperor Ashoka rejected Hinduism completely about 250 BC and wholeheartedly embraced Buddhism. Through this remarkable ruler and his descendants all India was converted to Buddhism. Many believe that Lord Buddha himself made pilgrimages into Nepal, and that Ashoka, in his travels collecting Buddhist manuscripts and spreading the Word, erected the great stone pillar at Lumbini in southern Nepal which reads, 'The Blessed One was born here.'

Through Ashoka and those who followed, Buddhism spread to Nepal, Burma, Ceylon, China and Tibet, where it was nourished through the centuries even as it faded from the Indian scene, leaving very few adherents there by the ninth century of our era.

Some say that Buddhism reached Tibet from China. Others believe it came up from Kashmir, Nepal and India. Perhaps the Word of Buddha came from all these areas, for by the seventh century Buddhism was the state religion of Tibet. Thousands of monasteries appeared in the mountains and on the great Tibetan plateau, harbouring an incalculable number of yellow-robed lamas and monks. There the gentle Way of Buddha was incorporated with native Tibetan superstition, magic rites and mystic incantations, and the Lamas held sway over great tracts of monastic lands, sealed off from the world almost as securely as it is today under Chinese occupation. This Tibetan Buddhism or Lamaism is the religion of the Nepalese in the high Himalayan regions near the Tibetan border, while the Buddhism of the central Nepalese hills and mountains was influenced from the south – a more all-embracing religion, well laced with their native and Hindu gods, rituals and festivals.

For since remotest times Hindu holy men and Buddhist ascetics have made pilgrimages from India into Nepal, known in the holy texts as the 'Himalayan Paradise'. With the dying of Buddhism in India the learned Brahmans gradually rose again to ascendency and regained royal patronage. Nepal was often ruled by Hindu kings driven from their lands from time to time over the centuries by invaders. The Arabs, Turks, Mongols and Moguls came to India with their unbending Muslim faith, inflicting terrible cruelties upon Buddhist monks while they lasted, and on Hindus throughout their centuries of occupation. From time to time Hindu Brahmans and the ruling warrior caste fled before the onslaught into the remote Nepalese hills and valleys, and those who came during the seventeenth century were to change the history of Nepal.

There was never wide disparity between Brahmanism and its caste system, brought in by the dominating Indians, and the mixed Nepalese religion of animism, Buddhism and Hinduism which they found here, for all these beliefs had common origins. While there are still individuals, clans and pocket regions in Nepal who profess to be either Hindu or Buddhist, these religions have blended, mingled and coexisted with a tolerance, mutual respect and a peacefulness seldom seen anywhere in the world. This phenomenon is evident everywhere in Nepal – with Hindu and Buddhist idols side by side in the same temple, Buddhist *chaityas* and Hindu pagodas together in the same temple grounds, Buddhist priests officiating in Hindu temples, in religious rites and ceremonies and festivals, and in the hearts and minds of the people.

As the ancient Nepala Mahatmya texts say, 'To worship Buddha is to worship Shiva', and the Swayambhu Puran reciprocates by recommending and sanctioning the adulation of Lord Shiva.

The Valley of Kathmandu

Lying in the central hills of Nepal is the lovely Valley of Kathmandu, long known to Nepalese in outlying regions simply as 'Nepal', for it has been considered the trading, governmental, cultural and religious focus of the country for many years.

Although the white peaks of the cold Himalayas can be seen in the northern skyline standing only thirty to forty-five miles from this valley, winters are mild and crisp and snowfall is all but unheard of. The summer monsoon brings profuse semi-tropical vegetation to the valley, lying as it does at a height of 4,500 feet, but in the same latitude roughly as Egypt and Florida.

Completely surrounding the fifteen-by-eighteen mile valley is a protecting ring of hills that rise steeply another 4,500 feet above the valley floor made uneven by stream and river beds cutting through terraced fields, and by smaller hills poking up throughout. These terraced rice plots throughout the valley, cupping gracefully around the slopes and climbing in steps up over the hilltops, herald the rotating seasons with their ever-changing colour – yellow with mustard blossoms in the spring, turning to pale green with growing rice seedlings in early summer. Monsoon rains bring vivid greens to the terraces, which gradually blend into the gold of October's harvest. And finally the dry brown plots in winter are brightened with a patchwork of emerald wheat-fields and clumps of leafy bamboos.

Dotted amongst these terraces are clusters of mudbrick and stone houses of two and three stories, their mud-plastered exteriors washed white over the lower half and rusty ochre over the upper level or levels – or possibly the other way around for variation. Their thatched and weed-grown tile roofs, sloping outward near the bottom eaves, are somehow vaguely similar to the alpine cottages of Europe. Villages perch on the slopes and hilltops where houses and temples are bunched together along crooked, rocky lanes.

Near the centre of the valley, at the junction of the two sacred rivers, the Bagmati and Vishnumati, sprawls the capital city of Kathmandu, with its jumbled skyline of ragged tile rooftops and pagoda spires at the heart of the old town. Mudbrick walls line the streets that spread out to residential areas of both Nepali-style and modern Western homes, with here and there massive ornate mansions falling into disrepair – the dwellings of the former ruling class, copied from those of neo-classical Europe.

Just across the Bagmati River to the south is Patan, an ancient 'city of temples', while Bhadgaon town lies six miles to the east, its hundreds of homes and temple shrines piled upon a plateaued hill. Two hundred years ago these three cities housed the royal palaces of three different kingdoms which divided the valley – palaces surviving today, their open squares crowded with temples and bazaar stalls, where honking vehicles, sacred cows, heavily-laden porters, pariah dogs and jostling humanity vie for right of way.

Often it is said there are more temples than houses in Kathmandu Valley, and indeed they are found in incredible numbers of every size and description: along the streams and footpaths, crowding the winding village lanes, among the rice terraces, clinging to the hillsides and choking crowded city streets. Great temples with heavily carved exteriors under many-tiered rooftops of ornate brass; massive white-domed stupas and hundreds of smaller Buddhist *chaityas*; small temples with low, ornate archways guarded by chiselled stone animals, and tiny temples containing one lone idol sheltered beneath a sacred tree or gracing a spring flowing from a carved stone serpent's mouth.

For the temples house the images and statues of the beloved gods and goddesses, countless in number, small and large, depicted in sculptured stone, brass and wood. Some sit yogi fashion, with benign and gentle faces. Others stand in exotic or erotic poses, their many arms fanned out on either side. Many are fierce gods and demons, holding terrible weapons, garlanded with strings of human skulls, standing upon their mangled victims with bulging, glaring eyes and gaping, fanged mouths. And everywhere are carved animals, especially serpents – on every temple and shrine, twined about the bodies and necks of many deities, and around the edges of every sacred pond and village water spout.

In these temples and idols and holy places of Kathmandu Valley are to be found the stories and legends of an ancient oriental culture.

In the Beginning

Far back in remotest antiquity, the ancient chronicles reveal, all the Valley of Kathmandu was filled with water, a lake of idyllic beauty completely surrounded by hills covered with great forests, flowering plants and fragrant herbs. It was called Nag-hrad, Abode of the Snake Gods, inhabited by a pantheon of serpent deities known as Nagas. To this day Nepalese people worship the Nagas and they were not at all surprised when geologists ascertained that water once stood in the valley.

As ages passed the lake of Nag-hrad became a place of great sanctity where pilgrimaged holy men and saints from far to the south and from beyond the northern snowpeaks.

One day a magnificent full-blown lotus blossom appeared upon the surface of the water at a point just above the sacred Swayambhunath hill, now covered with monasteries, temples and a massive white stupa from whose gilded spire four pairs of all-seeing eyes look out across the valley. This miraculous lotus flower took root, it seems, on a hillock at the bottom of the lake some two miles to the east, where is now located, just beyond and above the Bagmati River, the most sacrosanct temple of goddess Gujeswari, which shelters a sacred and bottomless hole.

As epochs passed Buddhas and aspiring Buddhas came to the lake to meditate and pray. One day they saw emanating from the lotus a brilliant, radiant flame which was none other than Adi Buddha, the Self-Existent One called Swayambhu – the God Supreme. For long ages the Bhodisatvas and Buddhas worshipped the Eternal Flame, until one of them thought of making the area into a valley habitable for mankind.

This thought was transplanted into the mind of Manjusri, a divine saint from China, who pilgrimaged to Nag-hrad to worship the Swayambhu Flame and the goddess Gujeswari. Manjusri walked the peaks around the lake three times and then, with one blow of his mighty scimitar, struck a deep cleft in the southern hills, allowing all the water to drain from the valley. This ravine is now called Chobar Gorge, the only water escape from the valley, through which the Bagmati River flows to the south.

With the escaping waters, all the Nagas were driven from the valley except Karkot Raja, King of the Serpent Deities, who was induced to remain. Manjusri granted to Karkot Naga power over the wealth of the valley and a permanent home in Taudah, where he dwells to this day, the people say, in a pond a short distance from Chobar Gorge.

2. Rural home, Kathmandu Valley
(Mary M. Anderson)

Carved wooden windows of the old
royal palace, Bhadgaon
(Betty Woodsend)

3. Lingam ceremonial pole being raised, unfurling 'snake' banners, during Bisket celebration of New Year in Bhadgaon   (Shridhar Manandhar)

Towering spires of Lord Machhendra's chariot followed by that of Min Nath during his Patan festival   (Betty Woodsend)

Khats, decorated roofed palanquins carrying the goddesses of Thimi village during New Year festival, the men covered with red ceremonial powder (Shridhar Manandhar)

Disciples and followers of Manjusri settled the valley, cultivating the land, building monasteries and temples, learning the
'mysteries' of the Tantras and worshipping Swayambhu and
Gujeswari, as Manjusri taught them. From time to time the gods
themselves came to this Himalayan paradise to dwell among the
valley people and their kings, mediating with the Snake God Karkot in times of drought and famine, warring among themselves
and the demons, with problems and adventures much the same as
those of ordinary people.

It is written that the Hindu gods Brahma, Vishnu and Shiva
themselves visited the valley in the form of deer. One Buddha
pointed them out to the inhabitants as three gods who also worshipped Swayambhu and Gujeswari, and who had come as protectors of the people.

As ages passed one Buddha prophesied that in time the name of
Pashupati would be greatly celebrated, and it was Lord Shiva who
was called Pashupati. His great temple, Pashupatinath, on the
Bagmati River not far from Gujeswari's shrine, houses the sacred
Shiva lingam, holiest of holies, before which kneels a tremendous
'golden' bull. Here thousands of devotees come each year from all
over Nepal and India in a festival to honour Shiva's name.

Vishnu was known as Narayan, whose temples now grace all
four sides of the valley, where crowds of faithful worshippers
walk many miles from one to the other each year in a pilgrimage
festival to worship this beloved deity. Some say it was Vishnu himself, rather than Manjusri, who cut the ravine draining the valley,
while others smile and say they are one and the same.

In the ensuing eras a certain Buddha, needing water for a holy
ritual, thrust his thumb into one of the surrounding hills, and from
this hole emanated a goddess who miraculously turned into water
– which now flows into the valley as the sacred Bagmati River, and
eventually runs into the holy Ganges.

The population of the valley increased, and so did the gods and
goddesses. Festivals were held in their honour, and their adventures
were told down through the generations in folklore and legends
which seem to indicate, some think, that the Newar people who

33

still dwell in the valley were the original inhabitants, as they themselves believe.

Dwellers of the Valley

Of the 500,000 inhabitants of Kathmandu Valley today, more than half are Newars who have been here, records show, for over 2,000 years and nobody knows how long before. Proud of their ancient heritage, the Newars made the valley what it is today – a terraced vale, filled with graceful temples and idols, where age-old traditions, rituals and festivals have remained unchanged despite a long history of rule by invaders.

The Newars believe that they themselves were the original dwellers of the valley, and no amount of research has conclusively proven otherwise. Theories have been advanced that in the beginning they were a Mongolian people from the north; that they are closely akin to the ancient tribes of southern India; that they migrated through the Nepalese hills from the eastern mountains; or that they came with a dynasty of cowherd kings from the Indian plains – a people much discussed in ancient Hindu scriptures. In the wide variety of Indo-Mongolian facial types to be seen among the Newars, and in their legends and traditions, may be found links with all these peoples; certainly now they are a blended race. And with the present-day lowering of social and caste barriers, this age-old blending of cultures and races is on the increase.

The fun-loving, frank, hospitable Newars have since remotest times been owners and tillers of the soil, still cultivating today with the few hand implements of their ancient forebears. Through the ravages of time much of their lands have been lost, but almost all Newars, no matter what their occupation, still cling possessively to a tiny plot of ground. Land means rice, and so strong is his pride in landownership that a Newar of the older generation to this day is ashamed to be seen in the bazaar purchasing rice, for this may indicate he owns no land.

Tradesmen and merchants have always been prominent among Newars, from vendors in small bazaar stalls to highly successful marketers of Nepalese, Tibetan and Indian produce. Nowadays Newars operate some of the most thriving business concerns in the valley.

But the Newars are best known to the world for their amazing artistic creativity and skilled craftsmanship, which was usually channelled toward expressing their fervent religious piety, producing a culture which a few centuries ago ranked among the highest in Asia. In their remote, secluded valley the Newars developed their own distinctive art style which is now thought of as 'purely Nepalese'.

Every clan, every household it seems, has its own musicians, whose crashing cymbals, many-toned drums and mournful, blasting trumpets are heard at every festival. Their highly stylized pageants, dramatic presentations and ritualistic dances, performed with grotesque masks and ancient ornate costumes, reflect their love of beauty and grace, their pride in tradition, and their aptitude for mimicry and humour. The spontaneous songs and lively dances of the Newars were noted hundreds of years ago in the travelogues of ancient globe-trotters.

Their sculptured ornaments and religious idols, lovingly wrought by skilled craftsmen in bronze, brass, wood, stone, silver and gold, often embossed with precious and semi-precious stones, were sought by far-away India, Kashmir, Tibet and China, and today are found in museums around the world. Despite this sad depletion, hundreds of these images still remain in Nepalese temples, where they belong.

Old Newari woodcarving ranks among the finest to be found anywhere, still seen throughout the valley in a rich profusion of heavily ornamented windows, doorways and balconies of homes, temples and ancient royal palaces. Large panels of intricately carved wooden filigree, gargoyles, demons, serpents, peacocks, flying horse dragons and many-armed goddesses are remarkably well preserved.

Of less fine workmanship, but of great curiosity to visitors, are the small scenes carved into the base of the slanting temple struts, depicting animals and humans combined in amazing postures and in positions of sexual play and intercourse, the original purpose of which defies explanation. Many theories have been advanced, including the well-known supposition that these scenes were designed to scare away lightning, giving the temple protection from adversity. It is doubtful that the Newars ever thought that sex would scare anything away, for they have an open-minded, healthy approach to such matters. And it is doubtful if it was the Western visitor who taught the Nepalese that these erotic carvings were 'naughty'. Rather, they seem to be an expression of the fertility cult which has fully survived from ancient days to this. Perhaps they were carved on places of worship to please and honour the gods and goddesses who, after all, have the same appetites as humans and animals.

The heavily decorated, many-tiered pagoda temple style peculiar to Newar builders and artisans is generally believed to have originated with them. Records show that emperors of Tibet and China sent for Newari craftsmen to build temples in their lands, whence the style eventually spread to Japan.

Fortunately for the Nepalese, and for the world, the old Newari dynasty of Malla kings that ruled for many centuries before the 1700s were tolerant of the traditions and mixed religious beliefs of their Newar subjects, and encouraged their craftsmanship in all the arts. It was during the long reign of these Hindu Malla kings that many of the existing palaces, temples and sculptured idols were created, although hundreds of existing works of art date back to far more ancient times.

One tribe of Brahmans and high-caste ruling warriors of Rajasthan in India, who fled from the Muslims in the 1600s, took refuge in the hills of Nepal, and finally settled as rulers of Gorkha, forty-three miles north-west of Kathmandu Valley. Before long these Shah kings were casting their swords about for new lands to conquer, and by the middle 1700s their realm bordered the valley. Here they found the ruling Malla family divided into three hostile camps, with three feuding Malla kings reigning from their palaces in Kathmandu, Patan and Bhadgaon – a situation much to the advantage of the Shahs. The Newar people were weakened and oppressed by interminable strife and intriguing among the Malla rulers.

The King from Gorkha, Prithvi Narayan Shah, was at first defeated in the valley by the inhabitants of the little hilltop village of Kirtipur a few miles south-west of Kathmandu city. Smouldering with rage, the Shah King withdrew, returned later with heavy reinforcements, overcame Kirtipur and ordered the noses of all men and boys in the village to be severed, excepting those who played musical wind instruments. Records exist of travellers who saw the two great baskets of amputated noses, and who in the ensuing decades encountered the brave victims of Kirtipur, whose horrifying, skull-like faces served as a grim reminder to all would-be dissenters.

Despite the travail amongst their own kings and the threat of the Shah forces in the valley, the autumn of 1768 found the Newars celebrating in Kathmandu their great annual festival of the Living Goddess – the day chosen by Prithvi Narayan Shah to lead his forces into the city. They say the old eratic Kathmanda King, failing to muster his troops from among the inebriated holiday revellers, fled to Patan and the victorious Shah King magnanimously allowed the celebration to continue. When the Living Goddess symbolically bestowed the right to rule upon the conqueror, following an ancient tradition of this festival, story has it that the tipsy populace rejoiced, so tyrannized had they been under the three feuding Malla kings.

Today Prithvi Narayan Shah is hailed as the Father of the Nation, having within his reign conquered all of Nepal and fixed the present frontiers. The British marched into Nepal in the interests of maintaining peace on the northern border, and after minor skirmishes came to terms with the new Shah King, whereby certain lands were deeded to the British in the south-west, and they were allowed to establish a one-man diplomatic mission in the capital city of Kathmandu. To all others King Prithvi sealed his borders, and for almost 200 years Nepal was a Forbidden Land.

The present King of Nepal, Shri Panch Mahendra Bir Bikrim Shah Dev is a direct descendant of Prithvi Narayan Shah.

In the 1840s strife once more rent the valley when the Shah dynasty was debilitated by a shocking succession of murders, plots and jealousies within the court in which the queens, courtesans and paramours played an active part. At last one enterprising young nobleman, whose forebears had come to the valley with Prithvi's troops and who was influential in military circles as well as the palace, usurped the power of the throne through a series of intrigues, murders and bloody massacres of his own. Jung Bahadur Rana titled himself Prime Minister and Maharaja of Nepal, stripped the royal family of all ruling power confining them to the palace except for public ceremonial appearances – for in Nepal the King is regarded as a deity, the incarnation of Lord Vishnu.

For one hundred years this remarkable Rana family held absolute power in Nepal, marrying almost exclusively into the royal Shah family and into families of noble birth in India.

When the winds of revolt raised the dust of India in the 1940s the message of Mahatma Gandhi seeped into Nepal and political unrest grew. This was the beginning of the end of Rana rule. Concerned with the instability of government in Nepal, and the weakening of their only buffer against the threat of Chinese Communists, the Indian Government arranged for the 'spy-thriller' escape of the then King Tribhuvan and members of the royal family to New Delhi in November 1950.

The Rana regime, faced with strong dissension at home and heavy pressure from the Indian Government, agreed to reinstate the Shah King on the throne, and finally surrendered their powers altogether. Eventually the vast holdings and mansions of many of the Ranas were confiscated by the Nepalese Government. The progenitors of their royal marriages, together with the hundreds born through the decades to countless second and third wives and concubines, form a goodly section of the population of the Kathmandu Valley today. Many of the Ranas now are businessmen, government officials or military officers earnestly concerned with the welfare of their developing nation, still treated in general as nobility, almost a class unto themselves.

Tribhuvan's son, the present King Mahendra of Nepal, is

reigning monarch of a planned democracy in which local, regional and national 'Panchayat' organizations represent the people, and tremendous efforts are made to overcome grave problems and difficulties in bringing a small, landlocked Asiatic nation into the modern world.

Thus today over half the people of Kathmandu Valley are Newars, while the remainder are descendants of the Gorkha conquerors, smaller ethnic groups of Tamangs and Gurungs from the highlands, Brahmans who settled from the south long before the Gorkhas, and immigrants from outlying hills and plains who come seeking education and a better way of life. And still the year-long succession of festivals goes on, celebrated in the age-old tradition by Nepalese of vastly differing origins who live, work and worship together in a tolerance and understanding which could set an example to much of the world today.

Nowhere is this more clearly pointed up than at New Year in mid-April, when the King radios his message of goodwill to some ten million subjects throughout the land, while thousands converge upon Bhadgaon town to celebrate the year's beginning as it has long been celebrated by their ancestors.

APRIL-MAY

1 NAWABARSA AND BISKET

Nepalese New Year in Bhadgaon and Thimi

Year after year the Nepalese festivals follow round the old 'religious' lunar calendar in the same sequence. An exception is New Year Day, which always falls in the middle of April, observed throughout Nepal as the first day of the official Nepalese solar calendar. It should be remembered then, when observing the festivals as chronological events, that other annual celebrations which occur at this season may in some years fall a few days before and in other years a few days after *Nawabarsa*, the New Year.

The most important New Year festival in the valley is held at Bhadgaon town, a picturesque jumble of weed-grown, tile-roofed houses and temple spires crowning a plateau six miles east of Kathmandu, one of the capital cities a few centuries ago, when the valley was divided into three kingdoms. Old records indicate that the Malla kings of Bhadgaon – or Bhaktapur as it is also known – lent their royal patronage to promote the Newari celebrations of the New Year.

It is believed that the Bhadgaon festival is called Bisket in reference to the Newari words *bi* for 'snake', and *syako* for 'slaughter', forming the term which eventually became *bisket*, a celebration to commemorate the death of two serpent demons.

It seems that one of the ancient Bhadgaon kings had an only and beautiful daughter who was so excessively passionate that he eventually resorted to conscripting from among the inhabitants a different man each night to satisfy her needs. Soon the males of the city came to regard this duty, as it rotated from one household to the next, with mortal fear, for each morning the Princess's lover-of-the-night was found dead, an inexplicable mystery.

It so happened that a foreign prince, having become separated from his hunting party, found lodging in Bhadgaon at the home of a kindly old woman. During the night he was awakened by the sound of weeping and learned upon investigation that the grieving mother's only son was destined next night to attend the Princess. Now with patient insistence the Prince convinced the woman that the mysterious deaths could be solved only if he himself be allowed to serve in the boy's place.

At the palace the following night, after he had satisfied the Princess and saw her sleeping soundly, the Prince hid himself in the room sword in hand. At last he beheld two dark threads emanating from the girl's nostrils which rapidly expanded into monstrous serpents writhing about in search of their usual victim; but this night, when they attacked, they were slashed to death. At daybreak pallbearers and mourners came to carry away the corpse and were astounded to find the foreigner chatting calmly with the Princess.

Word of his marvellous deed spread, bringing townsmen in such numbers to view the snakes and gallant Prince that the palace could not accommodate them. The mutilated serpents were hung from a tall pole in the city square, the King bestowed honours on the Prince and instituted a gay festival on the first day of the year, when an immense ceremonial chariot was pulled about the town, carrying Goddess Bhadra Kali, so that she, along with the multitudes, might witness the lofty victory pole and applaud the death of the evil snakes.

In a different version of this story, Bisket celebrates the marriage of this Bhadgaon princess to Prince Bhadra Malla, the first of many royal suitors to remain alive after spending the night in her room – a pre-wedding practice in those days. When Bhadra became ruler, he and his descendants were known as the Naga Mallas – the Snake Kings of the Malla dynasty – in remembrance of his heroic extermination of the serpents.

Legend has it that originally Goddess Bhadra Kali alone was

fêted in the chariot procession, until one year Kala Bhairab from Kasi (Black Bhairab from Benares, India) came to witness the New Year festivities disguised as a mortal man. When the celebrating populace saw this tall foreigner in their midst, they suspected at once that he was some illustrious personage and notified their priests. They, through the arts of Tantric 'mysteries', divined that he was indeed Lord Bhairab, the powerful deity who represents the awesome, destructive force of Shiva. Eager to detain him in the valley, the priests cast *mantras* or magic spells about the great God of Wrath and Terror who, finding himself immobilized, attempted escape by sinking into the earth, returning to Benares by the underground route. But just as he was about to disappear the people cut off his head, and that is all of Bhairab the Bhadgaon people were able to save.

Now he is depicted as a glowering brass mask enshrined on the upstairs landing of his great three-storied temple on a main square of the city. This omnipotent guardian deity gazes through five miniature golden windows toward the west that he may ever be watchful of approaching danger. The actual severed head of Bhairab from Benares, they say, is kept hidden in the temple, seen and worshipped only by the Tantric priests. But once each year, during Bisket festival, its mysterious locked box is brought out to ride in the chariot beside the shining mask of Bhairab, and to this day the people of Bhadgaon say the head of Kala Bhairab in Benares is not the original.

As he is prone to do when neglected, Bhairab of Bhadgaon once became angry and created such havoc and distress that the Raja, on the advice of court pundits, placated him by enshrining near his temple an idol of one of the Shakti Mother Goddesses. Her towering temple with five pagoda-tiered roofs is called Nayatapola, still the pride of Bhadgaon, where this mysterious 'hidden' goddess – actually an ancestral family deity of the former Malla kings – can be worshipped only in the dark of night and only by those of the higher castes.

It is Bhairab's wife and female counterpart, Goddess Bhadra Kali, however, who rides in the Bisket procession. Four days

43

before the New Year her eight-inch brass figurine is carried from her shrine, deep in the heart of the crowded city, to the open square before Bhairab's temple. There two enormous temple-shaped *raths*, vehicles of the gods, are waiting. Bhairab's chariot is the larger, its four solid-wooden wheels regarded as sacred representations of the *Vedas*, ancient Hindu holy books. The heavy upward-curving beam extending to the front represents a snake god, while the dwarfed human metal figure attached at its head is the *betal* who accompanies Bhairab on all his journeys. The massive, ornately-carved, three-tiered chariot is designed in the shape of '*sri jantra*', a mysterious, sacred Tantric symbol.

Bisket celebration officially opens when Bhairab and Bhadra Kali are enshrined in their respective chariots and pulled by ropes through cheering, worshipping crowds up ancient, stone-block streets so narrow that the great wheels must roll through garbage-strewn gutters on either side. Now when Bhairab's vehicle reaches a sloping open square, the inhabitants of the upper part of town vie with those from the lower in a hair-raising tug-of-war, each side straining with all their might at ropes tied fore and aft, while swarming mobs of celebrators cheer and shout in their midst. Swaying and bouncing precariously, the towering chariot is yanked this way and that until one team finally succeeds in moving it in their direction – a most auspicious omen predicting good fortune for their townsmen during the coming year.

For several nights there is celebrating in the streets. Hundreds come to leave gifts and offerings to Bhairab and his wife – rice, red ceremonial powder, lighted oil wicks, holy water, flowers and garlands. Music blares and masked dancers, costumed to represent various divinities, perform by the light of flaming torches. Now, and for the next two days, people make the rounds of all the temples with gifts for the gods and goddesses of Bhadgaon, seeking their blessings in the New Year, for it is believed that during Bisket festival the spirits of all the deities actually descend to Bhadgaon town.

The third day of the festival is called *Syako Tyako*, when each household sacrifices a fowl or other animal – usually a goat –

before the idols, later consuming the meat in a great ceremonial family feast, one of the many held throughout the year in Newar homes. Seated cross-legged around the room they are served an endless variety of foods ladled into pressed-leaf plates on the floor before them. All is eaten dexterously with the fingers, washed down with home-made rice wine in tiny clay bowls – liquor of often the finest quality.

On the day before New Year the chariots are pulled to a large open area at the lower outskirts of the city so that Lord Bhairab and his equally powerful and terrifying wife, together with hundreds of inhabitants, may witness the erection of the *lingam* ceremonial pole, a thick, shorn tree-trunk some eighty feet in length. This is an exciting, dangerous operation, for the *lingam*, supported by bamboos and pulled by heavy ropes, must be made to rest in the centre hole of a large pile of cemented rocks. The crowds alternately cheer and watch in tense silence as hordes of scrambling, straining men pull and hoist the mammoth pole to upright position, often labouring for hours through many fruitless attempts. Not infrequently a man is killed when the sacred *lingam* comes crashing back to earth. There are years when the operation fails entirely. Then tempers run high, while others are uneasy and fearful, for such failure signifies a dark omen which may bring disaster to the nation.

But the *lingam* is erected, unfurling from the crossbeam or 'arms' at its tip two banners which sweep the ground – the male and female snake demons killed in ages past. Now cheering mobs swarm in with flowers, lights and blood sacrifices to the *lingam*, a phallic emblem representing the power of Shiva and Bhairab as well as a symbol of victory and the New Year, thought to bring protection and prosperity to the people of Bhadgaon. Some enthusiasts shin up the heavy guide ropes, swaying daringly over the crowd to secure blossoms and greenery affixed to the lofty 'arms', for these decorations act as a powerful *prasad*, or blessing, from the gods, bringing good fortune to stout-hearted devotees.

In the afternoon of New Year's Day thousands upon thousands come from far and wide, crowding into the field around the *lingam* pole, filling the side streets, windows, balconies and roof-tops – a sea of human heads. Two teams of celebrating men pull and strain at the ropes, causing the towering pole to sway first one way then another, while the crowds surge away or run for their lives. When at last the *lingam* thunders to the ground a great roar of approval arises, for most believe that only now does the New Year actually commence. The old year is dead and so are the evil snake demons.

For four more days the people celebrate in gay processions, carrying gods and goddesses through the streets with bands of musicians and crowds of worshippers in their wake. Daily parades honour Brahmayani the wife of Lord Brahma, Ganesh the Ele-phant God of Success, Maha Kali the Great Goddess of Terror (another of Bhairab's consorts), and Mahalaxmi the Goddess of Wealth.

In another part of town people of the pottery-making caste hold their own celebration, raising their *lingam* pole, this one without 'arms', four days before New Year, sending it crashing to the ground on the fourth day of the year. Now, with the ending of Bisket, the Bhadgaon people believe the divinities ascend once more into Heaven.

Two miles west of Bhadgaon the village of Thimi celebrates the New Year in a spectacular gathering of all their deities, when Bal Kumari – yet another consort and female representation of Lord Bhairab – is the honoured goddess. Throughout New Year's Day her aging pagoda-tiered temple in the heart of the village is thronged with musicians and worshippers bringing to Bal Kumari, their guardian and protector, gifts of flowers, rice, fruits, vege-tables and coins. Of vital importance is the offering of scarlet ceremonial powder, for all the Shakti Mother Goddesses are exceedingly fond of the colour of blood.

Far into the night worshipping throngs celebrate and keep vigil in Bal Kumari's temple square holding aloft hundreds of *chirags*, burning ceremonial oil torches, the flames of which light up the night sky, the jagged rooftops of surrounding temples and the faces of clay-brick, many-storied buildings. The *chirag* of

Goddess Bal Kumari, distinguishable from others by its four combined torches, must be kept alight throughout the celebration, for
its extinction forecasts danger and hardship not only for the people
of Thimi, but for the king and entire nation. It is believed that the
tremendous accumulated heat from the massed flames will drive
the winter away and hasten the advent of crop-nourishing warm
summer days.

A few of the pious undergo special penance for Bal Kumari by
lying immobile all through the night at her temple, flaming oil
lamps glued with cowdung to forehead, chest and limbs.

The second day of the New Year brings Thimi's greatest
annual festival. At dawn the narrow, rough stone lanes are alive
with spectators through which pass teams of men from each *tole*
or city division, carrying heavy, temple-like *khats* – ornately
canopied ceremonial palaquins affixed to two bamboo poles which
ride upon their shoulders. The tiered brass roofs are decorated
with garlands, greenery, fruits and gay festoons. The deities ride
within while a long-fringed, many-coloured ceremonial umbrella,
its base resting in a bamboo cup strapped to the waist of its bearer,
is kept whirling high above each *khat*.

They converge at the temple of Bal Kumari, thirty-two *khats* in
all, each accompanied by perhaps three dozen men and boys
throwing clouds of brilliant orange-red powder over themselves,
the khats, idols and passers-by, and into upstairs windows over
laughing girls, women and children. For to drench one's elders,
friends and neighbours in vivid red powder is a token of respect,
just as it honours the gods and goddesses. Soon the courtyard is
filled with *khats* borne round and round the temple and through
the crowds on the shoulders of barefoot men whose faces, peaked
topi caps, home-spun shirts and baggy-seated, drawstring trousers
are all but obliterated in vermilion powder.

Excitement mounts when the *khat* bearing Ganesh, the elephant-
headed god who brings success to all ceremonies, comes from
near-by Nagadish village, supported and surrounded by several
hundred men covered with the same vermilion powder, carrying
flaming torches above their heads. Troupes of musicians pound

47

drums and crash cymbals in wild abandon as the *khats* of Thimi deities join Ganesh from Nagadish to parade up and down the narrow main street, some making their heavy palaquins igzag, turn in circles, and veer dangerously close to buildings, scattering spectators.

At mid-morning all the *khats* chase down the street after homeward-bound Ganesh in an attempt to induce him to stay, thus prolonging the celebration. Failing this, they are rushed back to congregate before the old Taleju temple where once stood the 'royal palace', playfully prohibiting Bal Kumari from entering, for with her disappearance the *khat* procession is over. At last the sweating, joyous *khat*-bearers, shouldering their gods and goddesses, disperse down the alleys leading to their home areas.

Now chickens and goats are carried through the streets for sacrifice, the gift of blood from their slit throats drenching the idol of Bal Kumari, the meat to be used in clan and family feasts. Tradition says that on this day no person in Thimi may refuse an invitation, even from an enemy. Thus, if a man invites his rival neighbour to his home, succeeds in getting him dead drunk and deposited unceremoniously into a gutter or garbage-clogged street, the host may consider himself winner of the feud.

Hundreds walk across the highway, along the raised path separating terraced fields, to the near-by village of Bode to see a smaller New Year procession of seven *khats* and to witness the awesome 'tongue-boring' ceremony at the temple of Goddess Mahalaxmi.

Usually a man of Bode volunteers to undergo this sacred religious atonement. If not, one is chosen who did it in past years. For the last four days this man has undergone a 'cleansing' ceremony during which beard, eyebrows and hair are shaved away to remove all 'unclean body growths'. He withdraws alone to one room of the house so that no person may touch and defile him, eating one sparse meal each day of 'clean' foods only – no meat, garlic or salt. He should be a man of means, for his family must give food and drink to all villagers who call at his home. For twenty-four hours preceding the ceremony he abstains completely from all nourishment.

Now around midday the temple *pujari* or priest, holding the man's extended tongue in a piece of cloth, thrusts a long metal spike through its centre. With the needle piercing his out-thrust tongue the penitent walks about the lanes of Bode shouldering a bamboo structure of several sacred flaming torches that all may witness and admire his piety and painful religious penance. When he returns, the *pujari* removes the needle inside the temple and fills the wound with mud from the floor, thought to have special healing powers.

The slightest sign of bleeding is an ill omen which portends that no merit has been earned; that the man, who evidently has broken some rule of the 'cleansing' period, will be punished by the gods. If however, no blood is seen, this marvellous display of religious zeal will surely bring such merit to the performer that at death he will be taken straight to Heaven, escaping thereby the punishing burden of repeated reincarnation.

2 MATA TIRTHA PUJA

Looking upon Mother's Face

Although the people of Nepal are exposed increasingly to foreign cultural influences and to the ways of so-called 'progressive societies', they cling to the proud and ancient tradition of the closely-knit family unit. Only a few 'moderns' are forsaking the joint-family system. Evident everywhere is a demonstrated reverence, respect and affection for parents, senior kinfolk, ancestors, brothers and sisters, sons and daughters, and always little children. To some degree this phenomenon may be attributed to religious teachings, but also to the numerous ceremonies and festivals designed to foster and maintain these vital bonds.

Such a festival is Mata Tirtha Puja on the last day of the dark fortnight of April or early May when every Nepalese must 'look upon his mother's face'. This same phrase is used on Father's Day, and again when parents visit their newly-wedded daughter to 'look upon her face' and take her back, for a short while, to her original family home. The term implies a formal duty when affection and respect are displayed.

For those whose mother is living, the household bustles on this day with the preparation of special foods and gifts. Everyone participates, regardless of age. Small children dip into savings to buy gifts for mother, possibly a present of the traditional sweets, eggs and fruits. Families with married daughters especially relish Mother's Day when laughing, chatting girls and women are re-united at the place of their birth. They bring presents and dishes, usually of sweetmeats prepared by their own hands to vie cheerfully with sisters displaying their own culinary skill.

While many use automobiles, taxis and buses these days, it is still common to see women dressed in their most colourful saris and blouses, ribbons and flowers bouncing in their hair, wearing ornaments of gold or brass, or perhaps a single gem, gleaming on the nostril. They are followed by porters who carry gifts and food, for rare is the household in the valley without at least one servant child to perform simple tasks.

One of the warmest, most touching aspects of the day is when a man or woman bows before the mother to receive her blessing – the touch of her hand on the forehead in an ancient ritual in which honour and respect are displayed, and her benediction of good fortune and love is received.

Those men, women and children whose mother is dead consider it their sacred duty to make a pilgrimage to Mata Tirtha, *mata* meaning 'mother', and *tirtha* a sacred site usually of pilgrimage and holy bathing. Mata Tirtha, six miles south-west of central Kathmandu, just off the Thankot road, actually has two ponds or pools, the larger for bathing, and the smaller just up the hill, famous as the place where one 'looks upon one's mother's face'.

Legend says that when the ancient cowherd kings ruled this region one of the cowherds became deeply depressed by the death of his mother. On Mother's Day he went into the forest to pray at the edge of this water-storage pond. As he offered gifts, his mother's beloved face miraculously appeared in the water and her hand accepted the food. Now it is called Mata Tirtha, where many hope to see the mother's face in the water. It is said, however, that long ago a certain girl, when she beheld her mother's image, jumped into the pond to join her and disappeared in its depths. Since that event it is a matter of doubt that one will see the mother's countenance, but worship performed and gifts left in her memory will bring peace to her departed soul.

Some families come from distant places, often walking many days to spend the night lighting wicks, singing and praying for the mother's soul, performing *sraddha*, intricate prayer and offering ceremonies for the dead. Many arrive in the dark of early morning to bathe 'while stars are still seen in the heavens'. By daybreak the worshippers form an endless stream of humanity bathing in the larger pond, stooping to murmur prayers before climbing stone steps to Mother's *kunda* or sacred pond, which is fed by springs channelled down from the hilltop. On the way they stop to pray to Mahadev, Lord Shiva portrayed as the usual phallic stone lingam, leaving bits of food, ginger and coins.

Now they crowd around the mother's pond, tossing in rice, sweetmeats, fruits, coins and red powder, bowing to pray over the water for a moment and to leave small clay dishes of lighted oil wicks in her memory. All circumambulate the sacred tank, a display of adoration which Nepalese perform at all their idols and holy places. They leave gifts to near-by idols of Narayan and Buddha, and present coins and gifts to waiting priests who ask the mother's name. Many believe their gifts will reach the dead mother, confident that her soul 'knows' her offspring have come to honour her memory.

They say that one day a child of the merchant class was so desolate over the loss of his mother that he cried out to Lord Vishnu, beseeching him for the sight of his mother's face, without which he felt he could no longer live. Vishnu appeared before the distraught child disguised as a Brahman priest, and on Mother's Day led him by the hand to Mata Tirtha for holy bathing. When the mother's face shone forth in the sacred waters the boy pleaded, 'O Brahman, by your kindness I have seen my mother. Allow me to take her home.' Vishnu assured him that he was asking the impossible, but promised that in his next incarnation he would again have the same mother. He assured the boy that by his pious performance of holy bathing and by offering gifts in his mother's name, her soul was now at peace. Then the boy experienced a great sense of tranquillity as he felt the warmth of his mother's blessing, a boon so long-lasting that he eventually became an emperor.

3 RATO MACHHENDRANATH RATH JATRA
The Chariot Ride of Red Machhendra

One of the most famous and perhaps most spectacular of all Kathmandu Valley festivals takes place in April or early May, when Lord Machhendra's towering, massive chariot is hauled through the narrow streets of Patan town, just across the river from Kathmandu. Since its inception the Newar people have religiously preserved all the old traditions and ceremonies of Machhendra's gala procession, celebrated today by tens of thousands of Nepalese – farmers, villagers, city dwellers and royalty alike, regardless of caste or creed.

Rato or Red Machhendra of Patan is distinguished from Seto or White Machhendra of Kathmandu by the colour of his features, but many believe they represent the same god. Some Hindus worship him as the historical saint who bears the same name. Thousands call him Karunamaya, the compassionate God of Mercy. Learned Buddhists identify him as Padma Pani, the fourth of the five Buddhas who represent the elements. Because he created and watched over the universe, protecting and teaching the gods themselves, he came to be called Aryavalokiteswar Padma Pani Bhodisatva, or simply Lokeswar.

Legend says that at one time even Lord Shiva was a disciple of the great *guru* Lokeswar and learned from him the secret of attaining union with the Supreme Being through prolonged meditation. It seems that once Shiva's wife Goddess Parbati fell asleep as Shiva recounted all he had learned from Lokeswar, while the divine *guru* took the form of a fish and secretly listened. When Shiva questioned Parbati and came to know she had not heard his recitation, he divined that there must be an eavesdropper.

'Whoever is lurking in this place must appear at once,' said Shiva, 'or I shall put a curse on him.' With this Lokeswar manifested himself in his true form and Shiva fell at his feet begging forgiveness. Ever since, the great Lokeswar has been known as Machhendranath – Lord Machhendra – from the word *machha* meaning 'fish'.

Again it is said a Brahman woman once gave birth to a son on a dangerously inauspicious day under such malignant signs that the child was cast into the sea. Instead of perishing, however, the boy entered the stomach of a great fish and continued to grow. When this matter came to Lord Shiva's attention he released the child, and ever after he was called Machhendra in honour of the fish that gave him life.

Why thousands look upon Machhendra as the patron deity of Kathmandu Valley is revealed in the Vamsavali texts and repeated by the old inhabitants with little variation. During the reign of old King Narendra Dev of Bhadgaon, they say, a twelve-year drought in the valley caused tanks, wells, ponds and fields to dry up, bringing famine and pestilence to animals and humans. At last, after long meditation, the King's spiritual guide divined that it was a disciple of Lord Machhendra, Gorkhanath, who had caused the drought by imprisoning all nine of the valley's rain-giving Snake Gods under Mrigasthali hill, near Pashupatinath temple. Gorkhanath prevented their escape by seating himself atop the hillock with the dual motive of punishing the valley people for neglecting to accord him due respect, and also to gain an audience with his divine Guru, Lord Machhendra, who was then deep in meditation in the hills of Assam. For Gorkhanath knew that, while he dared not interrupt Lord Machhendra in seclusion, this compassionate deity would surely appear when he learned of the people's profound distress.

Now the King's priest, too, knew that relief would not be forthcoming until Lord Machhendra was persuaded to come to the valley, for then Gorkhanath would be impelled to leave his stronghold over the Snake deities in order to bow before his Guru. Thus the King of Bhadgaon and a learned man, Bandhudutt, from Kathmandu, together with a farmer-porter from Patan, set out to fetch Lord Machhendra. According to legend this deity was the youngest of the five hundred sons born to the demon Shashi who ruled Assam.

Along the route the party was joined by Karkot Naga the Snake God, who enabled them to overcome obstacles and supernatural impediments placed in their path by powerful demons. As they neared the palace in Assam, Bandhudutt recited such powerful *mantras* and performed such efficacious religious ceremonies that Lord Machhendra, despite attempts by his mother to prevent his leaving, transformed himself into a large black bee and flew into Bandhudutt's golden ceremonial vase. Now the angry demons captured the golden vessel, but Bandhudutt invoked the aid of four powerful Bhairab deities, the most vengeful and wrathful of gods. Faced with the divine and terrifying power of the Bhairabs, the demon king and his subjects capitulated and allowed Machhendra to leave Assam.

Now when the returning party entered Kathmandu Valley, carrying the sacred bee, they stopped to rest two miles south of Patan near the Nakhu River. When Gorkhanath arose from his hillock and came to pay homage to his revered guru Machhendra, all the Snake Gods were released and sent torrents of rain over the parched land and to the rejoicing people. It seems Bhairab came again, this time to the camp site and, barking once, said, '*Bu*', which in Newari means 'birthplace'. Then and there the King ordered the town of Bungamati built. The sacred vessel containing the Machhendra bee was enshrined, priests were appointed to worship it as God of Rain and Harvest, a great land endowment was granted for his maintenance, and ever since Bunga village has been known as Machhendra's birthplace.

Among the farmers of the valley, Machhendra is adored under his ancient name of Bunga Deo, the God of Bunga who presides over agricultural prosperity through his agents the Snake Gods. Most people at all costs avoid killing a black bee, regarding it as a form of Machhendra, and he is often worshipped as the ceremonial water vessel in which he reached the valley. Deep and abiding affection for this merciful God of Rain reflects the isolated valley's complete dependence in former years upon local food production.

Although Machhendra is a male god, he is attributed also with feminine characteristics, an adoring parent and sustainer who loves and feeds the people when they pray to his image, 'O Mother, give me to eat the rice grains left to mould on the harvest stalks and a bit of fermented radish', both greatly relished by Nepalese, especially farmers. During his festival Machhendra undergoes certain rites for Newar men, but also others peculiar to women only.

They say that once the mother of Machhendra, testing his benevolence, secretly hid an insect wrapped in many folds of cloth within a small box. Next morning she found a grain of rice beside the insect, for Machhendra allows no creature to suffer from hunger. Then the mother knew her son was the deity responsible for existence of life on earth, and manifested herself as a peepul tree which grows today at Lagankhel in Patan.

In time a handsome temple was built for Machhendra at Tahabal near Patan's Durbar square. Clay was brought from the sacred hill of Mhaipi near Balaju to form his image, which was given life and soul through the recitation of magic *mantras*. A mammoth festival was instituted wherein the image was drawn in a chariot around the streets of Patan each year before being carried to his temple in Bunga village for an annual stay of several months.

Initial ceremonies start two weeks before the actual chariot procession, on the first day of the dark fortnight in April, when Machhendra's five-foot image, with red face and eyes benevolently lowered, is carried from his temple in a small palanquin to an open field, Lagankhel, in Patan where the party is thought to have rested when bringing him into the valley. Here, amidst thousands of cheering, adoring devotees the idol is bathed in holy water. The ancient sword of the King of Bhadgaon is carried here in procession, representing his presence as in olden days. An invitation also goes to King of Kirtipur, nowadays presented to the headman of this village from whence come the men who pull Machhendra's chariot near the end of the festival.

Now the idol is handed over to those who during the next few days perform ten ritual ceremonies for Machhendra which Newars themselves undergo. Idol-painters, always from a certain family, recolour Machhendra and repaint his features. Now he is carried back to his temple in the dark of night to await his installation in a splendid chariot waiting at Pulchowk area, ceremonies which take place on the first day of the bright lunar fortnight in April or sometimes early May.

Before this ornate chariot or *rath*, vehicle of the gods, protrudes an upward-curving horizontal beam of great length, ornately carved with the serpent head of Karkot the Snake God, who helped procure Machhendra from Assam. Above the temple-like throne room containing the idol, rises a fifty-foot steeple or spire of wooden cross-pieces lavishly bedecked with evergreen branches, flowers and coloured festoons. This massive vehicle moves on tremendous primitive wheels of solid wood in each of which dwells the spirit of the four Bhairab deities who frightened off the demons from Assam so long ago.

On the fourth day of the same bright fortnight Machhendra begins a spectacular journey from Pulchowk area through the narrow, rough stone streets of Patan aboard the creaking, cumbersome chariot whose towering spire sways precariously close to the several-storied buildings. Machhendra's chariot is always followed by another, only slightly less grand, containing the idol of Min Nath, popularly called Chakuwa Dev, considered to be Machhendra's daughter – or often his son. When Chakuwa Dev's *rath* is pulled from his temple which stands across the street from Machhendra's Patan shrine, people say 'he is going to Pulchowk to receive Machhendra'.

As the procession inches along the narrow lanes, hundreds of celebrating devotees swarm alongside and in its train to worship the God of Harvest. Those who pull the thick ropes of the chariot, or push it from the rear, consider it a sacred duty. Hundreds who cannot share this honour surge in just to touch the ropes, hoping thereby to receive the good fortune which befalls those who do the work. Bands of barefoot musicians and marching soldiers provide noise, music and colour, while excitement and religious fervour seem to charge the very air.

The great lumbering vehicles may progress only a few hundred yards each day and reach the final destination at Jawalakhel perhaps months later, depending upon the auspicious moment carefully calculated by astrologers as to when they may move forward, and also on the number of breakdowns and repairs the raths may undergo. In 1969 one of the great chariots was set ablaze, probably from ceremonial lamps left by devotees at the idol's feet, and it remained in the middle of the street for days waiting for the spire to be repaired and recovered with foliage. Incidents such as this make the people uneasy, for they consider them ill omens.

In certain predetermined areas – Gahabal, Sundhara and Thati in Patan – the chariots remain overnight, or perhaps for several nights, depending upon the chariots' condition and whether or not they can be moved. At each halt the inhabitants of that neighbourhood swarm out to present offerings to Machhendra, to touch the heavy wheels of Bhairab, and the long wooden yoke which represents the Snake God. They gaze at the splendidly decorated tower, which may be slightly askew by this time, and watch or join the wildly celebrating crowds. Animals are sacrificed to pacify the Bhairab gods in each wheel whose motion this deity controls, for these wrathful Bhairabs have been known to crush a straining rope-puller who may slip and fall under the wheels. Each night surrounding householders indulge in merry gatherings for feasting, drinking and celebrating with relatives and friends.

When the procession again passes Lagankhel, the chariots are made to circle three times the tree representing Machhendra's mother, an ancient form of honour and respect. On reaching Thati area there may be a delay of several days while astrologers calculate with particular care the timing of the last move to Jawalakhel, for upon arrival there 'the sun must be in the northern hemisphere'. During the stop at Thati two men climb to the uppermost section of the chariot's spire and drop a coconut into the crowd. Hundreds eagerly await this moment, for they say the person who catches it in the mad scramble will be blessed with sons. It is commonly repeated that when Lord Machhendra stops near Pode Tole the women of that area sleep the night without clothing, for Machhendra is supposed to come for a nocturnal rendezvous.

The climax of the celebration takes place in an open field at Jawalakhel any time between May or August. When the auspicious day arrives the word travels far and wide, as in all festivals where the timing is fixed by astrologers. They come by the tens of thousands, many keeping an all-night vigil, burning oil-wick lights in Machhendra's name. For this is the day of *Bhoto Jatra* when the sacred waistcoat, or *bhoto*, will be displayed for the entire populace to behold.

It seems that Karkot Naga the Snake God once gave a dark velvet, jewel-encrusted shirt or *bhoto* to a farmer who was also an eye-healer who had cured the 'eye sore' of his serpent queen. After some time the splendid garment was stolen by an evil spirit. One day, at the Machhendra festival in Jawalakhel field, the eye-healer saw someone wearing his long-lost shirt. A great quarrel arose between the two. Karkot Naga, who happened to be attending the ceremonies disguised as a human, settled the matter amicably by presenting the disputed garment to Lord Machhendra for safe keeping for ever after. Now each year the *bhoto* is fluttered from the archway of the chariot, that the straining, excited populace may catch a glimpse of this sacred relic and be assured of its safety.

For this occasion Kumari of Patan, a little girl deified as a living goddess like the famous one in Kathmandu, is carried to Jawalakhel to witness the exhibition of the *bhoto*, where she is surrounded by admirers swarming to make offerings. The King and Queen of Nepal, government officials and military officers join their countrymen to pay homage to Machhendra and to see once again his sacred shirt.

People say during this holy day some rain 'must' fall as a sign of Machhendra's benevolence, and it invariably comes, bringing roars of joy from ecstatic crowds. Many who spend the day picnicking on the grounds dance with glee, faces raised to the gathered clouds, while others fall prostrate before Machhendra's chariot to kiss the dust on which it rests. No matter how fair the skies may be at the onset of *Bhoto Jatra*, it is a mistake to attend without an umbrella.

Now a ritual is performed in which Lord Machhendra bids farewell for another year to his companion Chakuwa Dev whose chariot stands near-by. Sweets of native brown sugar and rice, called *chaku* and *wa* respectively in Newari language, are offered to Chakuwa Dev in Machhendra's name, even as a mother pacifies her child with gifts of food at leave-taking. Now Machhendra is removed from his chariot and receives a smart military honour guard while a volley of gunfire cracks in salutation.

Before Machhendra leaves the field a priest climbs to the top of the chariot spire and drops a copper, bowl-shaped disc to the ground in an ancient ritual which is watched with great trepidation, for if it falls to the ground face down this is a good omen, foretelling rainfall and prosperity for the valley. But if it lands 'mouth open' to the skies, the people may suffer from hunger and want.

The great God of Harvest is now carried in a small, gilded palanquin back to Bunga village with singing crowds and a joyous fanfare from country musicians. He is installed in his 'birthplace' temple with the same ceremony required of Newari men during their 'initiation' rites into their old and powerful social organizations, guided by a long iron key down a path sprinkled with holy water.

Once in twelve years – the next in 1980 – the festival of Machhendra is held on an even grander scale; he is then pulled in his chariot all the two miles to Bunga village across the Nakhu River. On these occasions the 'showing of the Sacred Garment' is here performed at his original home.

Popular legend tells of a snake who kept closely to his home near the Nakhu River at Bunga to avoid the money-lender to whom he was hopelessly indebted. When April came, however, he ventured out to watch the chariot procession of Red Machhendra, leaving his wife with a warning to reveal his whereabouts to no one. No sooner had he departed than the creditor appeared at the snake's hole and the foolish wife blurted out that her husband could be found sitting atop a certain temple of Buddha, easily discernable in the crowds of spectators by his white clothing.

When the money-lender accosted his debtor, the snake was so angry with his wife that he surrendered without an argument, telling the man he could do with him as he liked, since there was no possibility of payment. Then and there the creditor decided to present the snake as an offering to Lord Machhendra. When the wife learned of her husband's fate she went crying to the Bunga temple, begging the snake's forgiveness. The resentful husband not only sent her away but forbade her to see him but once every twelfth year.

Today the serpent remains with Machhendra in Bunga, and once in twelve years, when the great lumbering chariot is pulled across the Nakhu River, the snake-couple meet for one brief moment. But sometimes in the dead of night people from villages around the river hear the she-serpent weeping, alone in her underground home.

4 BUDDHA JAYANTI PURNIMA
The Full Moon of Lord Buddha's Birth

For 2,500 years the followers of Lord Buddha have consecrated Purnina, the day of the full moon, in late April or early May, as 'The Triple Blessing', heralding the day when their beloved Master was born, the day he later received enlightenment, and the day on which he passed away into Nirvana about 483 BC. Ever since The Blessed One's birth at Lumbini village, near her southern border, Nepal has been hallowed ground for millions of Buddhists round the world.

Prince Gautama Siddhartha was son of an Aryan Hindu king, born miraculously from between his mother's ribs as pictured in countless Nepalese stone reliefs. After a pleasant childhood he was early married to a cousin, the beautiful daughter of a neighbouring raja. During his twenty-ninth year, when the miseries of illness, old age and death and the merits of asceticism were revealed one after another to him, Gautama developed an abiding compassion for suffering humanity and a growing dissatisfaction with life and all its vanities. Ten years after marriage, on the night his son was born, Gautama unobtrusively left the palace and began his long, wandering search for Truth. Disillusioned by the teachings of Brahman hermits, he finally underwent solitary penance in the forested hills of northern India, but insight and enlightenment did not come.

It was during this lonely time of meditation and failure that the saint was assailed by terrible temptation, symbolized in legend as Mara, the evil disturber. Somehow Gautama found the strength to prevail against his tormentor and during the ensuing days his mind began to clear, doubt vanished, and the significance of all things became apparent. With the dawn of the day of the full moon came Perfect Knowledge. Then Gautama was recognized as the Buddha, the One Enlightened.

The remainder of his life was spent walking the dusty roads of India, and probably into the hills of Nepal, teaching the Word to thousands of followers, a philosophy embodied in human kindness. He taught that man is not judged by caste, creed or colour; that he is master of his Self. He believed in learning as opposed to blind faith, and the renunciation of all earthly desire to attain Nirvana, that exalted state of highest spiritual peace, for the souls of men will continue to be reincarnated again and again on this earth so long as anger, greed, jealousy and self-interest rule their hearts.

When Buddha passed away into Nirvana on the full moon day of his eightieth year he left behind a philosophy which would in time grip the minds of a third of the world's inhabitants. In centuries that followed he was deified by his adherents and though his basic doctrines remain intact, most Nepalese Buddhists embrace a pantheon of Hindu gods and Buddhist saints whom they worship through the mystic rites of Tantrism.

Now Buddhists come from foreign lands to visit The Compassionate One's birthplace in Lumbini, while Nepalese Buddhists make long pilgrimages into India, where he meditated and received enlightenment at Buddha Gaya, taught in Benares and passed away at Kushinagar.

On his birthday the focal point for Buddhist activities is the massive, white-domed stupa which crowns Swayambhunath hill just across the Vishnumati River from Kathmandu, the largest, most sanctified of all Nepalese Buddhist shrines. Erected by saints over 2,000 years ago, this tremendous circular hemisphere is said to cover and protect the Divine Light of Swayambhu, The Self-Existent One who radiated as a flame from a lotus blossom atop this hill when the waters left the valley in remotest times. Many believe this *chaitya*, or lotus-bud-shaped stupa, contains certain sacred relics of Lord Gautama Buddha. Subsequent saints, monks and kings have surrounded the great stupa with monastic cloisters and a forest of small idols, temples, statues and miniature *chaityas*, which today enshrine the entire sacred site.

From the white dome of Swayambhu stupa rises a tall, gilded spire, on all four sides of which are painted the tremendous 'All-Knowing' eyes which gaze out in each direction from this highest point in the valley. Lids lowered over half-veiled pupils, these wide, oriental, ever-watchful eyes may appear drowsy or benign, or again accusing and awesome, according to the conscience of the beholder. In lieu of a nose is a gigantic, spiralled red 'question mark', an ancient symbol denoting *dharma* – virtue – the only path to the 'ocean of happiness'. The tremendous *vajra*, or 'thunder-bolt', ensconced before the stupa is said to represent the power of Buddha's all-pervading knowledge over the divine strength of Lord Indra, King of the Heavens.

All through the night of full moon Swayambhunath is ablaze with light from butter lamps and electric bulbs. Its glowing spire, outlined in white moonlight, against the blue night sky is visible for miles around. Devout Buddhists come by hundreds, many from distant places, to spend the night fasting in Lord Buddha's name, chanting prayers for his blessing of World Knowledge, as they have done since time immemorial.

Sunrise finds the temple and hilltop gaily decorated with flowers, festoons, bunting and ancient religious tapestries. Hundreds of prayer flags flutter from streamers strung from the temple spire out over the great courtyard. A colossal, gilded figure of Lord Buddha is displayed, as are hundreds of smaller images to which fasting devotees bring offerings of rice, coins, flowers and flaming wicks, bowing to pray before each image. Gorgeously robed monks perform religious ceremonies with solemn, stylized, prayerful dances. Processions, led by yellow-gowned monks and followed by faithful adherents, carry Buddha down the long flight of steps to the cloister at Naghal where rituals of worship are performed before he is again returned to his hilltop shrine.

Parading groups march through the streets of Kathmandu, Patan and Bhadgaon with images of Buddha, prayers flags and banners. Religious symposiums are held at which the story of his life is reviewed, together with the world-wide significance of his message.

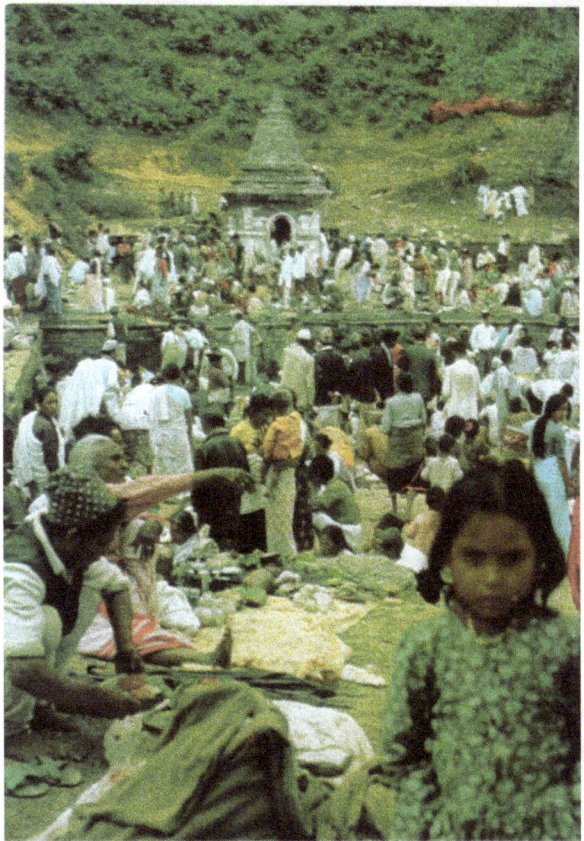

. Holy bathing at Mata Tirtha, six
miles southwest of Kathmandu, in
remembrance of deceased mothers on
Mother's Day   (Teeka Simha)

Picnicking and worship in honour of
dead mothers at Mata Tirtha on
Mother's Day   (Teeka Simha)

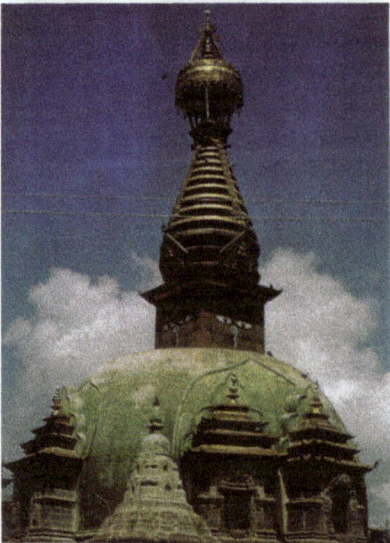

5. Spire of Swayambhunath temple glows on the full moon night of Lord Buddha's birth   (Teeka Simha)

Swayambhunath temple with 'All-Knowing Eyes of Buddha' (Betty Woodsend)

The *lamas* of the famous Buddhist stupa at Bodhnath, seven miles east of Swayambhu, mount an image of The Master on the back of an elephant and follow it around the shrine in solemn procession, their long maroon robes swaying majestically as they chant in unison praises to his name. They circle as well as a smaller shrine near-by, a replica of Bodhnath called Chabil in honour of the Indian princess Charumati, daughter of Emperor Ashoka, who converted all India for a time to Buddhism. She married a Nepalese prince and in her old age, it is thought, erected this lovely monument to Buddha some two thousand years ago.

Thus on Lord Buddha's birthday thousands of Buddhists, together with their Hindu brothers, pay homage to his exalted name, just as the tolerant Nepalese hold Jesus Christ in highest reverence.

MAY-JUNE

5   SITHINAKHA OR KUMAR SASTHI
The Birthday of Warrior-God Kumar

Ask any Nepalese to identify Kumar and he immediately portrays a handsome valiant young warrior-god who courses through the skies on a peacock. His brother is Ganesh, the elephant god who controls success, and his father is none other than the mighty Lord Shiva. Ask why Sithinakha Day is celebrated and he replies diversely that it is Kumar's birthday, the beginning of rice-planting season, the day for cleaning wells, the conclusion of Newar people's *Dewali* worship and the time for stone-throwing fights.

Sithinakha is known as *Kumar Sasthi*, Kumar's Sixth Day, marking the occasion of his birth in the bright lunar fortnight of May. Newars call it *Sithinakha*, possibly using *sithi* as a corrupt form of *Sasthi* or Sixth Day, while *nakha* implies a celebration. To many, however, Kumar is actually known as 'Sithi'.

Kumar's military prowess is legend, as is the earthy story of his birth.

It seems that in the dawn of creation the gods were once utterly vanquished in one of the titanic wars with the demon hordes which fill the pages of Hindu mythology. This humiliating reversal came about when the demons, by virtue of having practised abnormally severe penances, austere abstinence and pro-longed spiritual meditations, had accumulated such enormous religious merit and so many all-powerful boons that they became invincible – mightier than the gods themselves.

When the demon leader ousted Lord Indra from his throne, this King of Heaven called an assembly of the gods wherein Lord Vishnu predicted that nothing could be done until the advent of a saviour who would be born in time to the supreme god Shiva. Straight away Agni, the God of Fire, was dispatched to Shiva's celestial palace at Kailas, among the Himalayan snowpeaks, with an urgent plea for assistance.

It so happened that Agni, disguised as a common religious mendicant, found the great Lord Shiva bedded with his recent bride Parbati. After an interminably long wait, the importance of his mission overcame the God of Fire's patience and he burst into the bedchamber. When he discovered he had interrupted the divine couple's love-making, Agni was completely mortified, the goddess completely embarrassed, and Shiva was wild with rage. Just as the great Lord rose up to reduce Agni to ashes with a powerful flame from his Third Eye, the terrified Agni remembered his disguise and thrust out his hand begging for alms. Now the pious bride interceded, dissuading her husband from committing the cardinal sin of mistreating a religious beggar. Then Shiva, still burning with anger, ejected a handful of fiery semen into the beggar's cupped palms. This Agni accepted without a flicker and, devout Hindu that he was, gulped it down, bowed low in obeisance and beat a hasty retreat.

The semen of the enraged Lord so scorched the God of Fire's stomach that he vomited it into the sacred Ganges River. From this divine sperm the baby Kumar was born, Son of Shiva, the great messiah for whom all the gods had waited. He was reared by the Mother Ganges and in time went to live with his father, where he grew to manhood with his brother Ganesh and was trained for war. Eventually the mighty Kumar-Kartikeya led the divine forces of the gods against the demon hordes and completely annihilated them. Indra was reseated on his heavenly throne, the jubilant gods regained their prestige, and Kumar has since ranked high in the Hindu pantheon.

Above the entrance to many Nepali homes is carved the image of the elephant-headed Lord Ganesh. His brother Kumar is represented as a red circle traced on the ground before the doorway where the earth has been purified with a mixture of red mud and cowdung. In this sacred circle is drawn a lotus of six petals representing Kumar-Kartikeya, whose six different faces portray in turn the one who illuminates the world and removes ignorance, the one who grants boons to his devotees, protects the fire sacrifice, reveals the knowledge of self, destroys evil demons, and looks lovingly upon the face of his bride.

During important religious ceremonies of the year the sacred items of worship and offering are disposed of by placing them in Kumar's circle, later to be cleaned away by a person of the sweeper caste. Occasionally, this symbol, worshipped as Kumar himself, is decorated with seeds, sweets and beads in the belief that it furnishes protection from all distress. On Kumar's birthday, called Kumar's Sixth, religious ceremonies are performed with the offering of six types of cakes, six types of bread, vegetables and grains, all placed within his sacred symbol.

During the Kumar festival lotus-shaped miniature paper wind-mills are fixed on rooftops to spin in the breeze, or made to whirl by little boys as they run through the streets. This windmill on Kumar's day is symbolic of the end of evil times and the ushering in of an era of righteousness.

On Sithinakha day a curious mock battle is still waged in many villages, wherein the inhabitants meet on the river bank and hold a great feast. Then they separate into two groups and pelt each other with rocks and stones. Nowadays this is usually carried out by youngsters only, but many years ago it was a serious matter, for those on either side who were injured, captured or defeated were offered to Goddess Kali in bloody human sacrifices.

This strange practice allegedly originated when one of the ancient Malla rulers had a dream wherein the god Skadaswami divined that, if all the boys in the city should be assembled on this day and kept near Goddess Kankeswari Kali's temple on the Vish-numati River below Kathmandu, the King's subjects would never revolt and his enemies would be destroyed. The God suggested that he himself had been taught by his parents in boyhood to play at stone-throwing during this month. The Raja, taking this to be a warning from the great Lord Shiva, assembled the youths and established the custom of rock-hurling warfare whereby the maimed and vanquished were slaughtered and their blood offered to Goddess Kankeswari.

It is said this dangerous game was abolished, at least in Kathmandu, by Prime Minister and Maharaja Jung Bahadur Rana around 1870, when a non-participating onlooker, British Resident Colvin, was struck by a flying stone.

To Nepalese farmers, Sithinakha marks the beginning of the rainy season, when corn may be planted in the hills and rice sown in beds for later transplantation in the terraced fields. Many on this day place all their musical instruments, a vital part of Newari life, in the custody of Nasa Deo, Lord Shiva represented as the god of dance and music, and there they remain until the heavy work is done.

Nepalese, long considered the best of farmers, look forward to rice seedling transplanting, a time of strenuous labour alleviated, typically, by laughter, songs and rice-beer. Knee-deep in water. groups of men bend double to turn the muddy earth with the short-handled *kodali* hoe of their ancestors, while shouting an impromptu song. Behind them groups of brightly dressed, laughing women answer this tuneful jest with an impromptu song of their own as they stoop to thrust seedlings into the rich grey slush.

Sithinakha also marks the end of the one-month Dewali period, when Newars of related ancestry gather for great feasts and complicated rituals to honour their family gods and goddesses. Clans who have not completed this annual worship are seen on this day carrying baskets of freshly bathed idols on temple-like palanquins out through the open fields to the deities' aboriginal counterparts – usually a row of crude stones. Raw eggs are broken over them, cow's milk is dripped from a conch shell and goats are sacrificed to honour the gods of their forefathers. Now the clan is seated in a large square according to strictest seniority, to indulge in a huge meal served on traditional plates of pressed green leaves, a ceremony older than written history.

This, too, is designated as the day for cleaning wells, tanks and ponds, long considered the abodes of the Snake Gods, for now the pre-monsoon water levels are at their lowest point. This day is

chosen because the serpent deities themselves are away performing their ancestral Dewali worship, for in Nepal the deities
undergo the same religious rites as the people. Thus the wells can
be cleaned with lime when disturbing the Snake Gods can be
avoided. A little mica, the glittering mineral found so abundantly
in the valley soil, is tossed into the well as an offering to the
Nagas.

Chronicles tell how the city of Bhadgaon was once surrounded
by a thick fortifying wall and moat, the maintenance, renovation
and cleaning of which were the responsibility of every citizen of
the town, regardless of caste. Any person who failed to complete
his assigned section by Sithinakha day was duly punished.

Many perform the rite of cleaning wells to propitiate the
Mother Earth deities, especially Basundhara, Goddess of Agricul-
ture, who is worshipped before any well or watering place is dug.
Another tradition is that all construction should be completed
by Sithinakha Day lest calamity befall the project – usually coming
in the form of monsoon rains which quickly undermine unfinished
mud-brick buildings.

The actual festival procession or *jatra* for Lord Kumar is held
the day following his birth, the seventh day of the waxing moon.
In the morning thousands come to his temple near Jaisidewal in
north-western Kathmandu, bringing offerings in baskets and
trays, and to carry away *prasad*, blessings from their brave warrior-
god in the form of red powder for the forehead, or leaves and
flowers for the hair. Kumar is the ancestral Dewali deity of the
Newari *Bhakta* clan who comes in droves to pay him honour and
to watch his evening procession. Usually there is a long delay, for
the *Bhakta* people say that Kumar's *jatra* cannot commence until
'a million people have assembled'.

When the idol of Kumar is at last removed from the temple and
placed in an ornate, gilt-roofed palanquin litter, the long base
poles are hoisted upon men's shoulders and a joyful procession
moves around the winding city streets. Above the shrine where
Kumar rides surrounded with flowers, flickering lamps and food
offerings, one man twirls a heavy, fringed umbrella, that ancient

symbol of paramountcy. Troupes of happy musicians, thumping drums and clanging cymbals, follow in their wake.

Finally, when God Kumar has been sufficiently exalted for another year, he is returned to his temple home, the crowds disperse and the farmers put frivolity behind them for the next three months, for no major festival will interrupt their rice planting until the night when the mythical demon Ghanta Karna is carried to the river for joyous cremation.

JULY-AUGUST

6 GHANTA KARNA
The Night of the Devil

The Nepalese people are for ever haunted by evil spirits, fearful demons, witches and devils, who are said to infest their homes and roam the land. Some people live in mortal fear of neighbours possessed of the 'evil eye', who practise the black arts of malevolent curses and magic spells. But there is one certain night during the monsoon season particularly favourable to the evil activities of all these creatures of the Devil, and it falls on the fourteenth day of the dark lunar fortnight in July or early August, which is traditionally the last day for rice transplanting.

This is the Night of the Devil, when Nepalese celebrate their victory over the most dreaded of all demons to terrorize the countryside in ancient times.

Ghanta Karna, often known as Gathemuga or Gathemangal, was a devil of towering strength with glaring, evil eyes, the fangs of his gaping mouth dripping with blood of his victims. He was so corrupt that he vilified the gods themselves, defiled and destroyed homes and fields, roaming the land, stealing children, maiming the weak, killing and devouring his captives. His depraved sexual orgies and unspeakable excesses with his countless wives horrified the pious people.

He was a sworn enemy and rival of Lord Vishnu, the Great Preserver, and wore ear-rings of jingling bells to ensure that even the very name of this god should not pass his ears and thus weaken his powers of evil and black magic. The people therefore called him Ghanta Karna, Bell Ears, and prayed for his extermination.

In final desperation the populace held a great meeting and

prayed for help. One god complied, appearing amongst them in the guise of a common frog. One day, when Ghanta Karna was gloating over his latest orgy of cannibalism and destruction, singing and dancing in fiendish glee, he discovered that a tiny frog was imitating and mimicking his every move. Enraged at the creature's insolence, Ghanta Karna lunged at him, but the frog jumped beyond his reach. The maddened fiend gave chase, but with each giant step the frog leaped just far enough in advance, all the while drawing Ghanta Karna closer to a deep well.

On reaching the well the wily frog jumped in and the monster, thinking victory was his, plunged in after. Quickly the people swarmed about the trapped Ghanta Karna, stoning and clubbing him to death. Then in joyous procession they dragged the gigantic, repulsive corpse to the river for cremation, throwing his ashes into the water, and there was peace in the land once more.

The Nepalese still honour the common frog by special rites later in the year, but on the Night of the Devil they celebrate Ghanta Karna's death and beg their gods for protection against the curse of evil.

On the morning of Ghanta Karna groups of mischievous urchins erect simple arches and crosses of leafy branches at a street intersection in each *tole*, or city district, for it is well known that cross-roads are the favourite haunts of witches and evil spirits. '*Jagat? Jagat!*' they screech, begging a small toll from all passers-by, pedestrians as well as motorists, to defray the cost of a great mock funeral procession and victory feast to be held later in the day. They say Ghanta Karna left his wives penniless, and the wives had to enlist little children to beg for funds to cremate their fiendish husband.

During the afternoon, effigies of Ghanta Karna are erected at cross-roads around the city, and outlying villages as well, made from leafy bamboo poles, bound near the top to form a tall tent-shaped structure. A vividly painted, glowering demon's face is affixed to the body, and a pumpkin marked with evil sexual organs is placed at its feet. People come to hang tiny cloth devil dolls on the effigy, and toss coins to it, hoping thereby to avoid the ravages

73

of disease and the wrath of evil forces. Some say the bamboo poles for the effigies were carried into town during the previous night past tightly shuttered windows, for it is taboo for any person to witness their passing.

The main character in the festival is a Newar man of the untouchable *Pode* caste who has the dubious honour of impersonating Ghanta Karna, his near-naked body painted with lewd symbols and pictures depicting all types of sexual depravity. During the day he goes about town crying, 'Ghanta Karna is dead!' carrying a clay begging bowl hung from a pole. People are not likely to refuse him, for his curse can bestow all kinds of afflictions and misfortune.

Toward sundown an eager crowd gathers around the bamboo effigy awaiting the untouchable Ghanta Karna. Suddenly they scurry to make room for the garish impersonator as he strides through the mob, holding his begging bowl and shouting hoarsely, '*Om Shanti, Om Shanti*', promising peace on earth to those who give. The spectators whistle and jeer, but coins drop into the bowl none the less.

'*Aja de ha! Aja de ha*,' he cries, 'I am the father of your father!'

Suddenly flaming torches are thrust into the man's hands. The crowd draws closer as he circles the effigy three times and quickly seats himself between the bamboo legs. Men snatch the torches, set the leaves afire, and with one mighty shove cast the flaming effigy to the ground, forcing the wild-eyed Ghanta Karna to sit upon the bamboo poles. Then, roaring with victory, they drag the effigy off towards the holy river with the sweating Ghanta Karna riding amidst the smoke and flames of the effigy's burning leaves.

Along the way the rowdy crowd taunts him, threatens him with fiery torches, and showers him with shouted vulgarities, for it is generally believed that vile language may frighten or even kill certain evil demons. They look for excitement during this gay funeral procession, and usually find it when they enter a locality where the people of that *tole* are performing their own Ghanta Karna ceremonies. It so happens that some of the bamboo effigies represent male demons, while those of other localities are thought to be female. The crowd with the male demon attempts to place its effigy atop the female effigy and a great mêlée results amidst raucous laughter and streams of obscenities. Often fisticuffs and injuries result before the bedlam subsides and the two groups proceed toward the river, still drawing the living Ghanta Karnas on the bamboo pyres.

At the river banks the effigies are set fire in earnest, burned to the ground and the ashes thrown into the water to roars of approval from everyone. The bedraggled *Pode* man is threatened with the same fate, but eventually wrenches free from his tormentors and streaks away through the night. At least he has a bowl of coins for his trouble, which some say is a dependable yearly income for a man of this caste.

People who must be abroad on this dark night keep an eye out for witches and spirits, while many prefer to remain locked within their homes. They say that at midnight on Ghanta Karna night the evil spirits migrate to their favourite haunts and to their temples, their forefingers held up before them like a burning torch as they float along above the ground. The witches evoke their guardian goddesses, usually at temples of the mighty, bloodthirsty Kali, for success in the black arts and to initiate disciples into their gory cult. Favourite gathering places for witches and spirits, they say, are Singha Satal in Kathmandu and the hillock called Mhaipi on the road to Balaju.

Some housewives perform a strange ceremony called *Balipuja* on this night, filling an old clay pot with dirty husks, curdled blood and buffalo entrails, covering this unholy mess with fruits, flowers and rice, topped with a flaming cotton wick. This gruesome offering is left at the cross-roads in the hope that the gluttonous appetite of the witch will be appeased, and she will not search further for human victims.

To be avoided at all costs are those said to have an 'evil eye', those who wander aimlessly about weeping, uttering strange sounds, their bodies unclean and unkempt. They are said to have an unquenchable appetite and to walk with one hand held up before them – a sure indication of their affliction. Their evil spirits, if aroused, can enter one's body, sapping the strength and will. To provoke the curse of the 'evil eye' is a fate worse than death.

On Ghanta Karna day crowds gather around the streetside trinket-vendors, purchasing inexpensive iron rings thought to be magnetized by the touch of Ghanta Karna and to afford the wearer immunity from evil power. Old people believe that if such a ring is not worn on this day the cuticle of the ring finger will surely become inflamed.

In many homes rituals are performed to cleanse the premises of evil and drive away the haunting spirits. Iron pegs, especially made for the purpose, are nailed to the threshold to discourage their entrance. Effigies of wheatstraw, nettles and certain fruit leaves are burned through every room. A small area of mud plaster is scraped from a corner wall into an earthen pot, replaced with a mixture of cleansing cowdung and mud. Then the pot and burning straw torches are cast into the cross-roads dump where all unclean and 'impure' materials are disposed of. These dumps are known to be the haunts of certain dreaded goddesses who protect the neighbourhood under normal circumstances, but can bring calamity and disease if neglected and allowed to go hungry.

Finally, with the ending of the Ghanta Karna rituals, when everything possible has been done to free the people, their houses and the land from the menace of evil for the coming year, Nepalese families gather to celebrate in great, convivial feasts of thanksgiving, usually in the home of the senior clan member.

7 GUNLA

The Sacred Month of Lord Buddha

The fifteen days before full moon of August or early September, and the fifteen which follow, comprise the sacred lunar month of Gunla, as holy for the Buddhist population as Lent is for Christians, or Ramadan for Muslims, or the four months of Chaturmas for Hindus. During these auspicious thirty days Buddhists devote themselves with great enthusiasm to fasting, penances, pilgrimages and holy ceremonies, with a typically Nepalese climax of feasting, merrymaking and rejoicing.

The focal point for Gunla activities in Kathmandu is the massive, white-domed stupa called Swayambhunath, dedicated over 2,000 years ago to Adi Buddha, The Self-Existent One. To this lofty shrine the people come each day of the Buddhist holy month, starting long before sun-up, hurrying through the city streets in groups, thumping drums, clanging cymbals and blowing flutes in an ear-splitting but joyful cacophony. Fasting, singing and praying, the devotees climb the 365 steps that lead to the stupa where they slowly circle the sacred shrine, trailing their hands to spin the hundreds of metal prayer wheels set into its base. Each whirling cylinder is filled with printed paper prayers, and each is embossed with the mysterious, sacred phrase, *Om Mani Padme Hum*, the untranslatable benediction of peace.

Worshippers hurry among the temples and idols to leave their offerings, to stand silently for a moment in the milling, unnoticing crowd before each god, with eyes closed, palms together, whispering a prayer. Others recite the praises of Lord Buddha for all to hear.

Many enter the large *vihara* or monastic cloister that shelters a towering, twelve-foot gilded image of Buddha, to leave offerings among banks of flowers, smoking incense and small flaming oil wicks, tossing rice, red powder and coins over all. They bow before their Lord, while at one side seated rows of shaven-headed Buddhist monks or lamas in heavy wine-coloured robes keep their gentle, intelligent faces intent on prayer and the counting of their beads. The loud drone of their rapid chant is shattered periodically by deep, mournful blasts from several eight-foot Tibetan trumpets and the booming of a large drum which stands beside a man-high prayer wheel.

Hundreds queue before the temple of Sitala Ajima or Harti Ajima, Goddess of Smallpox, that powerful Grandmother of the World who, if angered and left hungry, harasses little children even unto death, but when appeased alleviates all sorts of troubles and disease. When a child is vaccinated against disease in the modern way, offerings are immediately taken to Ajima, so deep-rooted is the belief, among Hindus and Buddhists alike, in her efficacy.

Crowds mass before the near-by Buddha, enshrined in the ledge of Swayambhunath stupa, for he is the Supreme Lord of the Universe, the messiah who was born to redeem the world with his message of universal love, brotherhood and non-violence for all living creatures – a doctrine he pursued in action as well as taught.

Musicians and devotees ascend the steps again through crowds of new arrivals, pariah dogs and bold, bare-bottomed monkeys who never need fear ill treatment here. Nowadays foreign ascetics and pale-faced 'flower children' in flowing robes and sandals wander through the crowds, having come half-way round the world, some in earnest quest of the Gentle Way of Buddha. But others come to sample the readily-available drugs and stimulants judiciously used through the long centuries by the Nepalese, especially during religious meditation, pilgrimages and ceremonies requiring physical endurance and prolonged concentration, but used with a moderation and propriety little understood by visiting Western youths.

By mid-morning most worshippers are back at their homes, having perhaps stopped along the way to worship the Hindu idols of Ganesh, the elephant god of good fortune, Bhairab, the Terrifying One, or the mother earth goddess Kumari – for Lord Buddha, the Great Master, is a deity of utmost tolerance.

During all thirty sacred days devout Buddhists invite priests to recite the teachings of Buddha in their homes. Pious householders, their families gathered at their knees, read from the holy manuscripts; sacred hymns are sung; images of the compassionate Buddha are displayed; and musical bands blare forth at all hours of the day and night. Each evening the devout congregate at the *viharas* and monasteries, intoning hymns in Buddha's name amidst smoking incense and lighted butter lamps, their deep voices rising in a jargon of rhythmical choir-like chanting.

On each day of Gunla Buddhist housewives fashion tiny votive images – figures of Buddha, various deities, and toy *chaitya* shrines – from special clay pressed into moulds, each image 'given life' by the insertion of a grain of unpolished rice. At the end of Holy Month the number of these tiny idols is supposed to total at least one and a fourth *lakhs*, or 125,000. Then families and related caste groups form processions that move toward the sacred river, chanting hymns, escorted by local musicians, while women in their best finery and jewellery carry burning incense. At the river bank the votive images are dumped in a heap around which the procession passes three times, for circumambulation of idols and sacred shrines is a vital part of ceremonies of worship all through the year. With the completion of the rituals the idols are immersed in the sacred waters.

This month is traditionally a time of arduous fasting, especially for village women who come to the city *viharas*, take the vow of abstinence, and subsist, it is said, on a few handfuls of consecrated water administered daily by Buddhist monks. These pathetic, emaciated creatures huddle in rows in the shadowy gloom of the sanctuary, concentrating on the great Lord Buddha, arousing the curiosity, admiration and reverence of visiting devotees.

This severe fasting penance is endured in the hope of reaching Nirvana, the highest spiritual peace, or again to acquire prosperity, freedom from debt or other devastating troubles, and often for the return of an erring husband. Their pitiful appearance, sometimes their impending death, or the condemnation of family and friends induces the husband to come for his wasted wife at the end of Gunla, usually with a decorated palanquin in which to bear her home. There he decks her with new clothing, holds a feast in her honour and nurses her back to health, for it is believed that a wife's month-long fast is sure to bring wealth, good fortune, a son, or possibly all three to his household. Sad is the situation of the wife whose husband fails to collect her, for this indicates the end of their marriage.

Throughout Gunla are held Buddhist festivals such as Pancha Dana, the Ceremony of Five Offerings, on the eighth day of the light lunar fortnight – a week before full moon. This is a festival of charity and benevolence in old Patan town, a famous centre of Buddhism in earlier times, when five kinds of food – unhusked and polished rice, lentil seeds, wheat and salt – are offered to the revered 'begging' monks in a sacred, ancient ceremony of alms-giving. Legend commemorates this as the day when Prince Siddhartha commenced his ascetic period of meditation, after which he gained enlightenment and was called the Buddha. It is the day when the Buddhist priestly caste is honoured in remembrance of the time when they lived solely and honourably from the alms of their devotees.

For Pancha Dana homes and shops are decorated with flowers, festoons and sacred pictures. Women sit with large baskets of five offerings, dispersing them in handfuls to a procession of monks wearing sacerdotal robes and crown-like head-dresses, who pass by, begging alms and chanting hymns in the time-honoured tradition of their ancestors, even as Buddha did before them. The monks touch the forehead of each donor with their sacred books, bestowing the benediction and protection of Buddha.

Lord Buddha so loved the poor that he once blessed a child whose only offering was a handful of dust. During his legendary visit to Patan in ages past, when he was simultaneously offered the humble gift of an impoverished old lady and the sumptuous alms of the King of Patan, Buddha accepted the woman's gift and be-

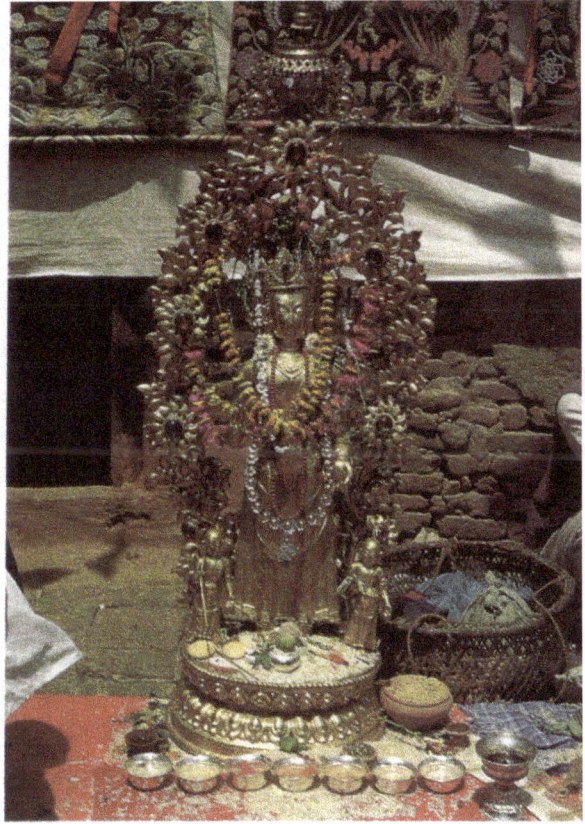

6. Buddhist deity displayed at Swayambhunath temple in honour of Lord Buddha's birthday (Betty Woodsend)

Buddhist Lamas perform a ceremonial 'prayer' dance on Lord Buddha's birthday at Swayambhunath temple (Betty Woodsend)

7. Bands of dancing musicians, with jingling ankle bells and carrying
flaming torches, parade in honour of the dead during Mata-Ya festival in
Patan   (Betty Woodsend)

Hill women in festival finery gather before Mahadev (Shiva) temple at
Kumbeshwar Pond in Patan for the Sacred Thread Festival

(Teeka Simha)

stowed his blessings upon her. Seeing how the hard-earned alms of the poor were so precious to Buddha, the King laboured for many days as a blacksmith, donating his wages to beggars. Only then did Buddha accept his alms and bless him. In remembrance of this day the grateful ruler built a *chaitya* called Dipavati, a stupa still standing in Patan. And in Guita Tole area of Patan where the old woman lived, people still make their Pancha Dana offerings in her name.

For this day the caste organizations of each *tole* or locality of Patan arrange a great feast to honour and worship the begging Buddhist priests, an event which brings women and children crowding on to balconies and housetops to watch the ancient, annual 'feeding of the monks'. At nightfall the arrival of a certain lama ringing a sacred bell announces that Pancha Dana is over, after which no Buddhist priest may accept food nor beg for alms in Patan. Two and a half weeks later, on the thirteenth day of the dark lunar fortnight, the same Pancha Dana ceremonies are observed in Kathmandu and Bhadgaon.

Bahi Doe Boyegu, the exhibition of the gods in the *viharas*, commences three days before full moon, on the twelfth day of the light fortnight, and may continue for several days, depending upon the whim of the community responsible for certain *viharas* or Buddhist cloisters. During *Bahi Deo Boyegu*, especially in Kathmandu and Patan, religious relics and idols of ancient Buddhism are displayed to the public, often behind wooden lattice screens in the courtyard porches.

Hundreds come to gaze with awe and reverence at these sacred objects. At Tham Bahal are ancient religious texts of musty parchment lettered in gold, by the 'thumb of Saraswati, the Goddess of Learning', they say, or perhaps by Manjusri, the Buddhist saint who made Kathmandu Valley habitable for man. Termite-ridden idols and images, carved from wood, reveal the artistry of ancient craftsmen. Cloth paintings and wide tapestries depict the adventures of saints and heroes of Buddhist scripture and legend. Over-size grains of rice, said to have been grown in the valley in remotest antiquity, are displayed, as well as moth-eaten ceremonial robes and silken costumes, and hundreds of lengths of wrinkled cloth donated by devotees to the gods, gifts to be returned to the donor after death so that he may be properly clothed in Heaven.

In the Tham Bahal temple at Kathmandu is displayed a crumbling three-foot wooden image of the goddess Nini Maju, who introduced the making of alcoholic spirits to the valley people in ancient times. In Patan's Guita Baha a strange manikin stares from an upstairs window – the poverty-stricken old lady whose alms Buddha accepted so long ago. Year by year these displays become more depleted, but what remains tells of the fine workmanship of the ancient religious objects. Throughout the celebration of *Bahi Deo Boyegu* both rich and poor file through. On the second day of the waning moon even the Living Goddess Kumari, in one of her rare public appearances, is carried around on a decorated platform to view the sacred antiquities of Buddhism.

On the day of the full moon, when Buddhist and Hindu alike don the 'sacred wrist thread of protection', to be described in a later chapter, devout Buddhists hold special religious ceremonies at an ancient, grass-grown stupa on the eastern edge of Patan, one of four such monuments thought to have been built by Emperor Ashoka, the great Buddhist ruler of India, when he visited Nepal two hundred years before Christ.

Of great importance during Gunla month is the remarkable Mata-Ya or Festival of Lights, always held two days after the full moon, when hundreds of Buddhist men, women and children carry lighted lamps and flaming tapers to honour their dead in a gruelling, day-long pilgrimage through the maze of streets and alleys in old Patan town. Accompanying them are countless groups, dressed identically in their distinctive caste attire – their very finest – singing the praises of Buddha at the tops of their voices, crashing cymbals and thumping drums in the name of their dead. This day commemorates also the joyous victory over the evil Mara, the Disturber, who tried unsuccessfully to tempt Lord Buddha from his meditations. Traditionally one should change one's dress or costume and partake of various feasts nine times during Mata-Ya day in celebration of Buddha's victory.

Starting near dawn, the parade sets off at a run along a pre-scribed route through rough winding lanes, crooked alleys and nar-row passages of the crowded residential areas. Ankle bells jingling, torches smoking, the devotees toss gifts of rice, coins and clouds of sacred red powder on hundreds of Buddhist idols, shrines, *chaityas* and holy places which are to be found in private courtyards and in the alleys and pavements throughout the town. Bearers trot after them, carrying heavy baskets of offerings and supplies of oil for the lights, suspended on poles from their bouncing shoulders.

The faster they run, the hotter the day becomes, and the greater their suffering the greater will be the comfort which comes to the souls of their dead. Breathless paraders rush past crowds of spec-tators on temple steps, in the doorways, or leaning out of upstair windows. By midday the panting, sweating pilgrims have slowed to a trot, their hair, ears and clothing blood-red with sacred pow-der, and still they come, some soberly tossing coins and offerings in the name of their dead while others shout songs to honour Buddha's victory. By afternoon many a pilgrim is exhausted.

A number of half-naked men suffer special penance by pro-strating themselves in the dust before each and every shrine, and by sundown, hands and knees bleeding, they can scarcely pick themselves up. Others are fortified with quantities of home-brewed liquor; or dressed as scarecrows, or clowns, or demons with cloth faces, or as massively-muscled women, or as mendicant Lord Shivas in mangy tiger skins, or as ogres in bearskins. They cavort and dance in wild celebration to entertain the crowds or to gain religious merit for the souls of their dead. Undoubtedly this freakish costuming is a continuation of the previous day's 'cow procession for the dead', which is described in a later chapter, as are other festivals which happen to fall during the month of Gunla.

On the day following the close of Gunla, the first of the bright lunar fortnight, hundreds of celebrating Buddhist families gather on the holy Swayambhunath hill, beneath the All-Seeing Eyes of Buddha. There, literally covering every level of the hillside, with lightened hearts and purified souls, crowds indulge in an all-day picnic, with merrymaking and a lively outburst of music – the final celebration of the Buddhist faithful.

8 NAGA PANCHAMI
The Day of the Snake Gods

Though one seldom sees a live snake in Kathmandu Valley, they are very much with us, as evidenced by the wood, stone and metal carved serpents which adorn the idols of gods and kings, the temples and shrines, water taps and sunken ponds and even homes and shops. For since time immemorial the Nepalese have respected, feared and worshipped snakes, believing there are Serpent Gods who for six months inhabit the face of the earth and the remainder of the year dwell far underground as a pantheon of Nagas or Snake Deities. Down in Patal, the Netherworld, the Nagas have their own kingdom, called Naga-Lok, the Realm of the Snake Gods. In Naga-Lok the Nagas maintain an organized society, accepting the rule of a Naga Raja or Snake King, dwelling with their families in homes or palaces, displaying both human and superhuman qualities much as the higher echelon of gods and goddesses.

The Nagas, like all the gods, require propitiation, respect and devotion, and when properly assuaged they bring the vital rains, grant increased wealth and give protection for jewels and treasures. But an angered, unappeased serpent deity can cause drought and famine, death from snake bite and disease, loss of possessions, and that awful calamity, the collapse of homes and buildings.

Many a foreigner has been startled to hear a Nepalese home-owner's distraught announcement that 'his house has fallen down', a relatively common occurence during the monsoon rains. Often the foundations of mud and clay-brick dwellings are set in rice fields and if the underground Snake Gods are not properly and faithfully assuaged, their angry writhings and gyrations are sure to bring destruction. Traditional precautions must be taken to pacify the Nagas before starting constuction, for when a site is chosen for a new building, the ground area must be divided into eighty-one geometric portions. After studying these divisions in relation to the position of the celestial bodies at that particular time, the astrologers can determine the location of the underground Snake Deity. At this specific point a paper image of a snake with a human face must be placed, and the foundation can be constructed without fear of offending the Nagas.

While Naga Panchami is the annual day set aside for the worship of snakes, many people perform small *pujas* throughout the year in places where Snake Gods are said to dwell, in the corners of gardens and courtyards, in drains and near water spouts, pools, springs and streams. To avoid disturbing the Nagas, wells are cleaned only on one certain day each year, Sithinakha, when the Nagas, like the people, are out worshipping their ancestral deities. For most Nepalese it is taboo to take a life, and to kill a snake lends the added danger of angering the Snake Gods. Some believe that when snakebite occurs, magic words and incantations may charm the snake to return in secret and withdraw the venom from the wound, restoring life to the dying and sometimes the dead.

Snake Gods are widely worshipped as controllers of rainfall. When there is a dearth of moisture, special ceremonies are directed at the Nagas, imploring their blessing of rain, while many milk their cows into the sacred Bagmati River to feed and appease the Nagas. Farmers perform *pujas* at Taudah Pond chanting, '*Pani dio Naga Raja*', beseeching the Snake God Karkot Raja, who has always made his home in this tank, to send water to the land.

Long ago, before human memory, all Kathmandu Valley was a lake called Naga-hrad or Naga-vala, the Abode of the Snake Gods. When the Buddhist saint Manjusri came from China and with his sword struck a deep ravine in the encircling hills and let the water drain away as the Bagmati River, all the Nagas were driven out except Karkot Raja, King of the Snake Gods. He was induced to remain, given power over the wealth of the valley, and a permanent home in Taudah Pond beyond Chobar Gorge, where he dwells to this day.

They say that the early descendants of the valley people suffered from prolonged drought inflicted by the gods as punishment for the sins of their ruler, who had committed incest. This king, however, had been initiated into the Tantric 'mysteries' by a teacher from Swayambhunath monasteries, and with his magic powers he had summoned all the Snake Gods and forced them to produce rain. When all the Nagas appeared at the King's command, except their own Karkot Raja, the ruler proceeded to Taudah Pond and overcame the Snake King by surrounding him with *mantras* or magic spells, impelling him to attend the gathering. Seeing this miraculous feat, the Snake Gods fell down before the King, each presenting him with a picture of himself drawn in his own blood. They further declared that a dearth of rainfall could be dispelled hereafter by the worshipping of these images, as is done to this day during Naga Panchami.

The day of the Snake Gods falls during the monsoon rains on the fifth of the brightening lunar fortnight late in July or early August, actually within the Buddhist holy month of Gunla. Every shop, temple, mansion and hut honours the Serpent Deities by displaying pictures of Nagas over the doorways and holding cere-monies of worship before them. First the lintel beam over the entrance door is cleansed with water and cowdung by a Brahman or the head of the family. Using a dab of dung for adhesive, a vividly coloured paper drawing depicting the Serpent Gods is affixed to the area, strings of cotton-wool balls are festooned around it and a paste of red powder and rice is applied to the Naga's forehead as a sacred *tika* blessing. The family gathers to perform a *puja*, offering flowers, incense, burning wicks and a sprinkling of holy water. Food is set out for the snakes – milk or rice water, honey, curds and boiled rice. Prayers are intoned to pacify the Nagas and to evoke their protection and blessing.

Legend says that a demon king, Danasur, once ruled the valley and managed to steal the wealth of Indra, King of the Gods and Heaven. Indra enlisted the aid of powerful Karkot Raja, who retrieved the treasures by causing them to be floated into the Bagmati River. When Karkot returned the stolen valuables to Indra, he kept one-fourth of the bounty for his reward. Perhaps this explains why Karkot now lives deep under Taudah Pond in a fabulous palace of gold and silver, the walls studded with gems.

Although the Snake Gods are thought to have the power to cure or cause disease, the legend persists that Karkot's wife once suffered from 'eye-sore'. Finally Karkot transformed himself into a Brahman priest and ascended to the surface of the valley in search of an eye-healer. In this disguise he had no difficulty in persuading one such man to follow him to the edge of Taudah Pond. There the eye-doctor was asked to close his eyes and miraculously found himself transported to a glittering subterranean palace where the Naga Queen, Karkot Rani, was seated on the throne. Within a few days he healed the Queen's eyes and was whisked back once more to the surface of the earth. In payment, the Snake King bestowed priceless gifts upon the healer, among which was the famous *bhoto*, or jewelled shirt, which is displayed during the Machhendra chariot festival in Patan.

Karkot's queen had lapses of character, like other goddesses and humans. Once a Newar farmer came upon her committing adultery with another Naga, and he dealt her such a blow with his bamboo pole that she fled in pain and terror. When she recovered her dignity, the Queen reported the incident to King Karkot, neglecting to point out the act which prompted the farmer's deed. Soon thereafter the farmer was confronted by the monstrous Karkot Raja, whose raised hood and fiery eyes signalled that he was about to strike. But the man demanded to know why he was to die. In the ensuing discussion, the Queen's misdeed came to light. Karkot Naga returned to his underground palace and dealt his wife many more blows than had the farmer.

Other Snake Gods are well known to all Nepalese. Takshaka Naga, angered at being driven from the valley when the waters receded, developed the sinful habit of striking people without provocation. However, he contracted leprosy and was duly punished. To atone for his sins and thereby rid himself of the disease, Takshaka returned to Kathmandu Valley to perform a severe penance and abstinence in honour of Lord Shiva. Now it seems that the Bird God, Garuda, ever jealous of any oversight of

88

his master Lord Vishnu and long renowned as an enemy of all the Snake Gods, attacked Takshaka and held him under water. Immediately Lord Machhendra, here called Lokeswar, came riding on a lion to rescue Takshaka. This in turn brought Lord Vishnu to assist his faithful carrier, Garuda, and there ensued a mighty quarrel.

When peace was established, Takshaka Naga coiled himself about Garuda's neck in mutual friendship, Garuda took Lord Vishnu on his back, and the lion lifted them both upon his shoulders and flew to a hill five miles east of Kathmandu, where the Changu Narayan temple is located. There, to this day, is the image of a lion, the Bird God, Lord Vishnu and Lokeswar, one atop the other. They say the image of Narayan, another name for Vishnu, enshrined in this temple periodically becomes damp with 'sweat'. It is then said that Garuda is fighting the Nagas again. Temple priests carefully wipe away the beads of moisture from Narayan's face with a cloth, and in former days this consecrated linen was presented to the King of Nepal. Now, it is said, when the cloth is cut into strips and worn by devotees, they become immune to snakebite.

Lord Krishna often appears in the pictures of Nagas over doorways on Naga Panchami day. According to the scriptures, Garuda the Bird God harassed the famous serpent deity Kaliya Naga, driving him from his rightful home in Dwipa. Kaliya was forced to take up residence in the Jamuna River near Brindaban where Krishna lived with the cowherders, and for four leagues around a whirlpool of water boiled with the poisonous venom spewed from this angry Naga's 110 heads.

One day, when the herd boys were playing, Krishna jumped into the river to retrieve their ball. Immediately, Kaliya Naga rose up and vomited poison from all his hoods, wrapping himself about Krishna again and again, but each time the mighty boy Krishna made himself so huge that the snake lost its hold. Suddenly Krishna, who himself is an incarnation of Lord Vishnu, jumped atop Kaliya's head and performed a dance before the anguished cowherds. Then he assumed the weight of the whole universe, immobilizing the powerful Kaliya, who dashed his hoods about, spewing blood and poison from every fang. At last, when he saw that Krishna was unaffected by this powerful venom, the Snake God capitulated, knowing at last that this was the Lord himself. When Kaliya prostrated himself before Krishna and all the Naga's wives begged that his life should be spared, Krishna, true to his teaching, forgave the Naga and sent him back to his home in Dwipa with the promise that never again would he be endangered by the Bird God, once Garuda beheld the awesome footprints of Krishna on Kaliya Naga's head.

To devotees of Shiva, the snake worn about his neck or coiled at his waist is a symbol of the eternal cycle of the ages. On Naga Panchami day many visit his temple at Pashupatinath to worship the snake images. Here all who worship Shiva must first do obeisance to the fearless Basuki Naga, whose temple stands adjacent to Shiva's. Ancient chronicles reveal that Basuki Naga was appointed to guard the fabulous treasures of Lord Shiva which are said to be locked still within Pashupatinath temple.

Once when this temple of Shiva was inundated by the flooding Bagmati, a greedy water goblin stole two of Shiva's most prized possessions: the sacred *rudraksha* nut which he wears on a necklace and his 'right-sided' couch. When the goblin swam away in the swift current, however, the vigilant Basuki Naga chased him down and after a violent struggle recovered the invaluable keepsakes for a grateful Lord Shiva. Old people say the valley formerly was free of theft and snakebite due to the vigilance of Basuki Naga at Shiva's temple, and many believe a snake stays coiled within their own money and treasure box, usually thought to be a small white serpent protecting the contents from theft. Regularly small dishes of milk are set near the box, a food offering for the guardian snake.

They say that once the old Newar king, Jaya Prakash Malla, lacking sufficient funds to raise an army against the threat of invasion, cast his eye upon the fabled wealth stored at Pashupatinath. When he ordered the chief priest to unlock Shiva's treasure room, the King was terrified to see the enormous Basuki Naga coiled about piles of silver and gold. The snake glared at the King with crested hoods raised, flames darting from his eyes. Immediately the ruler ordered the doors to be locked again and story has it that never again did this King covet the divine treasures of Shiva.

On the outskirts of Bhadgaon is a large, cemented water pond called Sidha Pokhari, where a wicked Naga once dwelt who floated objects of shining gold on the water's surface to entice people to their death. A Tantric holy man from nearby Thimi village devised a plan to overcome this serpent, bringing to the pond a companion to whom he had given careful instructions. The Tantric was to enter the water and transform himself into a serpent; if the companion saw milk rising to the surface he would know the Tantric had been killed by the Naga and all was lost, but if blood rose in the water, this was a sign that the Tantric had overcome the Snake God, and when the Tantric emerged from the pond the companion must immediately shower him with magic rice to restore him once more to human form.

With all this understood, the holy man slid into the water. Now when the companion saw blood rising to the surface, he forgot all his instructions and ran screaming for Thimi. The Tantric, still in snake form, followed, pleading with his friend to throw the rice, but the terror-stricken man merely ran faster. At last the holy man resigned himself to life as a snake, returned to the pond and is living there still. But to this day the people of Thimi cut a wide swathe around this pond, fearing the Tantric snake may still take his revenge.

The story long associated with Naga Panchami day is of a poor peasant who accidentally killed three baby snakes while tilling his field. The bereaved mother serpent, filled with rage, entered the farmer's house and struck dead the farmer, his wife and two sons with her venomous fangs. When she turned glowering upon the one remaining daughter, the awe-struck girl suddenly snatched a bowl of milk and set if before the snake. Surprised and pleased, the mother serpent drank the milk and said, 'Good daughter, on this Naga Panchami day you have fed me milk and therefore I shall not kill you. For your kindness and devotion, ask of me any boon you like.'

At this the girl gasped, 'Let my dead parents and brothers live again. Let no Naga kill anyone on this day. This is my prayer.' Immediately the pacified snake, saying 'Let it be so', restored life to the family and departed in peace.

Small wonder that the Snake Gods are well fed and their images are so widely displayed on Naga Panchami day.

9 JANAI PURNI OR RAKSHA BANDHAN
The Sacred Thread Festival

Janai Purni, on the full moon day of August, is a time crammed with festivities that begin the preceding evening, continuing all through the day and lasting far into the night.

For high-caste Hindu men, Janai Purni means the annual changing of the Sacred Thread, a yellow cotton string worn about the neck and underarm beneath the clothing of Brahmans, the learned priestly class, and Chetris, who were originally warriors and rulers. This thread is bestowed upon males only, usually during youth, in impressive religious rituals which officially initiate them into Hinduism and must be worn thereafter on every day of their lives. The 'triple cord' symbolizes body, speech and mind, and when its knots are tied the wearer is supposed to have gained complete control over each. This Sacred Thread may be changed during the year if it becomes frayed or defiled, for example, by the wearer touching a woman in menstruation, at which time she is considered 'unclean'. But according to Hindu rules the cord must be changed without fail by a Brahman on Janai Purni day, *janai* meaning sacred thread, and *purni* stemming from Purnima, the day of the full moon. Some believe it was on this very day in late summer, far back in antiquity, that Hindus first donned the thread and vowed to wear it for all time.

On the preceding day the wearer makes himself 'clean' by shaving, cutting the hair, paring the nails and bathing. He must observe a partial fast, taking only one meal of foods considered 'clean' – no meat, onions or garlic. Next morning, on Janai Purni day, a Brahman, usually the family priest, comes to the home. The entire family gathers round while he reads from the holy book, performs a ceremony which sanctifies the new thread in the name

93

of Lord Vishnu, and places it about the recipient's neck. In payment the priest is given foodstuffs and money in an amount commensurate with the family's means.

Now for men, women and children of every caste, regardless of station, Hindu and Buddhist alike, Janai Purni is the day when the sacred yellow thread called *Raksha Bandhan* is tied about the wrist – the left for females, the right for males. *Raksha* means 'protection', while *bandhan* signifies a bond or restriction. The wearer believes that it will endow him with good fortune. Tradition says that this sacred wrist-string should be worn for three months – until Laxmi Puja, during the Festival of Lights, when, no longer yellow, it is removed and tied to the tail of a sacred cow. Thus when death comes to the donor he has a better chance that a cow will be waiting to assist him across the River Bhaitarna, and through various other barriers along the route to the Gates of Judgment, by allowing the dead soul to cling to her tail.

On the night before Janai Purni hundreds of worshippers gather at the sacred sunken square pond called Kumbeshwar in Patan. This *pokhari* lies in the courtyard of the five-tiered temple of Mahadev (another name for Shiva) which houses two three-foot Shiva lingams. These phallic idols represent Lord Shiva himself and are found in great number throughout the valley. All are sacred, but certain ones, such as Kumbeshwar, possess greater powers and attributes than others. The first lingam in this temple is a pillar of gilded metal with five faces of Shiva carved around the head. Beside it stands a second, the entire body of which is covered by a coiled snake carved in gold. It is this second lingam which must be moved into the sunken pond the night before Janai Purni.

For this ceremony crowds pack the Mahadev courtyard, covering the steps leading to the temple's open archway behind which the lingams stand. Reflected in the glow of oil lamps is the ascetic face and shaven head of the scarlet-robed officiating priest. His lips move in prayer as devotees reach over the shoulders of the throng to hand him garlands for the lingams, toss in coins and offerings, and receive Shiva's blessing from the priest in return. Hundreds crowd about the adjacent Kumbeshwar pond, watching young men rough-house in the sacred water, diving, splashing and shouting up to the spectators.

Suddenly there is a long, mournful blast from a great ceremonial trumpet and the mob surges back towards the temple. Nine musical troupes, each in turn, circle Shiva's shrine, pushing through the eager crowds with a blowing of trumpets and a frenzy of beating drums. From her temple bordering the courtyard the image of the goddess Bagala Mukhi Ajima, borne on the shoulders by several men, is carried through the spectators, and is 'presented to Lord Shiva'. Now the officiating priest carries the heavy, gleaming lingam, wreathed in garlands, through the courtyard, assisted by a surrounding throng. Before each slow, ponderous step is taken toward the pond a guiding priest reads a phrase from an ancient holy text, often drowned by the blare of music.

When the procession finally reaches the pond's edge, the lingam is suddenly rushed down the steps, out over the wooden walkway and deposited under a canopied platform in the centre of the water. The crowds roar their approval, boys in the pond throw water high into the air, drenching the lingam, the priests and the spectators. Now at last the stage is set for the early morning Janai Purni festivities. Most people surge through the courtyard door, but hundreds remain far into the night, listening to the weird, rhythmical tunes of several musical groups, the most accomplished in the area.

On the morning of Janai Purni the worshippers arrive long before daybreak and by sunrise a mass of humanity covers the lingam platform in the water, the wooden walkway leading to it, the cement steps and the surrounding walls of the pond. They come in thousands. Men clad in loincloths submerge in the murky water, bowing with palms together to the sacred lingam of Shiva before clambering up the slippery steps to retrieve their clothing. Boys splash about for coins tossed to Shiva by the crowds. Offerings of flowers, rice and scraps of fruit float on the water. Women scoop up handfuls of the liquid to sprinkle over their heads before moving off through the throng to receive the sacred *raksha* thread.

95

In the courtyard pandemonium reigns. People crowd around Brahmans squatting on the verandah below a great peepul tree, absorbed in the sale of yellow string which he ties deftly about the wrist of the buyer, intoning a quick prayer and reaching for the next customer. The prescribed blessing he gives is, 'Thus I tie the *Raksha* round your wrist, the same which bound the arm of the mighty Bali, king of the Danavas. May its protection be eternal.' Perhaps this is a subtle reminder to the people of the extraordinary acts of charity performed by King Bali, as recorded in the ancient texts.

It seems Raja Bali had taken a sacred vow to grant every wish and request made of him, a vow considered the highest form of charity. His boundless benevolence, piety and devotion finally won him a place superior to Indra, King of the Gods, and all the deities ruling the Three Worlds. Seeing their realms under Bali's rule, the dispossessed gods appealed to Lord Vishnu, who came to their assistance disguised as a dwarf. Knowing Bali had taken the holy vow of charity, the dwarf begged from him as much land as the tiny man could cover in three full strides. The moment Bali granted his wish, the dwarfed Vishnu swelled to the size of a tremendous giant and in two mighty strides stepped across Heaven and Earth. When the giant demanded where he might take the promised third step, King Bali said, 'I have no more lands to give you than you have legs to measure with.' With this Vishnu caused a third leg to grow from the giant's navel, and demanded an answer.

At this miracle King Bali knew he faced the Lord himself and in deepest reverence placed the giant's third foot atop his head and was pushed far into the bowels of the earth. Thus Vishnu restored the Three Worlds to the rightful ruling gods and repaid Bali for his last act of earthly charity by making him King of Patal, the Underworld, where he is believed to be ruling still. Legend explains the gods' success by the fact that one of them wore a silken *raksha* about his right wrist.

By mid-morning of Janai Purni most people at Kumbeshwar pond have received their wrist threads, but groups continue to

8. Snake-decorated lingam, phallic symbol of Lord Shiva, installed on a platform in the middle of the sacred Kumbeshwar Pond at Patan for the Sacred Thread Festival
(Betty Woodsend)

Devotees throng to leave offerings to the Snake-encrusted lingam in the Kumbeshwar Pond   (Terry Bech)

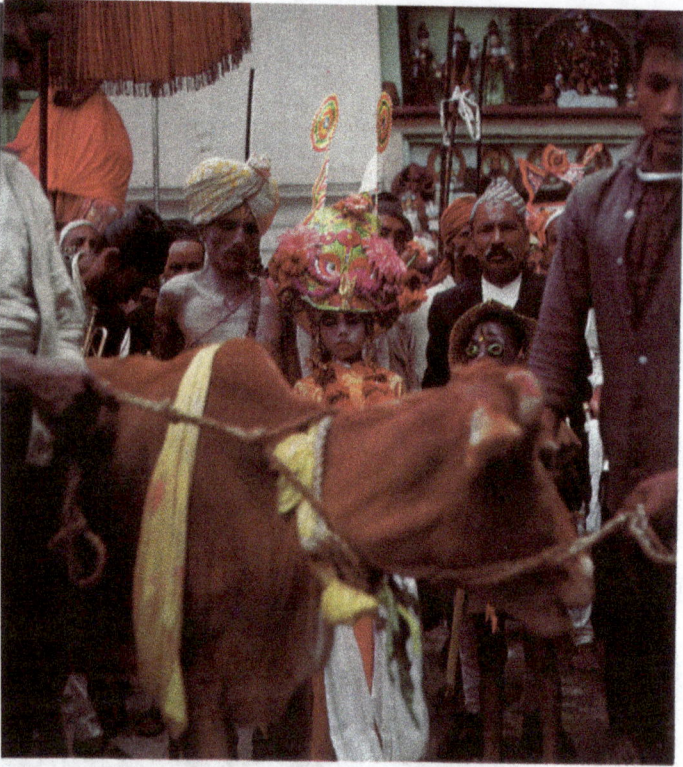

9. Live sacred cows, and boys costumed to represent them (with flower headdress), accompanied by yogis, parade to honour the dead in Kathmandu   (Teeka Simha)

Hill women in festival finery wait to receive sacred thread at Kumbeshwar Pond   (Teeka Simha)

come throughout the day. Later that night the Shiva lingam is carried from the pond back to its temple with the same pageantry that accompanied its going. Here it remains until the next year's Janai Purni festival.

To Lord Shiva's great temple at Pashupatinath, north-west of Kathmandu, crowds also converge long before daybreak on Janai Purni. Worshippers give alms of rice and coins to beggars and cripples on the walk that leads to the temple gates, take holy baths in the Bagmati River, do *puja* to the sacred Shiva lingam and receive the *raksha* thread for the wrist. People say on the day before Janai Purni this famous temple is closed, the only occasion in the year, for on that day Lord Shiva visits the sacred lake of Gosainkund.

This beautiful lake, twenty-five miles north of Kathmandu Valley at an altitude of about 16,000 feet, was created, legend says, by Lord Shiva himself. It seems he drank poison which threatened to engulf the world and all mankind, and in search of fresh water struck with his trident a glacier at Gosainkund. Water gushed forth to quench his thirst and formed this sacred lake. On Janai Purni thousands of pilgrims trek, sometimes from great distances and for several days, to attend the religious *mela* or fair, camp on the sacred shores, take holy baths in the waters, and worship in Shiva's name. On the climb through rarified air to Gosainkund, awe-struck pilgrims become weak and dizzy, and their sight blurs; then they know they have been 'possessed' by the poison which Shiva drank. Some faint and have to be carried back to their homes, never reaching the lake. Returning pilgrims tell of seeing an image of Shiva 'lying in the water', while others tell of seeing his long-handled trident or the vessel of holy water he often carries.

It is believed that in ancient times a Shiva temple actually stood on the rocks in this lake, since there exists today a reddish-brown stone which resembles a great kneeling bull, the same Nandi, servant and companion of Shiva, whose image is found before all Shiva temples.

A legend persists that long ago a devotee, while bathing in Gosainkund lake, dropped his brass water pot and it sank out of sight. Some time later it miraculously appeared in Kumbeshwar Pond in Patan, mentioned above. People believe the vessel made its way from the mountain lake through some subterranean river into Kumbeshwar Pond, a belief given further credence by the fact that the water of the Patan Pond remains abnormally cold throughout the year. Thus on Janai Purni day thousands of devotees, unable to make the long mountain trek to Gosainkund, are content to bathe at Kumbeshwar.

Janai Purni is also a day which honours the common frog in a ceremony called *Byancha Janake*, Feeding the Frogs, observed mostly by those from farming communities. Food is left in the fields and ditches, especially *quati*, a dish linked by tradition with Janai Purni. People believe the frogs bring the life-giving rains, since their croaking is heard by Lord Indra, Ruler of the Heavens. Country people think that their fields, like humans, are subject to the influence of evil spirits, such as the wicked demon Ghanta Karna, who was finally led to his death by a frog. A similar legend relates how the demon Daitya was lured by a frog into a muddy rice-field where he became hopelessly bogged, so that the people were spared once more.

The frog is held in such high veneration that its dried meat is offered throughout the year to the dreaded goddess of smallpox, Sitala, whose curses have long harrassed the people of Nepal. But on Janai Purni day the frog is honoured as a friend to all mankind.

For the Nepalese people the special dish *quati* is mandatory on Janai Purni day. It is a wholesome, tasty gruel, made from boiling nine varieties of dried beans after they have sprouted by soaking in water. Much relished, *quati* is said to sooth intestinal ailments prevalent during the hot, rainy season. Perhaps on this day, when people cleanse and purify themselves with holy bathing, they also hope *quati* will purge disorders from within.

Thus the day of the August full moon means many things to many people and the Janai Purni ceremonies enhance the welfare of the living, bring comfort eventually to the souls of the dead, and sustenance to the frogs in the fields.

AUGUST-SEPTEMBER

10   GAI JATRA
The Procession of Sacred Cows

Everyone knows of Yama Raj, the God of Death who decides at what level the souls of the deceased shall be reincarnated again on earth. He maintains a great ledger in Patal, the Underworld, wherein is recorded every mortal's birth, his good and bad deeds, and the predetermined date of his death. When one's time is up Yama sends a henchman, perhaps a black crow, to see that the released soul sets out for the judgment gates of Patal, which are opened only once each year, the day of Gai Jatra.

The route to Yama's gate may be exceedingly difficult, leading possibly through rivers of fire, and most bereaved families pray that a sacred cow may guide and protect the spirit of their dead along this dangerous journey by allowing it to cling to her tail. Most families also aim to ensure, by the performance of good deeds on Gai Jatra day, that a sacred cow will be in readiness at Yama's gate, where thousands upon thousands of souls are waiting, to push open the portals with her horns and assist the soul to enter for judgment.

This is why on Gai Jatra, the day immediately following the sacred thread festival of the August full moon, every recently-bereaved family must honour the soul of their dead by sending a religious procession through the streets along a route prescribed ages before. The Gai Jatra, or cow procession, consists for each family of a live, decorated cow or a young boy gorgeously costumed to represent one, together with the family priest, a troupe of musicians and a small boy in the guise of a *yogi* or holy man. After early-morning rituals for the dead at the home, each parade starts on its way to join hundreds of similar groups in an endless procession past temples, idols and holy places along the narrow, winding streets. Householders give food and coins to members of each procession, including the cow, real or impersonated. All must pass by the ancient royal palaces – Hanuman Dhoka in Kathmandu – and it is believed the old Malla kings kept census of the annual death toll by counting each group. When the cow processions return to the bereaved households, religious ceremonies are again performed and the cloth 'tails' of the cow-costumed boys, which drag along the ground during the pilgrimage, are cut into strips and tied about the necks of family members to protect them from misfortune.

Gai Jatra ceremonies vary with financial status, religious inclination and locality. In Patan town the processions do not parade as separate units as in Kathmandu. Instead, all the costumed boys meet at a central point and proceed around the shrines and rocky streets, accompanied by as much noise as the blaring musicians, beating drums, clanging domestic utensils (tied to the cloth 'tails' of the cows), and huge stone-filled metal rollers, which are dragged over the cobble-stone lanes, can produce. It is thought that this commotion may appease some irate deity and perhaps frighten away evil spirits or the wrathful souls of the dead who, through neglect, return to haunt the homes of their kinsmen.

Bhadgaon inhabitants stage spectacular processions, in which bereaved families engage persons to parade for their dead with heads encased in huge, cloth-covered baskets to which horns of straw and a painted cow's face are affixed. Families of means make enormous cow-heads by wrapping long bamboo structures with cloth and having them carried through the streets to a din of local music.

In some villages the entire populace participates in one long procession in which the masked inhabitants hold the tail of the preceding masquerading 'cow', carrying ploughs and other rural implements. They parade through a number of neighbouring villages, return for tremendous family feasts and at night gather in the town square for religious rites, to watch performances of local dancers, and to sacrifice animals to their gods.

One example of village Gai Jatra rituals took place in the hamlet of Tikanpur near Thankot. A rural family had lost both father and son some months earlier, at which time the bodies were cremated and the ashes scattered upon a near-by stream. On Gai Jatra day the entire bereaved family and clan gathered in a small upstairs room around two young boys ornately costumed to represent cows. From vividly coloured woven cane caps two bamboo sticks protruded, topped with brilliant circular festoons signifying the horns, between which the white paper mask of a cow was fixed. Garlands of flowers and jewellery hung about the boy's necks. Draped around their waists over flowered sari skirts and trailing the floor were widths of white cloth representing tails. Their dark sombre eyes, ringed with lampblack, looked enormous above perspiration-streaked dabs of yellow on their cheeks.

In a haze of burning incense and smoking cotton wicks an old priests intoned a prayer from a frayed holy book while sprinkling the 'cows' with holy water, rice, red powder and flower petals. In the background the ageing mother sobbed hoarsely, while mourning women murmured prayers. Suddenly a drum sounded outside and the smoke-permeated crowd clomped down the ladder stairs in procession, out across the muddy courtyard, up slippery stepping stones and a narrow footpath leading through the village. Behind trooped the grieving relatives, neighbours and a band of musicians blowing horns, clashing cymbals and frantically beating drums. Bringing up the rear was a gaily costumed troupe of 'actors' to perform rice-planting pantomimes at each halt along the route.

At the temples of Narayan, Ganesh, and Natisuri (the goddess of music and dancing), and at countless homes the procession paused for an outdoor performance, receiving from each household scraps of food and some rice-beer. Needless to say, things became livelier as the morning progressed.

As a 'first act' a comically dressed man representing a lowly field worker, one leg painted white and the other orange, mimed the pulling up of young rice seedlings, moving rhythmically with the beat of the music. Next the two little 'cows' were driven round and round, miming the tilling of the soil, guided by a colour-fully costumed young ploughman representing the *yogi* or ascetic. His graceful gyrations under the reins, in a fancy series of side-steps, brought cheers from the crowding throng of spectators.

Now the 'ploughed soil' was ready for hoeing by a lively farmer, who chopped away in stylized, exaggerated steps. When the music blared forth again, four slender young men leaped into the circle, dressed in bright saris and the headscarves of women rice planters. Moving backwards, they stooped in unison, mimick-ing the thrusting of seedlings into the mud. Twisting and dancing among them, two 'overseers' shouted directions, delighting the spectators with their song, 'If you women plant the rice well, we'll give you your pay.' Through all the acts an energetic master of ceremonies cavorted and pranced, slipping in the mud, announc-ing the numbers and swaying under upstairs windows to catch in his hat coins tossed down by laughing women and children.

Four hours (and many drinks) later, when the procession returned for a last performance at the bereaved family's courtyard, the effects of a long and strenuous day began to show. Two of the 'rice planter girls' quarrelled, one standing with tears streaming down his muddy face while amused adults held off the angry younger boy. Each maintained the other had pushed him and torn his sari. Then the master of ceremonies, after a particularly lively performance, threw his hat in the mud in disgust and pointed out the meagreness of the offerings tossed down from the windows. However, when the band struck up again everyone returned to his act and all was forgotten.

A married daughter of the bereaved family performed the final rites of washing the 'cow's' bare muddy feet, bending to touch them with her forehead. The grimy cloth 'tails' were washed in water which, now considered sacred, was sprinkled over the family members. Finally, when the last prayer was intoned and the smoke and incense died away, the happy crowd joined the bereaved family in a long and joyful feast. What matter if the Gai Jatra festivities brought the family into debt? More important that the gods were appeased by the pious generosity of this simple family, for a sacred cow would be now waiting at the judgment gates to assist the souls of father and brother into Yama's kingdom.

All over the valley similar rites are performed during the morning of Gai Jatra, but the late afternoon offers entertainment of an entirely different nature, which may continue for the next eight days. In all the streets, but especially in the Kathmandu bazaar streets of Indrachowk, Asantole, and before the old royal palace at Hanuman Dhoka, the spirit of carnival is in the air. Crowds gather on the temple steps and in balconies and at the windows of surrounding houses to watch outrageously garbed citizens blatantly burlesquing Nepalese institutions, social and religious customs, the government, political leaders, the army, foreigners and sometimes the gods themselves. Anyone may join the parade to lampoon one and all.

Men dress up as freakish ladies, or as monsters and animals under mangy hides. Some wear ludicrous masks or plain white cloth over their faces, while others come black-faced or paint their cheeks and foreheads in garishly coloured streaks and designs. They parade with bands, happy very often under the influence of home-brewed libations, to clown before the waiting crowds. Farmers and villagers, free for frivolity with the completion of the rice planting, flock into the city. A man in women's attire carries a rag doll in his arms, crying that he has no milk to feed the baby and bares his breast to prove it. Another laments having to wait on his wife, bring tea to her bed and do the housework, both very improbable in Nepal. Others carry placards decrying social ills – real, exaggerated or entirely imaginary.

Local newspapers participate in Gai Jatra satire, with stories announcing a great increase in salary for the superfluous masses of government workers. Others tell of the release of all political prisoners, who are now to be absorbed into the ranks of officialdom. Again it is reported that the abolished caste system has been replaced with rank 'according to wealth'. On this day, supposedly, citizens are free to express themselves without fear of reprisal.

They say this tradition originated during the reign of King Pratap Malla in the eighteenth century, when he was desperately searching a means to quell the inconsolable grief of his queen at the death of their son. He sent out a great procession of sacred cows to parade in the boy's memory, but the queen remained despondent. He ordered the citizenry, those who had had a death in the family during the year, to do the same, pointing out to his wife the number of others who had suffered as she had done, but to no avail. At last the King announced that a sizeable reward would go to any person who could bring the slightest joy to his wife, granting the people complete freedom to go to any lengths.

When the populace appeared in droves before the palace, garbed in preposterous costumes to mimic and lampoon all aspects of social injustice and the accepted order, the watching queen could not refrain from laughing. Then and there the King ordained that such parades would be repeated every Gai Jatra day.

People still remember when those of wealth engaged great dramatic and musical troupes to enact fabulous pageants, legends, dramas and religious stories, to which they invited the general populace. It is believed that such charitable and generous deeds, performed in the name of the recently dead, will earn for the donor great religious merit – all duly recorded in the God of Death's ledger.

Some orthodox Buddhists, absorbed in ceremonies for their holy month of Gunla, do not involve themselves in Gai Jatra celebrations, and some frown upon the antics of the afternoon revellers, likening them to the demons who disturbed and tempted Lord Buddha during his long meditation in search of enlightenment.

In general, however, judging from the vast numbers of dazzling processions leading live cows or lavishly costumed youths to represent them, the clowning of hordes of afternoon merrymakers, and the size and enthusiam of the watching crowds, the majority of Nepalese follow Gai Jatra traditions as handed down by their forefathers, thereby fulfilling time-honoured obligations to the souls of the recently dead.

11 KRISHNA JAYANTI
Lord Krishna is Born on Earth

In Nepal the great Lord Krishna is one of the most adored of all deities. The stories of his miraculous birth, fabulous childhood, endless romances and many deeds of valour have sunk deep into the imaginations and hearts of the Nepalese people.

Krishna is their ideal of manhood, his doctrine of *bhakti* promising salvation to all who devote themselves completely to him while dedicating themselves to the unselfish fulfilment of earthly duties. His is a promise of the ultimate triumph of good over the ever-present evil in the souls of men.

During the seventh day of the dark lunar fortnight in August or early September, the day preceding the midnight hour glorified by Krishna's birth, worshippers carry his garlanded and ornately clothed idols in procession through the streets in their arms, on platforms on their shoulders, or in open trucks crowded with revellers. Troupes of musicians follow, while groups carry tall banners proclaiming that 'Krishna is God!'

Everywhere are colourful pictures depicting Lord Krishna in babyhood or as a handsome, dark-faced nobleman, *krishna* literally meaning 'dark'. His idols sit in shop windows and recesses banked with flowers and jewellery. Arrays of pictures affixed to walls, archways of temples and entrances of bazaar stalls tell of his fabulous loves and adventures. Pundits sit cross-legged on cloth-covered benches along the streets and in the temple grounds, reading stories of Krishna to flocks of eager listeners.

Toward evening throngs of women literally cover the great temple called Krishna Mandir in old Patan square to keep vigil through the glorious night of his birth. Their shawl-shrouded forms are silhouetted in the darkness by rows of flickering oil-wick lamps as they sit huddled along every tier of the magnificent pagoda-roofed monument, overflowing on to near-by temples as well. Their faces lit by the oil lamps and the incense burning at their knees, their bodies rocking in humble obeisance, the women chant the many names of their Lord, 'Narayan, Narayan, Narayan' or 'Gopal, Gopal'. Some sing ancient hymns to Krishna, others clap hands to the rhythm, while some bow over the oil lamps in prayer. Many end their twenty-four hour fast by sharing bits of food, munching and gossiping.

Crowds of men and women edge their way slowly up narrow steps through the seated devotees to the temple's dark interior and along the balcony on the second floor to where the main Krishna idol stands. There they offer flowers, food and coins while an old temple priest gives them a dab of red paste on the forehead or a wilted blossom as a blessing from Lord Krishna. Then they make their way down through the crush of bodies to join the multitudes in the streets.

Most people believe that Krishna was born on earth to save men's souls as a direct incarnation of Lord Vishnu, who, together with Shiva and Brahma, completes the Hindu Trinity. Thousands worship Krishna as God Himself, Lord of the Three Worlds, the primal male. The holy books, Puranas, *Prem Sagara* and *Mahab-harata*, relate his birth and the incidents of his life. Followers of the Vishnu sect celebrate his birth at midnight, while Shiva adherents worship especially at sunrise next morning on the eighth day of the dark half of the moon. Thus the day is known as Krishna's Eighth.

He was born at the stroke of midnight, bathed in a heavenly radiance, a lotus-eyed child with azure-blue complexion of such beauty that the parents were struck with awe. At birth he wore a crown of jewels and robes of yellow silk, and immediately stood before his parents – such was his strength – with four arms posed about him, holding a sacred conch shell, a disc, a mace and a lotus blossom of radiant light. Lightning flashed, trees blossomed and bore fruit, heavenly music was heard, and the gods filled the forest pools with water and rained down flowers upon the land.

But tragic events had foretold this birth.

In those times there ruled a cruel and tyrannical king, Kansa, who in reality was a demon, having been violently begotten upon his mother. Kansa gave his lovely sister, Devaki, in marriage to one Vasudev, a good man descended from the same Moon God as Kansa and Devaki, and during the lavish wedding the evil Kansa was terror-stricken to hear a celestial voice announce, 'O Kansa, thy death will come to pass at the hand of the eighth son born of this marriage union.'

Through the ensuing years the demon king put to death six boy children born to Devaki. The seventh was saved by the all-pervading power of Lord Vishnu, who caused the foetus to be transferred from Devaki's womb to Rohini's, one of the wives of Vasudev who had taken refuge with a childless couple among the cowherding people some distance away. The cowherd's good wife reared this boy, Balarama, never realizing that he was actually the earthly form of Vishnu's loyal Snake God, Shesha, sometimes known as Ananta.

Now when Devaki and Vasudev were expecting their eighth child, the cruel Kansa kept them chained and guarded in their palace and planned to murder the baby at birth. When this beautiful child was born one midnight, Lord Vishnu, watching, caused the chains and gates to be opened and the guards to be drugged with sleep. The father Vasudev, terrified for the baby's safety, carried it in a basket through the stormy night to the home of the same cowherd in Gokhul.

Crossing the Jamuna River, flood waters would have swept them away had not the infant reached his foot from the basket, touched the waves and caused the river to recede. Vasudev left his son with the cowherd's wife, exchanging him secretly for a girl child which had fortuitously been born to her that very night. Returning home, he handed the changeling baby to his wife, and they found themselves once more in chains.

During this night the demon Kansa was awakened by the terrifying warning, 'Thy enemy is born, and thy death is certain.' He rushed to Devaki, but when he found her with a girl child and turned to leave, the voice said, 'Do not disdain the girl child. She, too, can take your life.' When Kansa snatched the baby and tried to dash it to the floor, the child flew from his hand and went straight to Heaven, for she was in reality Devi, the goddess Durga. Kansa heard her voice again from above, 'You cannot kill me. The one to kill you is in Gokhul.'

The baby Krishna flourished, along with his brother Balarama, both tended by the gentle cowherd's wife. When rumours of Lord Krishna's birth persisted Kansa, in a fit of wrath, sent out his emissaries to murder all babies, sacred cows, Brahmans, and all worshippers of Lord Vishnu in the kingdom.

Nepalese love the stories of the baby Krishna withstanding his enemies. One of Kansa's agents was a horrible demoness who appeared at the cowherd's home in the form of a beautiful woman whose breasts were filled with poison. She feigned affection for the baby, but when she took him to her breast, the baby sucked with such might that he drained her very life away. Then, her original shape returned, and she fell lifeless and hideous. But as the cowherds cremated her enormous body it gave out a flower-sweet fragrance, proving that Krishna, despite the demon's wickedness, had granted her soul salvation. For, 'Blessed are all those whom Lord Vishnu slays.'

When only five months of age and lying on his mother's knee, Krishna was besieged by another fiend, who appeared as a whirlwind, which tried to sweep the child away. Krishna made his body so heavy his mother had to lay him on the ground. Enraged, the whirlwind became a roaring cyclone, but it could not move the child's weighted form. Then, seeing the cowherds weep and lament for his safety, Krishna allowed the whirlwind to lift him into the sky, from whence he dashed the demon to the ground, putting an end to the monster as well as the storm.

Krishna and Balarama lived a pleasant life among the cowherd boys and girls playing amid the grazing cattle, swinging from the calves' tails and idling in the forests. He learned to love all dairy products and often mischievously stole pots of curds and milk from the herd girls as they slept. He had a knack for climbing high shelves, spilling the curds and butter, eating some and hiding the rest. The herd girls laughed and called him 'Butter Thief,' and when they complained to his mother, Krishna always fabricated a convincing alibi. Today on his birthday the Nepalese still offer him butter and milk and sweets.

One day when playing in the courtyard, Krishna ate some clay, but denied having done so when his mother approached. Opening his mouth to look inside, she stood transfixed. There she saw the whole universe – The Three Worlds. Soon the sensible woman recovered her faculties and deemed herself most foolish to imagine that the son of a lowly cowherd could be Lord of the Universe. Thus Lord Vishnu veiled his Godhead again.

The boy Krishna's superhuman strength and bravery amazed and delighted the people of Gokhul. Through the years Krishna's feats caused even Brahma the Creator to humble himself before the marvellous boy; and Indra, King of the Gods, knew him for the Primal Male when Krishna with one finger held up the mountain Gobhardan to protect the cowherders and their lands from Indra's flooding rains.

Dear to Nepalese hearts are the tales of Krishna's prowess as a lover, with his hundreds of adoring wives and especially the thousands of cowherd girls who left home, duty and husband to follow the magic notes of his flute, hypnotized with love for this heavenly male. He stole their clothing as they bathed in the river, easily gained their forgiveness by dancing with them in the moonlight to the tune of his flute, making his presence manifold so that each love-sick girl knew she danced alone with her Lord. When he left them broken-hearted, he promised, 'Meditate upon me always, as *yogis* do, that I may always be near you.' This was Krishna's message to the world.

Once, on his travels, dressed in handsome clothes which he had pilfered from a passing washerman, Krishna met an ageing, hump-backed woman who prayed permission to rub sandalwood paste on his body. Krishna, touched by her devotion, placed his bare foot on hers, and with two fingers under her chin, lifted her up and made her straight and fair. Then he said, 'When I have slain Kansa, I will come and be with you.' Small wonder women swooned with love for him.

The *Mahabharata*, one of the supreme treasures of ancient Hindu literature, relates Krishna's endless adventures with Balarama which took him all over India and, it is thought, into Nepal, the Home of the Gods. During the great battle on the plains of Kurukshetra, near to the present New Delhi, when Krishna's friend Arjun, the most noble of warriors, became agitated and guilt-stricken at the terrible slaughter, Krishna spoke to him on the battlefield. In his advice to Arjun, Krishna pronounced the Bhagavad Gita in its entirety, that beloved epic poem with its gospel of faith in the Will of God, of devotion to duty without thought of reward, showing a practical way of life to all mankind.

Years passed, and when all plans for slaying Krishna had failed, the wicked King Kansa enticed him and Balarama to a great tournament during which he planned that Krishna should meet his death. But Krishna, despite Kansa's trickery, won every bout. Finally, when he had slain all the King's great wrestlers he sprang upon the royal dias, dragged the King off by the hair and killed him then and there. All the gods and saints and men rejoiced. Then Krishna proceded to the castle where he was born, setting his parents free from bondage, and when they embraced him, they knew him to be the Godhead.

Finally it came to pass that a strange madness seized the people of Dwarka, awhere Krishna was king, causing the citizens to fall upon one another so that they were slain to the last man. Thereafter Balarama went into seclusion in the forest, where Krishna discovered him seated under a mighty tree as a *yogi*, or meditating ascetic. As he watched, from Balarama's mouth a thousand-headed snake god issued forth, Ananta, which glided away to the ocean.

Krishna, seeing his brother departed from the human world, wandered alone in the forest and finally lay down under the influence of *yoga*. All his senses left his body. By chance a hunter mistook him for a deer and shot him through with an arrow. When the terrified man touched Lord Krishna's foot where the arrow had entered, Krishna rose and forgave him and immediately ascended into Heaven, filling the whole sky with glory. Thus ended his life on earth.

The scriptures ordain that whenever religion and virtue decline and vice threatens, Lord Krishna will reappear on earth to save the righteous and punish the wicked.

So the day of his birth is acclaimed by Nepalese throughout the land. Especially is his memory revered by cowherds and rural communities, some of whose tribal kings are said to have originated in India at Mathura where Lord Krishna was born to Devaki.

12 GOKARNA AUNSI
Nepalese Father's Day

Deeply ingrained in Nepalese religion, tradition and culture is a reverence for one's father both in life and after his death. No man relaxes until he has produced a son, for it is the responsibility of male offspring, usually the eldest, to perform the abstemious purification rites necessary to bring peace to the father's soul after his body has been cremated.

It is the son, shaven-headed and swathed in white cotton, who retires from his family and closets himself in a bare room for thirteen days of mourning, the length of time varying slightly with caste. During this period he eats sparingly and abstains from sleep, only resting at times on a pile of straw, to honour his father's memory. During the first year after the father's death the family performs monthly rites and thereafter annual ceremonies seeking peace and comfort for his soul.

These ancient ceremonies, which hopefully ensure that the deceased as well as the mourners may be reincarnated on earth at a higher level, may explain to some extent why Nepalese fathers while living, and their memories after death, are treated with such respect.

The most auspicious day for honouring fathers is Gokarna Aunsi, the last day of the dark fortnight in August or early September, when all who can go to Gokarna village, five miles east of Kathmandu, where is enshrined one of the most sacrosanct of all the countless Shiva lingams in the valley. This cylindrical, carved stone phallic symbol of Lord Shiva is worshipped as Gokarneswar Mahadev, renowned for his singularly close communion with souls of the dead.

To the pious Nepalese, ever awed by natural curiosities, the

10. Women devotees keep vigil through the night of Lord Krishna's birth on the steps of Mahadev temple in Patan   (Teeka Simha)

Women devotees wait for hours with gifts and flower offerings in plates of leaves for Lord Krishna's birthday in Patan   (Betty Woodsend)

11. Year's most important holy bath for women on the steps of Pashupatinath temple on the Bagmati river during women's festival of Tij
(Betty Woodsend)

Women and children on temple steps at Hanuman Dhoka Square in Kathmandu, watching the chariot procession of Kumari, the Living Goddess, during Indra Jatra festival. Men mass in the street
(Shridhar Manandhar)

sanctity of this shrine is greatly enhanced by its location on the banks of the southward-coursing Bagmati River, where it follows a sharp bend and flows for a short distance back towards the northern hills. This oddity, coupled with the tranquillity of the near-by forest, has made Gokarna a centre of pilgrimage since ancient times. It is depicted in old Sanskrit geography as a sanctuary of verdant loveliness, named, no doubt, after the holy city of Gokarna in South India, as are several holy places in Nepal. Now a small village, Gokarna, according to Nepalese chronicles, was once a teeming, fortified capital of the Kirata Dynasty which ruled Nepal some 1,900 years ago.

Mythology places the origin of the Gokarna shrine in prehistoric times when the capricious Lord Shiva hid himself from gods and men, frolicking his days away in the Pashupatinath forest just north-east of Kathmandu in the guise of a one-horned, golden deer. All the world suffered from his absence and neglect. Finally Lord Vishnu, always the conscientious Preserver, Brahma the great Creator and Indra, King of the Gods, took matters quite literally into their own hands.

It seems that, after they had searched everywhere, a certain goddess told them of Shiva's disguise. The three gods proceeded to the designated forest, decided that a particularly docile deer was Shiva and began to chase him. By chance all three gods caught hold of the deer's horn at the same time which, to their horror, broke into fragments, so that each was left holding a fragment in his hand. Then Lord Shiva revealed himself before them, accepted their apologies and replied, 'O Brahma and gods, establish my horn in the sky, the underworld and on earth – the Three Worlds.'

In compliance Vishnu installed his section of the sacred horn at his abode in Vaikuntha, Indra's was taken to his realm in Heaven, and Lord Brahma enshrined his section at the sacred site where the temple now stands and called it Gokarneswar – Lord Shiva of Gokarna. That was on the fourteenth day of the lunar fortnight. On the following day, the last day of the waning moon of August, all the gods and goddesses descended from Heaven, bathed ritually in the Bagmati River near by, paid homage to the image of Shiva and established the present-day tradition of annual ancestor worship at Gokarna.

According to legend Ravana, the ten-headed demon king of Lanka, desiring to become impervious to attack from the gods and other demons, withdrew to Gokarna. Here he sat for years performing severe penance, meditating in deepest devotion upon the glories of Shiva, thereby acquiring tremendous religious merit, whereby he could receive powerful boons from Lord Shiva, even though he was a demon. Thereupon the fiendish king became so mighty that he conquered all Three Worlds, since he was impervious to the divine and terrible weapons of the gods. Such is the merit of devotionals performed at Gokarna.

Now on Father's Day people flock to this sacred shrine of Shiva to honour the memory of their father and promote the welfare of his soul. Those with living fathers come as well – men, women and children of all creeds – to pay tribute to the spirits of their ancestors. They come in cars, taxis and on cycles, spraying the dust over the hundreds who follow time-honoured tradition and walk the entire distance. Women in sarong-like bathing garments and men in loincloths prostrate themselves in the shallow waters, and rise to pray, letting the liquid flow from between cupped palms. Others squat on the bank of the river to splash their face and hands. Then, their hair dripping, they reclothe themselves, seemingly oblivious to others around, and make their way to the temple with trays and small baskets of offerings.

On this day fruits, eggs and sweets are especially auspicious to Shiva. *Pindas*, small pastry balls of rice or barley flour, are offered to the souls of the dead, either by immersing them in the river or giving them to a sacred cow. Coins and bits of food are tossed to beggars, cripples and the destitute who sit in the temple grounds, for the giving of alms on this day brings special concessions to one's father's spirit. Offerings are made to the priest and gifts are set before Lord Shiva's stone sexual emblem in the name of the dead, with a prayer that peace, comfort and happiness will be granted to their souls.

114

Those unable to travel to Gokarna take holy baths in near-by rivers or even in their homes, but there is no proof that the same amount of religious merit is gained. Legend specifically designates Gokarna in the story of the prostitute's son, Dantur, who was hounded for years by the taunts of others demanding to know who his father was. Finally the miserable boy went to a *rishi* and was advised to bathe in the Bagmati River at Gokarna and to perform ceremonies there for the dead. As he underwent these rituals, all the souls of the dead came before him to claim the offerings and the boy's paternity. When Dantur became confused, the Brahman priest pointed out his father's soul and the boy, happy at last, directed his worship to this spirit. In later years, evidently as merit earned for performing these good deeds at Gokarna, Dantur became an emperor.

Gokarna Aunsi is also a day to honour one's living father with gifts and a visit to his home. Married daughters bring sweetmeats and confections, competing laughingly with their sisters in the lavishness of their gifts. Children spend their hoarded coins for small offerings of food, the gift which traditionally expresses reverence, honour and love. Father's Day ends with an enormous family feast, at which the father's blessing is bestowed on one and all.

Thus Gokarna Aunsi is another in the continuous procession of holy days, wherein the poor and maimed are fed, the temple priests' pockets are lined, the shopkeepers do a thriving business, religion and ancient traditions are promoted, and the precious bonds of family and kinship, always strong in Nepal, are once again renewed.

13 TIJ BRATA

The Fasting Festival for Women Only

Every year, in August or early September, there is a three-day festival, which always ends on the fifth day of the brightening moon. Nepalese women claim it for themselves alone. In observing the required rituals and ceremonies, Nepalese women strive for what is desired by women everywhere – a happy and productive marriage, good fortune and long life for her husband, and the puri-fication of her own body and soul.

While observing this festival of Tij, women must undergo penances and rigid fasting, the severity of which is alleviated by lavish feasts, laughter and dancing in good fellowship with sister devotees. On the first day they indulge themselves and their appe-tites to the fullest in preparation for the all-important second day of strictest fasting. Because the last day of tedious, ceremonial holy bathing must take place on the fifth day of the waning moon, during some years a day elapses between the Tij day of fasting and the final bathing day. In other years the three days follow conse-cutively.

The first day is called *darkhana*, when the women of each house-hold prepare for a feast, the most sumptuous that can be produced: all kinds of curry – mutton, chicken, fish and vegetable, with chutneys, eggs, fruits and sweets, an indulgence which often strains the family purse. Tradition says the husband must meet this expense even if it means pawning valuables, taking a loan or selling part of his store of grain. Thus some men, alluding to the next day's fast, claim that 'a woman observing her yearly Tij fasting often consumes a whole bushel of corn'.

In the afternoon people are seen hurrying through the streets and along the footpaths carrying baskets and trays of edibles, the customary gift mothers must send this day to the homes of their married daughters. Along with food, according to her means, she may also send scarlet saris, red glass bangles and crimson cotton yarn for her daughter's hair.

Some women may hold their feasting party during the day; but when the children are sleeping and men out of sight, the women often congregate in one room and seat themselves on the floor around a spread of many dishes, laughing, bantering and gorging themselves with all they can hold, for at midnight begins a time of arduous fasting. Often the jollity goes on until morning, for many consider it a special penance to stay awake through the entire night.

Next is the most important day of the festival, when Tij fasting is performed on behalf of one's husband. Not one morsel of food nor drop of liquid may be taken for twenty-four hours. Extremely pious women will not swallow their own saliva; it is expectorated instead, to avoid a sin likened to drinking their own husbands' blood.

The rules of this fast are revealed in the holy books, citing how the saintly goddess Parbati, daughter of the god Himalaya, fasted in deepest humility, praying fervently that the great Lord Shiva would become her spouse. Shiva, touched by her piety and devotion, made her dreams come true and took her as his wife. In gratitude Parbati sent her emissary to preach and propagate this type of religious fasting among women on earth, promising that she who observes it will not only beget many children, but will live with her husband all the days of her life.

Traditionally the rites of Tij fasting are obligatory for all Hindu married women, and girls who have reached puberty. Only those are excused who are seriously ill or physically infirm, in which case she must engage a Brahman priest to undergo the day's fast in her stead.

In some households on Tij day the penitent women wait upon their husbands with even greater solicitude than usual, carefully tending his every need. In others, it seems, the woman becomes queen-for-a-day, master of her husband for a change, lifting not a finger to her household chores, while the hapless man undertakes her duties, grumbling good-naturedly at this complete turn of affairs.

All through this day and evening, groups of gaily dressed women flock the roads and pathways leading to the great temple of Lord Shiva, Pashupatinath, on the Bagmati River, chattering like bright-feathered birds in their blood-red marriage saris and wedding jewellery. Decorations, flowers and scarlet ribbons bounce in their hair. Though they may be weak from fasting and loss of sleep, the women take pride in concealing any ill effects, many laughing, dancing, beating small drums or singing ancient hymns.

They troop down the wide steps to the river, cleanse their hands in the sacred water, sprinkle a few drops over their heads and into their mouths as a blessing. Some completely immerse before swarming into the holy temple area and up the steps to the archway of the inner, gold-roofed temple that enshrines the famous stone Shiva lingam, that sacred phallic symbol representing Lord Shiva himself. Since it is taboo to touch this lingam, devotees scramble to toss in their offerings, and soon the sacred phallus is smothered in gifts and garlands of flowers. Many throw coins at Shiva's feet, while some present sizeable monetary offerings. Then they follow the throngs along a prescribed path through a maze of 108 smaller Shiva lingams which sit atop a low brick wall, and on past groups of dancing, singing women and Brahmans reading out the story of Parbati's sacred fast. Now and then a woman faints, weakened from exhaustion, the long day's fasting, the excitement of milling crowds and a religious fervour which seems to charge the very air.

Now the women are ready to conduct the *puja* or religious ceremonies especially prescribed for the day of Tij fasting while seated before images of Shiva and Parbati, a ritual often lasting two hours. This *puja* may be performed at one of the many ornately carved images in the Pashupatinath area where Shiva holds his bride upon his knee or where they stand together with Parbati clinging to her divine husband in utmost devotion. Some women enact their *puja* along the river banks, or return to their homes to worship before a small idol of the revered couple, fashioned with their own hands from cleansed and sanctified sand.

In this Tij fasting *puja* the gods are specially invoked on behalf of the husband. Grains of rice, flower petals and bits of fruit are carefully counted out, often by the woman herself, but sometimes by the family Brahman priest or female servants, for there must be no less than 108 of each. These she offers to Shiva and Parbati, beseeching their blessing upon her spouse. When completed, she must ensure that the flame of one of the oil lamps remains alight through the night, for it is a bad omen if it dies.

Early next morning she must complete this *puja*. To her husband she presents a bit of food which she has offered to the gods, usually a banana or other fruit, which he is required to eat. She touches his bare toes with her forehead, washes his feet and, according to tradition, is required to drink this consecrated liquid. Now the woman is allowed to break her long fast, but only after obtaining her husband's permission.

If astrologers ascertain that this is the fifth day of the waxing moon – for in some years it may be the fourth – then it is declared the day of *Rishi Panchami*, when partial fasting must be observed and long ritual holy bathing performed according to very strict rules. These bathing ceremonies are mandatory for all who have undergone the Tij fast.

After she has completed her husband's *puja*, usually very early in the morning for greatest privacy, women flock to any one of the shrines and holy places along the sacred rivers. Hundreds gather near the temple at Tekudhoban where the Bagmati and Vishnumati rivers meet just south of old Kathmandu, for the confluences of rivers have long been considered the holiest of places.

Red mud, especially that found at the roots of the sacred *datiwan* bush, must be smeared 360 times on many areas of the body, including the hands, elbows, shoulders, knees, feet and private parts. Then the hair is washed and women sprinkle themselves 360 times with 360 leaves of the *datiwan* shrub, brushing their teeth 360 times with a stalk of the same plant. This ceremony of atonement for female sin is attributed to the same merciful goddess Parbati, who prescribed the rites when she herself performed them to purge her body and soul on behalf of her divine spouse.

Those unable to travel to the holy waters must bathe in their homes in accordance with the same ceremony. Having undergone this purifying bathing ritual, women are absolved from all sin, real or imagined, including that awful transgression of touching a man during menstruation.

Now the women's Tij Festival is over, leaving those who have undergone the severe requirements serene and tranquil in the knowledge that all possible has been done to ensure a good husband for the unmarried, and security for those whose husbands will now live a long life of prosperity and conjugal happiness.

14 GANESH CHATA

The Elephant God curses the Moon

Lord Ganesh may be the wisest, kindest and most appealing of all the deities, but he is far from being the most beautiful. His runty, pot-bellied human body and heavy, long-trunked elephant's head prove no hindrance, however, to his vast popularity, for all prayers and petitions to any god or goddess must be preceded by the worship of Ganesh if results are to be expected. No religious ceremony, whether private prayer or public festival, and no undertaking, be it a business venture, a journey or the building of a new home, may begin until his blessing is sought. Printed at the beginning of all Hindu books is an honorary salutation to this beloved deity. For when Ganesh is pleased, he is generous and amiable, removing all obstacles to human endeavours, but when he is slighted, this wily, irrascible elephant god thwarts men's undertakings and aspirations without compunction.

An idol of Ganesh is worshipped in every home regardless of caste, creed or status. Each neighbourhood, village, city or region has its own Ganesh temple and holds an annual festival in his honour. Women fast every Tuesday, the day set aside to honour Ganesh. Unmarried girls seek his assurance of good husbands; pregnant wives seek his blessing for vigorous, clever offspring; while men beg him for success in all their pursuits.

At his Surya Vinayak temple, high on a hillside near Bhadgaon, even the Sun God Surya petitions Ganesh to remove obstacles from his daily circling of the globe by casting his first morning rays upon the image of Ganesh. It is to Surya Ganesh that children slow to walk and speak are brought in the hope that he may remove any unknown difficulty. Hundreds of myths and legends emphasize his shrewdness and wiliness, which are often strangely concerned with thieving and pilfering.

One of these tales records how a penniless Brahman – a common predicament among this priestly caste, it seems – whose wife's continuous complaint that she had not the necessary sesame seeds nor sugar to offer Ganesh on his festival day finally drove the husband to consider theft. However, that night, when he was about to pilfer a bazaar merchant's stock, the Brahman froze with guilt and stood praying aloud for forgiveness. This awoke the merchant who, fearing some evil spirit or even Lord Ganesh himself had come to harass him, called out that the interloper, if he would leave the premises at once, could take whatever he desired. The surprised Brahman helped himself to sugar and sesame seeds and departed. His wife made the required offerings on Ganesh Chata day, and the happy couple became very prosperous, because of the blessings bestowed by the flattered Ganesh.

Once when Ganesh and his brave warrior brother Kumar-Kartik went to Lord Shiva to settle their dispute over which was the elder, the famous father, hard put for a decision since Ganesh had not actually been 'born', decided on an impartial contest. The son who could circle the earth in the least time would be declared the elder. Kumar-Kartik flew off on his swift vehicle, the peacock, but crafty Ganesh, whose carrier is a lowly rat, quietly walked around his parents and bowed before them. When Shiva protested in puzzlement that Ganesh had not fulfilled requirements, Ganesh replied, 'No, but I went around my parents, and they represent the whole world to me.' For this bit of ingenuity, Ganesh has ever been known as the senior and therefore the privileged son of Shiva and Parbati.

Although in India Lord Ganesh is not considered a blood-thirsty god, in Nepal sacrifices are regularly made to his idol. He is always found near the goddess Saraswati, whom many consider another wife of Shiva, one of those who represent his female destructive power and are especially fond of blood. Ganesh and Saraswati, who is generally worshipped as the goddess of learning, are often found in images near burning ghats and in isolated places believed haunted by evil spirits. These unhappy ghosts and wandering souls bring suffering, especially to children, unless they are controlled with liberal offerings of blood from sacrificed animals and fowl.

Ganesh, for all his sagacity and good humour, often displays a crude and earthy vulgarity which most Nepalese – and not a few others – find amusing. When one poverty-stricken woman worshipped Ganesh on his festival day, offering a meagre handful of sesame seeds and sugar – items she could ill afford – the elephant god was greatly pleased. That night in compensation he paid a visit to her simple room. When his voice announced loud and clear, 'I want to ease myself', the woman awoke in terror. Thinking the intruder some dangerous lunatic whose anger must be avoided, she hastily instructed him to use one corner of the room. Hours later Ganesh cried out again, 'I want to make water', and again, 'I want to weep' and 'I want to laugh'. Each time the shaken housewife suggested another corner. At dawn when she fearfully opened the connecting door, she wept with joy to find heaps of gold and gems. Then she knew her offerings to Ganesh on his festival day had been very well received.

However, when a wealthy but envious neighbour learned of this miracle, she too performed *puja* for Ganesh, carefully duplicating every rite, offering the same meagre amounts of sesame and sugar given by her poorer neighbour. When Ganesh appeared in her prayer room that night the delighted woman cheerfully instructed him to use each of the four corners when he stated his needs. The next morning, when the greedy couple opened the door of the *puja* room, they were greeted with the horrible stench of urine and excrement. Thus the wily Ganesh repays those who succumb to temptation and envy, and those whose purpose is to deceive the gods.

Legend relating to the Ganesh Chata festival tells how Lord Brahma, the Great Creator, seeking success in his appointed duties, once underwent a strict fast in the name of Ganesh, which pleased the elephant god exceedingly. He appeared before Brahma and volunteered to fulfil his every desire. Brahma replied, 'O

Lord, it is my duty to create. Let there be no mishaps and mistakes in the process of creation.' Ganesh replied, 'So be it', and disappeared.

It seems Chandrama the Moon Goddess witnessed this episode and upbraided Brahma, criticizing a superior god who stooped to request boons from a deformed, elephant headed demi-god. When Ganesh learned of this defamation he was consumed with fury and pronounced a curse upon the Moon, saying that any person who dared even to look upon her would become an addicted thief. Thus the Moon Goddess was forced into hiding and without her rays in the dark of night both men and gods were uneasy.

Finally Brahma and all the divinities placated Ganesh with prayer and offerings of the finest foods, beseeching him to forgive Chandrama that the world might again have moonlight. The disgruntled Ganesh, in time, granted her pardon, but with one stipulation: on Ganesh Chata day the curse shall for ever remain effective.

Thus each year on the fourth day of the bright lunar fortnight in September, during the women's Tij fasting festival, Ganesh is honoured with offerings of sesame, sugar and radishes, and the sight of the moon is scrupulously avoided. After sunset people closet themselves in their homes, locking doors and windows, stuffing every opening with cotton lest moonlight should appear. Believers would never dream of venturing out on this night, for the sight of the crescent moon would invariably bring bad luck, the most likely misfortune being that they might be accused of theft. Stories abound of men who, mistakenly apprehended or accused, managed to prove their innocence with great difficulty. Many take the added safeguard against this possibility of carrying on their person on Ganesh Chata day a talisman, perhaps a green chilli pepper or citrus fruit.

Paradoxically, Ganesh Chata is the most auspicious time of year for robbers, for if a thief acquires much loot on this night he is assured of a successful career throughout the year. A burglar's failure to pilfer at least one item is considered an ill omen, foretelling his disclosure or arrest. However, anyone thought to show inclinations toward becoming a thief is encouraged to perform specific rites and make certain offerings to Ganesh on this day, that the elephant god may prevent his becoming an habitual criminal.

Late at night, after the religious ceremonies are complete, a great family feast is held and the story of Ganesh's miraculous birth is retold, in Nepal perhaps the best-loved of all tales.

Once while Lord Shiva was absent from home – this time frisking with a flock of ducks in a pond where he himself took the form of a great white king of this feathered species – his wife, Goddess Parbati, beautified herself by having the dead, dry skin massaged from her body. Collecting this scruff in a ball, the childless goddess miraculously transformed it into a small boy, breathing life and greater-than-average intelligence into his body. Delighted with her newly created son, Parbati asked him to guard the door while she bathed, instructing him to grant entrance to no one.

It happened that a certain man, Jalander, came seeking Parbati, having been told by his beautiful young wife Brinda that the Goddess Parbati was even fairer than herself. Jalander convinced the child confronting him at Parbati's door that he was the goddess's husband. The boy summoned his mother, and when Parbati came carrying a water jug to wash her returning husband's feet, Jalander was so consumed with desire at the sight of her that he fell unconscious.

Meanwhile Shiva rushed to Parbati's rescue and when a small boy – a complete stranger – barred entrance, the furious God of Destruction cut off the child's head. Only when Parbati asked how he managed to pass her son did Shiva realize the infamy of his deed. Promising to restore the boy's life, Shiva sent men into the forest to behead the first living creature they found sleeping with its head towards the north. This happened to be a white elephant, whose severed head Shiva affixed to the body of his son. Thus Ganesh has an elephant's head, and no right-thinking Nepali would sleep with his head toward the north – a position in which only the dead are placed. Furthermore, a man grievously offends the souls of his ancestors by sleeping with his feet pointing south towards the Abode of the Dead.

Now to bring complete solace to Parbati and to mollify their son, who will ever bear the head of an elephant, Lord Shiva ensconced Ganesh in a most prestigious position in the hierarchy of gods, ordaining that throughout eternity his name must be invoked before any deity is worshipped.

And so, besides the many festivals held throughout the valley in his honour every year, Ganesh is feted by one and all on Ganesh Chata, when people keep their eyes carefully averted from the Moon Goddess in remembrance of his curse. For it is of vital importance that the irascible Ganesh be kept happy, thereby preventing all unfortunate incidents such as the accusation of theft, for if Ganesh Chata goes well, if the day passes without adversity, this is a good omen, guaranteeing that the great ten-day festival of Dasain the following month will itself be a momentous success.

15 INDRA JATRA AND KUMARI JATRA
King of the Gods and a Living Goddess

In September Nepalese and foreigners alike look forward to the eight-day Indra Jatra festival, for few can but wonder at the story of Indra, King of the Gods, imprisoned by the inhabitants of the Kathmandu Valley. And rare is the person immune to the mystery and glamour surrounding a Nepalese girl child, who is deified and worshipped as Kumari, the Living Goddess.

Legend says Lord Indra, Ruler of Heaven, controller of clouds and storm, was fond of the white *parijat* flowers which grow abundantly in the Kathmandu Valley, but were not to be found in Heaven. When his mother requested a supply of these blossoms to perform her annual women's Tij fasting rites, Indra, hidden in a cloud of fog and mist, descended to the valley disguised as an ordinary mortal. It seems that the valley people, unaware of his divinity, apprehended Indra in the act of stealing their *parijat* flowers and, as is still the custom when a thief is caught, surrounded the Lord of Heaven, binding his hands and feet with ropes. They held him prisoner, it is said, in the locality of Maru Hiti in old Kathmandu.

Before long Indra's mother came to earth to investigate her son's disappearance and when the valley people learned the identity of their visitor and prisoner they fell down before them with profuse offering of foods and flowers. The Lord of Heaven and his goddess mother were fêted and carried in processions through the streets for a week, while the ruler of Kathmandu held lavish feasts and receptions in their honour.

Story has it that Indra's mother, in compensation for her son's release, promised to furnish the valley with the vital fog and dew during the autumn and winter season, moisture which the farmers still refer to as 'milk' for their ripening harvest. She further agreed to lead back to Heaven the souls of all who had died during the year. However, as she left the valley, followed by a long procession of souls each clinging to the clothing of the one ahead, the line broke and the spirits fell into Indra Daha, a lake on the hilltop eight miles west of Kathmandu. Strangely, Indra's mother continued on to her heavenly abode, leaving the people to mourn for the souls of their dead, a rite which has become a traditional part of Indra Jatra.

Through the ages scholars have come to identify Indra as the warrior leader of the ancient Aryan people who overran all India thousands of years ago, and there is conjecture that when Indra's forces approached this Himalayan land he may have been captured by the Nepalese king, Yalambar, and released after some agreement was reached.

A popular legend repeated during Indra Jatra relates that the ancient Nepalese king Yalambar journeyed to India to witness the epic Mahabharata war disguised as the great Lord Shiva in his terrifying Bhairab form. At the battle site Lord Krishna, knowing full well that Yalambar would certainly join Krishna's forces, none the less asked him on which side he intended to fight. When Yalambar or Bhairab ambiguously replied that he would fight on the losing side, Krishna chopped off his head with such violence that it soared through the sky route and landed in the Kathmandu Valley. It is this catastrophe, some say, which is commemorated each year by the Nepalese during Indra Jatra, when their headless ancestral ruler is worshipped as a great blue mask of Akash Bhairab whose eyes are turned 'for ever skyward'.

Indra Jatra officially opens on the twelfth day of the waxing moon in September with the raising of the flag of Indra before the old palace at Hanuman Dhoka in Kathmandu. This flag signifies that Lord Indra has come to the valley, and when it flies, peace, prosperity and unity are assured in the land. Mythology says such a flag pole was presented by Lord Vishnu to Indra, which unified his forces and gave him divine strength to overcome the demons.

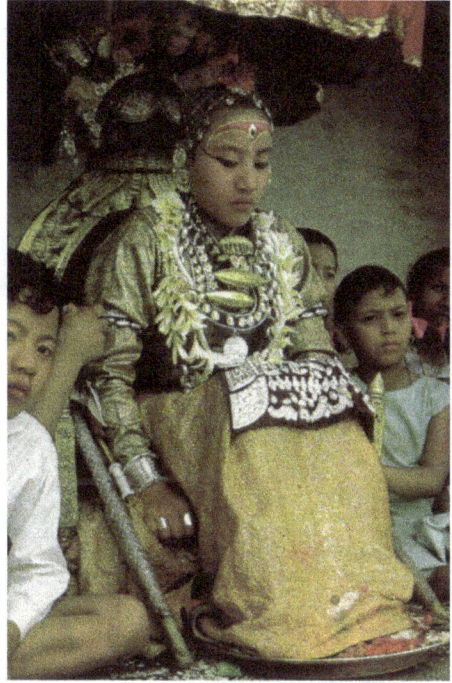

12. Kumari, the Living Goddess of Patan, comes to witness the showing of the 'sacred bhoto' or garment during Red Machhendra's chariot festival in Patan   (Betty Woodsend)

Officiating Buddhist priests, men of the same Newari caste as Kumari, at the procession of the Living Goddess, Hanuman Dhoka Square, Kathmandu (Teeka Simha)

13. Boy keeps vigil before the mask of the White or Swet Bhairab, recessed in the wall of Hanuman Dhoka, the old palace, its covering lattice removed only during Indra Jatra festival (Teeka Simha)

Children gaze upon the Blue or Akash Bhairab at Indrachowk, Kathmandu, displayed on the street before his temple only during Indra Jatra festival (Betty Woodsend)

Today it is worshipped, just as Indra worshipped it in ages past, as a symbol of unity, victory and power.

Some time before Indra Jatra begins a government-appointed priest and his porters go to Yosingu forest at Salaghari, four miles east of Bhadgaon, to select a suitable fifty-foot pine tree. It is sanctified with blood sacrifice and certain rites, felled, cleared of its branches and dragged in solemn procession into Bhadgaon town. A few days later people from near-by Thimi village pull the sacred pole into the Tundikhel parade ground in central Kathmandu. About four days before Indra Jatra, men of Kathmandu drag the pole to Hanuman Dhoka square, where they are given a feast in the old royal palace under the auspices of the Government. This practice of men from various villages participating in certain important festivals is very ancient and seems to enhance unity among the people.

For the pole-raising ceremony on the morning of the twelfth day, hundreds of spectators crowd into the palace square and on to the surrounding temples. The royal priest arrives accompanied by his detachment of elderly soldiers in ancient uniforms, bearing outmoded rifles and sabres which, together with an equally anti-quated military band, stand as symbols of the present ruling family's ancestral army. Present also are the scarlet-coated, modern palace guards standing at stiff attention.

Court astrologers announce the arrival of the auspicious moment. Music blares, guns roar in salute and a thrill of excite-ment runs through the crowd as the heavy pole, tugged and pulled with bamboos and thick ropes, is slowly raised. When the long banner of Indra's flag, displaying the moon as a symbol of 'intel-ligent planning' and the sun for courage and valour, is unfurled the crowd surges uncontrollably forward to leave offerings of sweets and flowers. At the foot of the pole is placed a small prison-like cage containing an image of Indra, along with a golden elephant – the mythical steed of the King of the Gods. Now the festival has begun.

Idols of Indra, with his outstretched arms bound like those of a thief, are brought from the temples and placed on high scaffolds around the town. Masks of Bhairab, the God of Wrath, some of ancient worm-eaten wood, others of gleaming brass, are placed along the streets inside elaborate canopies draped with garlands and finery. Images of other deities are displayed before their temples, for in Nepal the gods and the people witness their celebrations together.

At dusk on this day hundreds of people in whose family a death has occurred during the year proceed in long lines through the streets where houses have been cleaned, decorated and illuminated with butter lamps. All carry burning incense in the name of deceased relatives along a prescribed route said to mark the ancient road which once ringed the town. Some offer lighted oil wicks in small clay dishes to shrines and gods as they pass, while others chant religious hymns for their dead in a taxing three-hour procession.

Each night of Indra Jatra the shrines and ancient palace buildings crowding Hanuman Dhoka square are aglow with oil wicks, and each night in the shadow of the temple before the Living Goddess House an ancient tableau is enacted depicting the ten earthly incarnations of Lord Vishnu. Hundreds of worshippers crowd about to see the elaborate costumes and realistic, painted masks, and to hear again the beloved stories of Vishnu's marvellous visits to earth.

Nepalese folk dramas are presented around the city and ancient dances are performed in the streets by the light of flaming torches. Rich costumes and gawdy masks depict demons and deities dancing with remarkable grace and stylized precision. In contrast to the celebrating spectators, the dancers seem to be in a religious trance, and are thought to be possessed by the spirit of the deities they represent. Thus they are treated with great respect and reverence.

In the Sawo Bhaku demon dance a long-maned Bhairab, accompanied by two attendants, moves through the streets. Great care is taken along the route that no saris are left hanging from balconies – the traditional drying place – for if these demons spy such a garment they will climb the walls and tear it to pieces.

Anyone daring to open an umbrella will find it slashed to shreds by the demons' swords, and once aroused, these wild dancers can only be appeased by the sacrifice of a goat or chicken whose blood they drink. According to tradition, if bodily harm comes to those who offend, no legal action may be taken.

Prior to 1940 the Bhaku dancers staged a dangerous and exciting bull fight inside the old palace grounds each night of Indra Jatra. A horned water buffalo was made quite mad by feeding it with liquor, and was further enraged by stabbing it with curved Nepalese *khukri* knives, the wounds being inflicted by the dancing demons each time the animal charged. Finally, when the buffalo fell lifeless, the dancers drank his blood and were then thought to be possessed by the buffalo spirit. This practice has been discontinued, despite an old legend which says that long ago the God of the Skies smiled upon the ancient Nepalese and whispered to them, 'Sacrifice a buffalo to Lord Bhairab and Bhaku; peace will come unto you; prosperity will befriend you.'

In the famous Lakhe dance the sacred mask itself represents the demon Lakhe and is worshipped accordingly, and its spirit possesses its wearer. It is believed that if Lakhe happens to spy a man impersonating the demoness Dagini, he will kill him on the spot and great care is taken to prevent their meeting. This dance originated long ago, they say, when a man called Majipat Lakhe was discovered having illicit relations with a Kathmandu girl living in the Chikanmugal area. He was spared punishment when he agreed to perform the Lakhe dance each night of Indra Jatra.

Very popular is the elephant dance, depicting Indra's steed in search of his imprisoned master. Encased in elephant mask and a great basket-like body, the elephant swings a tail so enormous that spectators are knocked completely off their feet. His antics evoke roars of laughter, but no man dares to approach him wearing a hat lest it be snatched by Indra's elephant, who considers it an affront.

In the afternoon of the day before full moon ecstatic mobs gather near Hanuman Dhoka for the long-awaited Living Goddess procession and to glimpse the beautiful Newari girl who has been deified as the Vestal Virgin, Kumari, worshipped as a goddess by peasants and king alike. No doubt certain aspects of Kumari-worship and her annual festival parade existed among the Newars in ancient times, but it is generally believed that the ceremonies in their present form were inaugurated in mid-eighteenth century by Jaya Prakash Malla, the last of the 'Newar' kings.

It seems that during his reign a young Newari girl of Kathmandu became possessed by the spirit of Taleju, the divine Mother Goddess, who for centuries has been patron deity of Nepal and her royal families. The King, thinking the young girl a fraud, possibly afflicted with the 'evil eye', banished her from the city. That very night one of his queens went into paroxysms and declared that the spirit of the goddess had now entered her body. Losing no time, the worried King had the child returned to the city, publicly acclaimed her the Living Goddess Kumari, and worshipped at her feet. He further ordered an ornate home to be built for her, and instituted an annual *jatra*, in which she is drawn through the streets attended by two small boys representing Lord Bhairab and the elephant-headed god Ganesh, for these two deities are in attendance at almost every festival in the valley.

A related legend says that this same King wiled away many hours playing dice and other gambling games with the Goddess Taleju whose temple still stands inside the old palace grounds in Hanuman Dhoka. One day the King, overcome by her beauty, looked upon her lustfully – thoughts which the Goddess perceived – and she immediately vanished from his sight. That night Taleju appeared to the fearful ruler in a dream saying, 'O wretched King, your days are numbered and the fall of your dynasty is near. You shall no longer be blest with the sight of me. Select a girl-child from a Newar caste and I shall dwell in her body. Worship her as Goddess Kumari, for to worship her is to worship me.' Her prophecy was fulfilled.

How Kumari is chosen about every ten years remains a closely guarded secret involving the ancient Tantric 'mysteries'. She must be of the Newari Sakya caste, usually three or four years old, a virgin with no bodily marks or injuries. People say the child is led into a dark chamber deep within the confines of Hanuman Dhoka, and made to walk over severed animal heads which utter strange cries while their moving ears and staring eyes reflect the light of flickering oil wicks. Masked demons leap and shriek throughout, and if the child weeps or shows fear she is disqualified. If she remains perfectly calm and free of all emotion she becomes the next Vestal Virgin, Kumari, a form of Taleju, Kali and the Divine Universal-Mother goddesses who are all-powerful in Nepal. Her attendants, Ganesh and Bhairab, are said to be chosen by the same method.

It is generally believed that a child who displays such courage and emotional control is sure to have been some remarkable personage in former incarnations.

Kumari is taken from her family, installed in the ornate Kumari House, very close to Hanuman Dhoka, served by woman attendants, robed in silks and brocades, bedecked with jewels and crowned with a glittering tiara as the guardian and ruling deity of Nepal. People come daily to worship her, to propitiate her with money and gifts, seeking her advice and assistance in personal troubles, especially those of a financial or legal nature. All her moves and gestures are interpreted as good or bad omens; the royal family consults her before important ceremonial occasions; and her divine presence is required at important festivals throughout the year. During Indra Jatra, Kumari symbolically bestows upon the King of Nepal the right to rule for the coming year by placing the sacred red *tika* mark on his forehead as her blessing, while the King, in the traditional expression of gratitude, presents her with a golden coin, and touches her feet with his forehead.

Thus a girl-child reigns supreme so long as she meets with no bodily injury involving the shedding of blood. At her first menstruation she is automatically stripped of her divine status, replaced by a younger child chosen by the same secret Tantric rites and returned to her home as a common but wealthy citizen. An ex-Kumari is free to marry, providing there can be found a man who dares, for it is widely believed that whosoever breaks her virginity is doomed to an early death.

For her chariot procession every year during Indra Jatra thousands gather from all over the valley, completely filling the square before Kumari House, the steps and tiers of surrounding temples, crowding at the windows, balconies and rooftops for blocks around. Three huge and ancient chariots are waiting in the street, each bearing a 'mobile temple' heavily decorated with flowers, greenery and umbrellas of gold thread. Masked devil dancers cavort in the square, bands play, and five officiating Buddhist priests ring hand bells, their haughty faces immobile under heavy gilded crowns.

Foreign and Nepalese dignitaries line the balcony of the old administration building before Kumari House, and finally the King and Queen of Nepal appear on the balcony. The ecstatic crowd surges forward, very near to rioting, as Kumari emerges from her house carried in the arms of an attendant. She is enshrined in the chariot like a miniature oriental princess, robed in gold and scarlet, her enormous dark eyes exotically ringed with black. Next come little Ganesh and Bhairab, painted and costumed only slightly less lavishly, to be installed in their private chariots.

In the pressing crowds a goat is sacrificed to the heavy wooden tongue or yoke of her carriage to pacify the god Bhairab, controller of the physical power which moves all vehicles. If this is not done he may take a life by causing one of the heavy, wooden wheels to crush one of those who pull the chariot.

To the firing of military guns the three chariots inch forward, pulled and pushed by groups of shouting men, honoured to have this sacred duty. The parade stops below the balcony where His Majesty, regarded by the fervent multitudes as an incarnation of Lord Vishnu, bows solemnly to the little goddess, who gazes at him and the excited crowd with utmost poise and dignity. Then the unwieldy procession moves ponderously through milling humanity along the lower parts of the old city in a grand parade which will be repeated the following day through the main bazaar streets of Kathmandu.

With the passing of the Living Goddess, the King tosses handfuls of coins to the jostling spectators whose upturned faces are transfixed with adoration.

It was on this very day in 1768 that the present King's ancestor, Prithvi Narayan Shah, led his conquering army into Kathmandu from Gorkha. Jaya Prakash Malla, who then reigned in Kathmandu, unable to muster his forces from among the celebrating, tipsy subjects, fled to Patan in defeat, even as Goddess Taleju had prophesied. When the conqueror magnanimously ordered the celebration to continue, they say he himself led the Living Goddess procession, later seating himself on the throne amid a military gun salute and the rejoicings of the populace. Then, in traditional ceremony of Indra Jatra, the Living Goddess placed a red *tika* blessing on Prithvi's forehead, thus transferring the right to rule to the present Shah dynasty.

It is widely told that shortly before his death in 1955 the late King Tribhuvan, accompanied by his son, then Crown Prince Mahendra, went to receive Kumari's *tika* blessing during Indra Jatra. The Goddess Kumari seemed to be dosing, and, when prodded by an attendant, wrongly placed the sacred mark on the Crown Prince rather than the King. This incident was whispered through the town as a certain bad omen for their ruler, and like many omens in Nepal, this one was borne out when Tribhuvan died within eight months and his son Mahendra was crowned King.

In the evening, as the Kumari procession returns to Hanuman Dhoka, it pauses in Indrachowk before the great blue figure of Akash Bhairab in the street before his temple, and again before the twelve-foot mask of White Bhairab, recessed in the wall of Hanuman Dhoka. Behind each mask, jugs of rice beer have been installed with tubes leading out of Bhairab's snarling mouth. When this sacred liquor is made to run through the tube music blares and the crowd goes wild, trampling each other in a stampede to catch a few drops in their mouths or cupped hands, for the recipient thereby receives powerful blessings from Bhairab. Each fervently hopes to catch the tiny live fish, earlier placed in the beer, when it passes through Akash Bhairab's mouth, for he is then the luckiest man in the valley.

In the evening before the full moon a Newari farmer, masked and costumed as a female demon called Dagini, emerges from the dark streets at Maru Hiti, where Lord Indra was taken prisoner. Led by a musical band, supported on each side by attendants, this man is thought to be possessed by the demon's spirit. Hundreds of women from households where death has occured within the year form a procession behind Dagini, clinging to the sash or garment of the woman ahead. They are joined by a group of men carrying a long plank suspended on ropes from their shoulders, along which is set a series of flaming oil wicks. They light the way for Dagini and her procession as they file through the dark city lanes seeking the souls of those who failed to get to Heaven. Hundreds of spectators return to their homes only after they witness this 'row of many lamps' in a token of respect for those ancestors who fell when following Indra's mother to Heaven in the distant past.

Hundreds of women, having finished the parade, make a pilgrimage to Indra Lake, walking eight miles through the darkness, where at daybreak of the day of the full moon holy baths are taken to honour the souls of their dead. Many believe that Lord Indra himself accompanies them on this journey.

Countless others who have lost family members, many richly costumed, carry bronze ceremonial lamps in which a tiny oil wick blazes, and parade the route taken earlier by the Kumari procession. They leave small clay dishes of lights for Bhairab, Lord Indra and other idols along the way.

Long ago, at its inception, Indra Jatra festival lasted only seven days. It was extended through the eighth, they say, by King Jaya Prakash Malla whose amorous activities seem to have caused no end of upheaval. When one of his concubines living in Kilagal area of Kathmandu complained that she had missed the Kumari procession, the King dutifully ordained that the Living Goddess should be taken out in a third parade. Thus the people call the ceremony on the final and eighth day of Indra Jatra 'the procession of the half-wife', when hundreds assemble again to toss flowers, coins and her favourite red powder to Goddess Kumari.

On this last evening the great lingam pole bearing Indra's flag is lowered amid religious ceremonies, blood sacrifices and gun salutes. The moment it rests upon the ground hundreds of worshippers rush forward to touch it with their foreheads. Now it is dragged to the Bagmati River near Pachali Bhairab's shrine in a funeral-like procession and immersed in the sacred waters. Later it is retrieved and hacked into small pieces to feed the sacred flame which burns perpetually at Pachali Bhairab's place.

They say that late on the final night of Indra Jatra, after the last reveller has departed, singing loudly to the darkness, and before the idols of the gods have been returned to their homes and temples, a mysterious ceremony takes place. A small wooden puppet is brought from the confines of Hanuman Dhoka and used as a weapon to strike similar puppets placed beside the images of Indra. Could it be that the people of the valley harbour some dim memory of an ancestral king who was beheaded by the gods? Or is this an old anger at Indra or some Aryan leader who stole into the valley and was imprisoned by the inhabitants? Or an ancient resentment toward Indra's mother for deserting the souls of their dead when she returned to Heaven?

SEPTEMBER-OCTOBER

16 SORAH SRADDHA
Sixteen Days of Ancestor Worship

In Nepal, the most important of all earthly duties is ministering to the needs of and worshipping the souls of departed relatives and ancestors, for their spirits remain very much alive and require endless care and veneration. Ancestor worship is a part of daily life. One does not begin the morning meal until food and water has been offered to the spirits of the dead. Nepalese perform specific religious ceremonies and periodically offer gifts to these souls to assure their comfort, happiness and reincarnation at a higher level; but they also serve to bring the mourner himself enough religious merit to ensure him a better life when he dies and is reborn. In many homes ancestors are deified as household gods who, if given proper care, will protect the family against misfortune and who, if mistreated or neglected, may become malignant spirits, haunting the homes of the living and causing every kind of disturbance and calamity.

Almost any act of piety when performed in the name of the dead brings peace to his departed soul, be it the giving of alms to temple priests and beggars, making pilgrimages to holy places, offering food, clothing and money for the soul's comfort, or the observance of Sraddha, the ritual worship of the souls of dead relations at frequent and specific times.

At death, after the body has been cremated and the ashes strewn into a sacred river, a mourning period of about thirteen days is observed, usually by the eldest son, who sits alone and untouched by anyone while performing the meticulously prescribed rituals. On the eleventh day after death a priest comes to collect from the bereaved 'all the items which the deceased used while he lived' – bed, mattress, blanket, mud stove, cooking and eating utensils, food, jewellery and clothing. On the forty-fifth day a live sacred cow must be presented to the priest so that the soul may eventually reach Heaven. Specific gifts are made again six and twelve months after death. For the first year, every month, special Sraddha ceremonies are performed and food is offered to the dead; also on each anniversary thereafter.

Many can ill afford this outlay, and some resent the acquisitiveness of the priests, but most feel that unless these donations are made the souls of their kinfolk may wander cold, hungry and resentful. Few could withstand the condemnation of neighbours and kinfolk which would fall upon their heads if they neglected this sacred duty. And there is no doubt that the performance of endless rituals when a loved one dies does bring solace and comfort to those who grieve.

There is one fortnight during the year called Sorah Sraddha or Pitri Paksha, the entire dark half of the lunar month which falls in September and October, when it is believed that the spirits of departed ancestors leave their abodes in the regions of the dead and come back to the world to occupy the homes of their descendants, seeking their worship and homage. This fortnight immediately precedes the one devoted to the great Dasain holidays, and often includes the full moon day of Indra Jatra, making a total of sixteen days.

A well-known Sanskrit text says that 'each day of this holy fortnight is equal in point of sanctity to a day spent at Gaya', the holy city in India regarded as the most sacred of all places for performing rites for the dead. Hundreds of Nepalese journey to Gaya at least once during their lifetime to honour their dead. He whose father is living is exempt from the obligations of Sorah Sraddha fortnight, since all avenues to ancestors lead through the soul of the last deceased paternal kin. As long as the father is living, he himself will perform the obligatory rites to family ancestors. Thus the souls of the dead are perpetually cared for.

Each day during Sorah Sraddha finds hundreds of worshippers

at the temples, holy places, sacred rivers and especially at the great shrine to Lord Shiva at Pashupatinath near Kathmandu, performing Sraddha rites for their dead. On the ninth day of this fortnight, called Matri Nawami, special ceremonies are enacted for the worship of female ancestors, especially deceased mothers. A male ancestor's soul must be worshipped each day during Sorah Sraddha, but his special rites are performed on the day which corresponds to the day of the fortnight in which he died.

Sraddha means literally 'gift offered with faith', a pious offering to any deceased relative to whom honour is due in rites often performed in the home. In all forms of Sraddha the chief act is the offering of *pindas*, balls of rice or barley flour. Libations of water and the repetition of certain prayers are also essential. Before offering water as refreshment to the souls of the dead, libations are first made to the gods – Brahma, Vishnu, Rudra (Shiva) and Prajapati – and thereafter to the principal Hindu *rishis* or sages of ancient times. Next ancestors must be mentioned by name – father, grandfather, great-grandfather, mother, grandmother and great-grandmother in the paternal line, and on to maternal ancestors and others. In many homes ancestors are worshipped back to the seventh generation.

Next the votary bows down, head to the ground, and repeats a text which literally means, 'The father is heaven, the father is religion or duty, the father is the highest form of penance, prayer or meditation. It is by pleasing the father that all gods are propitiated.' This is the cardinal doctrine of ancestor worship. At the conclusion of Sraddha rites the *pinda* cakes are immersed in the holy rivers or they may be given to a sacred cow as food. The ceremony must be performed by the eldest son; hence the well-known Hindu and Buddhist necessity for marriage and procreation of male issue.

During this Sorah Sraddha fortnight many men refrain from shaving. Cutting the hair and paring the nails is forbidden on the anniversary of a father's death, but many abstain from these acts during the entire fortnight, a practice derived from the legend of King Karna.

Karna Raja had taken a vow to continue his daily fasting until his accumulated gifts of pure gold to the Brahman priests had reached certain immense proportions. After his death he was taken straight to Heaven, where he was lodged in a golden palace, and given nothing but gold to eat and drink, since throughout his lifetime his only gift of charity had been this precious metal. Finally in great hunger and distress the King asked as a boon to be allowed to return to earth for the fifteen days of Sorah Sraddha. His wish was granted and he spent the entire two weeks giving away large quantities of food to the hungry, a task which so engrossed him that he neglected to bathe, shave or wash his clothing. Thereafter he lived comfortably in Heaven.

Newar people, whose *pinda* cakes are made of barley rather than rice flour, offer oblations during Sorah Sraddha not only to ancestors but to kings of the nation and distinguished persons of their locality who might have died in the recent past, a tradition which honours kin, community and country.

Thus the traditional clan and family unit structure is vital for the eternal well-being of each person's soul after death, and conversely, the care and propitiation of ancestors preserves the closely-knit Nepalese family, in which several generations dwell together in one household.

17 DASAIN OR DURGA PUJA
The Universal Mother-Goddess triumphs over Evil

Dasain, like the Western Christmas season, is by far the longest, most auspicious and most joyous time of year, celebrated country-wide by all castes and creeds during the bright lunar fortnight ending on the day of the full moon in late September or early October. Families are reunited; blessings, gifts and glad tidings are exchanged, public parades, ancient processions and traditional pageants are held; and the all-powerful goddess Durga, in all her various manifestations and names and forms, is widely acclaimed with innumerable *pujas*, ritual holy bathing, profuse offerings and thousands of animal sacrifices, so that her many idols are drenched for days in blood.

The festivities of these two weeks glorify the ultimate and inevitable triumph of Virtue over the forces of Evil, commemorating a great victory of the gods over the wicked demons and devils who harassed mankind in ancient times. The Ramayana story is retold of the righteous King Rama, deified by Hindu mythology as an incarnation of Lord Vishnu, or again as God himself, who after epic struggles slaughtered Ravana, the fiendish king of the demon hordes from Lanka, a legendary country believed by many to have been Ceylon. Some say Lord Rama was successful in his battle with the demon only when he evoked the Shakti or Supreme Energy vested in Goddess Durga, the Divine Mother of the Universe. Others have it that Rama's saintly wife Sita, having been kidnapped by the demon Ravana, assumed the form of the Terrible Destructress, Goddess Kali – otherwise known as Durga – and destroyed this thousand-headed King of the Demons.

Greatly celebrated during Dasain, again glorifying the triumph of Good over Evil, is Goddess Durga's slaying of the terrible demon Mahisasura, who roamed the earth, terrorizing the populace in the guise of a ferocious water buffalo. Other accounts reveal how Lord Rama, having sworn to kill the evil Mahisasura of the Underworld, enlisted the Divine Energy of Goddess Taleju – still another of Durga's many forms – promising to take her to his Indian capital of Ayodhya and erect there a temple in her honour. It seems that Goddess Durga, as Taleju, was King Rama's ancestral family deity, eventually taken as clan goddess of the Nepalese Malla kings. She is to this day the Divine Protectress of Nepal and her rulers, her temples standing adjacent to all the old royal palaces.

No matter how the story is told, victory is celebrated during Dasain fortnight with great rejoicing, and Goddess Durga is adored throughout the land as the Divine Mother Goddess who liberated the suffering people from the miseries of Evil.

In preparation for Dasain every home is ceremonially cleansed with cowdung, decorated, painted and freshened for the visitation of Goddess Durga and the long-awaited return of distant and nearby family members. Footpaths and roads are congested with homebound travellers trekking overland, crowding into bullock carts, buses, trucks, automobiles and, in recent years, the airplane. Bazaars and shops are filled with holiday buyers seeking new clothing, gifts, luxuries, and tremendous supplies of temple offerings for the gods, as well as foodstuffs for days of family feasting. For weeks in advance droves of sheep, goats, ducks, chickens and water buffalo are herded into the valley from the southern Terai flatlands and outlying hills in preparation for the great slaughter. These are sold by villagers who return to their homes laden with the city produce necessary for Dasain.

All government, educational and military institutions and many business houses are closed for ten to fifteen days. Hiring of labourers is impossible. Workers expect bonuses, leave and salary advances; loans are often taken to cover the heavy expenses incurred by one and all. In recent years the Western innovation of exchanging greeting cards has come into vogue, and at every turn the traditional blessings 'Vijaya Dasami' and 'Subbha Dasain!' are heard.

The first nine days of Dasain are called *Nawa Ratri*, Nine Nights; Tantric rites were formerly conducted in the secrecy of night, but in Nepal are openly observed. Here the infinitely ancient mother-cult of Mother Earth and Mother Nature takes form in the worship of Shakti, where the Life Force is embodied in the Divine Energy or Power of the female, depicted as Goddess Durga in all her many forms. All Mother Goddesses who emanated from Durga are known as Devis, each with different aspects and powers, nine of whom, collectively called Nawa Durga, are listed in the scriptures, but many more are worshipped in Nepal.

Groups of devotees chanting sacred hymns, carrying lamps, accompanied by musical bands hurry through the darkness to bathe and purify their souls at a different *tirtha* or sacred bathing spot on each of the Nine Nights. It is vital to bathe 'while stars are still seen in the Heavens'. Men in loin cloths and women in bathing sarongs shiver knee-deep in the sacred rivers, bowing, praying, sprinkling themselves or immersing completely. Many light oil wicks on green leaf saucers and send them dancing down the current. Then with dripping hair and damp clothing they mass before the temples of Durga in the pre-dawn chill, holding their trays of offerings above the heads of the milling throng.

In many mother-goddess temples the deity is represented simply as a sacred *kalash*, or water jug symbolic of the Devi Goddesses, usually of baked red clay. In others, Durga, wife of Shiva, is depicted holding murderous weapons in all her eighteen hands, the Great Protectress who controls the mystery of life and death – of birth, procreation and fertility – with her terrible power. Especially is she worshipped and propitiated as Kali, the dark malignant Destructress wearing a necklace of skulls, standing on the mangled bodies of her victims, her long tongue dripping blood. In this awe-inspiring form she is also called Bhairabi, the female aspect of Bhairab the Terrible, who is one of the most ancient, powerful and venerated gods in Nepal.

Durga is the same as Taleju, family deity of Nepalese kings; and Gujeswari whose dreadful powers are so hidden and secret as to be beyond human understanding; Kumari, the famous Living

14. Men costumed to represent the Nawa (Nine) Durgas, powerful Mother Goddesses, parade through the streets of Kathmandu at Nar Devi Tole   (Teeka Simha)
Holy bathing, a vital part of Dasain festival, in the sacred Bagmati River at the temple of Gujeswari, one of the Mother Goddesses   (Betty Woodsend)

15. Idol of Maiti Devi, one of the blood-thirsty Mother Goddesses who receives animal sacrifices during Dasain festival, Kathmandu (Teeka Simha)

Fulpati, decorated flower bouquet, is carried from the old royal palace in Gorkha to Hanuman Dhoka palace in Kathmandu during Dasain festival. Here ladies said to dwell at the old palace in Hanuman Dhoka accompany its procession (Shridhar Manandhar)

Goddess and ruling deity of the Kathmandu Valley; Tara, the beautiful, frightening Buddhist goddess; Laxmi, Saraswati, Gauri, Uma, Sati and Parbati – all the daughters and wives of Lord Shiva. Durga, long associated with military prowess, is embodied in all the mother deities – compassionate, forgiving and all-protecting when properly assuaged with generous offerings of blood and intoxicating spirits, but inflicting terrible disease, evils and misfortunes if angered through neglect.

In old Bhadgaon town, where the Durga Devis have appeared through the ages from the bowels of Mother Earth at various places now considered holy, the Nine Nights are especially sacred. Each morning a community *puja* is performed at a different Devi shrine and the goddess is carried through the sloping stone streets with most of the inhabitants following jubilantly in her wake.

In the dark narrow lanes of Patan for nine nights is re-enacted the fantastic spectacle of the ancient Asta Matrikas, the Eight Mother Earth Goddesses, impersonated by slender male dancers in goddess masks, bedecked with jewels, flowers, head-dresses and glittering ceremonial costumes. They are accompanied by other deities, among whom Bhairab predominates in a great blue mask, robes and a long mop of matted hair. Amid a milling crush of humanity the goddesses are first seated at intervals along a narrow lane leading off Durbar Square, their hands held in exotic religious poses, their ankle bells jingling with a palsy-like shaking of the knees signifying that the spirit of the goddess has entered the dancers' bodies. The dancers are worshipped as real goddess, each fanned by solicitous attendants lest she be overcome by the rarity of oxygen in the fervent crowds which come to leave lavish food and flower offerings at her feet.

Sometime before midnight the goddesses, led by surrounding attendants, move in slow procession through the mobs with delicate posturing of bare feet and arms to the raised plinth of the Mahadev temple next to Krishna Mandir. There they present individual and group dances in the light of fiery torches and blinding gas lanterns, accompanied by thumping drums, blasting horns and the chanting of red-robed priests reading from ancient texts. These old traditional dances are re-enacted on each of the nine nights with a final afternoon performance on the tenth day in the courtyard of the Goddess Taleju's temple in Patan's old royal palace.

The first day of Dasain is called Ghatasthapana, which means 'the establishing of the holy water vessel', when the *kalash* water jug representing Goddess Durga, often with her image embossed on the side, is placed in the prayer room or some blessed and puri-fied area of the home. It is filled with holy water and the outside decorated with designs in cowdung into which are sown barley seeds and other grains. Surrounding piles of sand are also seeded with grain. The priest or householder intones a welcome, be-seeching Durga to bless the vessel with her presence. This *puja* must be performed at a certain auspicious moment determined by astrologers, when the spirit of Durga is thought to alight on the rim of the jug for only 'as long as a mustard seed can stand up-right on a cow's horn'.

Now the vessel actually becomes the Goddess and is worshipped as Durga throughout Dasain. The *kalash* and sand are blessed each day with a sprinkling of holy water and kept shielded from the light. By the tenth day of Dasain the seeds have sprouted to a height of five or six inches. This sacred yellow *jamara* 'flower' is gathered in small bouquets and bestowed by parents and elders atop the heads of the children as a token of their and Goddess Durga's blessing. During the last days of Dasain men and women wear the jamara sprouts behind their ears or in their hair as a decoration of Dasain.

All through Dasain the room where the Durga *kalash* has been established is kept purified and sacred and away from women. It is called the 'Dasain Ghar', House of Dasain, a place sacred to Durga, where daily religious ceremonies are performed. During Dasain wealthy Hindu families maintain Brahmin priests who stay in this room garbed always in blood-red cloth in deference to Durga's favourite colour, to perform the family ceremonies.

The seventh day of Dasain is *Fulpati*, meaning sacred flowers and leaves, when the *kalash* or sacred Durga vessel of the royal family is 'established' in the Dasain Ghar of the old royal palace at Hanuman Dhoka with pomp and ceremony befitting the might of the throne.

The royal *kalash*, filled with a bouquet of tall flowers, banana stalks, holy leaves and sugar cane tied with red cloth, is carried by men from the ancestral royal house in Gorkha forty-three miles and three walking-days over hills to the northwest. Following Tantric rites this Fulpati symbolizes the original family goddess Taleju whose idol is also enshrined in the Gorkha palace, the ancestral home of the present ruling family.

Mid-afternoon finds hundreds of government officials, meticulously attired in traditional formal dress -- black cap and coat, below which extends the snow-white, long Nepali shirt and tight-legged white jodpurs. They amass at Rani Pokhari, the large Queen's Pond in central Kathmandu, awaiting the arrival of royal Brahman priests with the Fulpati flowers from Gorkha. With their arrival, military guns boom from the nearby Tundikhel parade ground where Their Majesties are reviewing the troops, awarding medals and receiving Dasain greetings from foreign dignitaries. A short act of worship takes place, a goat is sacrificed to the sacred bouquet and the parade begins.

The Fulpati is carried by Brahmans on a decorated palanquin under a gold-tipped and embroidered umbrella, led by the antiquated military platoon of the royal priest, and accompanied by three or four ladies of the Royal family who are said to dwell in the old Hanuman Dhoka palace. The parade moves through the massed populace and narrow bazaar streets to Hanuman Dhoka, followed by a great procession of officials and marching bands. Cannons boom, volleys of artillery fire crack, and the smoke of military gun salvos from the Tundikhel drifts over the throngs of spectators.

On reaching the old royal palace the Fulpati is whisked past Hanuman, the monkey god who guards the door, into an inner chamber where the royal Dasain Ghar is established. Heavily decorated military men, government officials and the general public fill the square, waiting. Soon the sirens of security police on roaring motor cycles and a squadron of red-coated royal guards clear the way for the royal limousine. Hundreds bow with touching palms in the traditional *namaste* obeisance before Their Majesties, the King and Queen of Nepal; beribboned officers stand in stiff salute and the royal family enters the palace where the ancient Malla kings once lived, as well as the ancestors of the present dynasty, who conquered the valley from Gorkha two hundred years ago. The national anthem is heard, the King and Queen worship the sacred Fulpati flowers and kalash which represents their ancestral family goddess, and soon they are whisked away again through a crush of adoring subjects. Now the royal Fulpati has been officially established in rites simultaneously performed, it is said, at the old royal house in Gorkha.

With the arrival of Maha Asthami, the great eighth day, the fervour of worship and sacrifice to Durga and Kali increases. Orthodox Hindus fast all through the day in preparation for *Kalratri*, the Black Night, when hundreds of buffalo, goats, sheep, chickens and ducks are sacrificed at the Mother Goddess temples. Inside Hanuman Dhoka, at Taleju temple courtyard, countless buffaloes representing the demon Mahisasura are slaughtered under the auspices of the State in accordance with exacting, mysterious Tantric rites which must be followed to the letter of the ancient texts. Some are slashed and hacked, they say, while others are pierced through the heart, have their throats cut or their heads severed – all in the name of Goddess Kali.

One remembers that not very many decades ago human sacrifices were common, and though now outlawed, rumours persist that certain sects at certain temples, such as the one in Hari Sidhi village on the road to Godavari, this ancient custom is still occasionally and secretly performed. Many remember when legal human sacrifices were held at Dakshin Kali near Farping where today each Tuesday and Saturday innumerable animals and fowl are sacrificed, and where, on this Black Night of Dasain, Kali is today literally bathed in blood.

People insist that even now children 'disappear' seemingly into thin air, never to be heard of again. And a girl under the age of puberty is terrorized by tales and threats that if she wanders abroad unescorted she may be hypnotized or unknowingly put under a spell by certain *yogi* men who will lead her, powerless to resist, into their abode in some jungle thicket. There she remains, they say, in a state of religious bliss for a year, carefully trained and prepared in secret Tantric rituals before being led one day to the temple for sacrifice. Then by some unknown process her body is supposedly reduced to powder and used by the *yogi* man as sacred incense.

During Dasain certain followers of Lord Vishnu, vegetarians who perform no animal sacrifice, hack to pieces a *kubindo* pumpkin – two pieces of which, they say, if eaten by a pregnant woman, will cause her to abort. Some Newars break duck eggs over the idols and often drink the yolks as a *prasad* gift from Durga. Many believe their sacrifices, whether eggs, pumpkins or living creatures, represents Durga's slaying the demon Mahisasura. It is believed that animals sacrificed to the gods at Dasain, and during the year, are thereby relieved from the burdens of animal life and will be reincarnated as humans, so gaining their chance for ultimate salvation.

Most animals and fowls are sacrificed by slitting the throat, drawing the head back and holding the creature so that its blood spurts out over the idol and surrounding *puja* area. At Taleju temple, they say, the higher the blood spurts the more meritorious the sacrifice, and so the aim is for the highest tier of the temple roof. Failing this, the blood must shoot into the temple and wash over the *kalash* vessel which represents Durga as Taleju. Otherwise the efficacy of the offering is lost. Now the animal's head is completely severed, a portion of its tail is stuffed into the mouth, and it is placed on the ground facing the idol, humble and quiet. The head is often left for the temple keeper and the body is returned to the donor, which he considers a *prasad*, a gift from the gods, to be consumed in family feasting.

Goddess Durga prefers the blood of black, uncastrated male animals, especially water buffaloes, reminiscent of the buffalo demon she killed in ages past. While many householders perform their own sacrifices, others employ men of a certain caste traditionally thought to be brave, strong and immune to the repugnance of killing. Such men of the old royal palace are said to dance in the streets during Dasain singing, 'Mountains of flesh and seas of blood'. Brahmans, although they may officiate at the ceremony, do not perform actual sacrifices.

Thus, at night on the eighth day, great feasts are held in the home where large quantities of meat are consumed. Meat is also distributed to relatives and friends as a gift of *prasad*, in keeping with the tradition of generosity and good fellowship traditional to Dasain.

Again, on the great ninth day, *Maha Nawami*, called *Nawa Ratri* or Ninth Night, people rush to the temples with gifts, animals and prayers for the Mother Goddesses. Newars call this day '*Syako Tyako*' believing that 'the more you kill, the more you gain'. Especially on this ninth day, but also throughout the year at certain times, Newars have the head of their sacrificed goat cut into eight specific parts - two eyes, two ears, one nose, one tongue and two jaws - which are bound and tied back into place with a reed. This re-assembled head is cooked and carried to the home of the eldest male relative - usually the father. Eight men, seated on the floor in a row according to seniority, are offered the head. Each eats that portion which tradition allots to his rank - another of the countless ancient customs the Newars religiously follow to maintain the vital bonds of ancestral family organization.

Of significance on the ninth day is the early-morning official military sacrifices in the courtyard of the old armoury or *kot*, just across the square from Hanuman Dhoka, where animals, mostly black buffaloes, are slaughtered by the hundreds to honour Durga the Goddess of Victory and Might, and to seek her blessing of power upon the guns, bayonets and regimental flags. Foreigners with bulky camera equipment arise at dawn to jostle with hundreds of Nepalese for vantage-points on fences, rooftops and balconies. Military bands play lively tunes, guns boom and officers decked with medals, ribbons and full dress uniform stand at attention with their troops.

Before each display of regimental colours stands a post against which the animal's face is securely pressed and roped. The 'execu-

tioner' waits with a tremendous raised knife. An attendant sprin-
kles the buffalo with holy water, and suddenly, with one fierce
blow, the head falls and the body lies twitching, blood streaming
over the earth. The head is placed on the ground before the regimental flags, and the body is swiftly pulled aside by the leg and
thrust upon a heap of bloody carcasses to be used later in regimental feasts. Many officers perform their own sacrifice, and uneasy
is the man who does not accomplish the task with one stroke, for
this is an evil omen of certain misfortune.

Onlookers speak in whispers of another massacre which took
place in this same courtyard in 1846 when Jung Bahadur Rana, his
heart set on ruling Nepal, plotted with the Queen, whose lover
had been mysteriously murdered during evening prayers, possibly
at the instigation of Jung Bahadur himself. The enraged Queen
ordered the gathering of hundreds of unarmed noblemen in the
courtyard in the dead of night to find the murderer. Insults were
exchanged, shots were fired, a few were bayoneted, and before
long all who opposed Jung Bahadur were slaughtered – 500 in all,
some accounts say, while others maintain it was only 134 whose
blood, quite literally, ran into the streets. Thereafter Jung Bahadur
and his descendants reigned supreme for 104 years.

Also on the ninth day of Dasain sacrifices are made to Durga
beseeching protection for vehicles and their occupants against
accidents during the year. Blood from the severed body or gashed
throat is strewn over the vehicle, especially the four wheels, along
with intoxicating liquors, flowers, rice and red powder. Others
sacrifice to Bhairab, who, apart from his role as the male counterpart of Durga, is the divine instrument of locomotion and represents the moving force of vehicles. Each year at Dasain a goat is
sacrificed before each plane of The Royal Nepal Airlines for the
same reason.

The god Vishwa Karma, the Great Carpenter, producer of all
implements, tools and mechanical things, large and small, inventor
of handicrafts and the arts, is propitiated on this ninth day, when
factories, workshops and all tools must remain idle. Implements
are laid out with flowers, incense and flaming wicks. A bleating

goat or squawking duck is brought forward. A sacred, magic Tantric phrase is whispered in its ear, it is offered food, blessed with a sprinkling of holy water, and when it shakes its body, nods its head or flicks its ear the *mantra* has 'taken effect', the spirit of the deity has entered the goat's body and it has given consent for execution. Then the tools are drenched with blood. If the animal does not make the appropriate movement, he has been rejected by the deity as unacceptable for sacrifice, and is mercifully allowed to live. He is immediately replaced by another.

Thus the books of a student are blessed, instruments of doctors and craftsmen, weapons of hunters and military men – all implements of all professions are worshipped in the hope that Durga, or Vishwa Karma, will bestow power and grant perfection in their operation.

The peak of celebration, and the official conclusion of Dasain, is reached on Vijaya Dasami, the Great Tenth Day of Victory from which Dasain takes its name. This is the day on which Lord Rama slew the demon Ravana, and Durga appeared in a great fury, riding on a lion to vanquish Mahisasura in response to fervent prayers from gods and men. Their triumphant victories sent waves of jubilation through heaven and earth, marking the triumph of the power of righteousness over all that is evil. Holy baths are taken and there is a last-minute rush to the temples of Durga with offerings and gifts for the gods.

It is obligatory for Hindus on this Day of Victory to visit all elder relatives and superiors in strict order of seniority or rank, starting with parents. Unless one has a vital and valid excuse, failure to appear is an offence of utmost gravity, signifying that all relationships are severed. Some Newars, who throughout Dasain have been celebrating traditional feasts and ceremonies where the entire family clan is involved, may not observe this custom, paying instead an honarary visit to their employers or superiors.

The purpose of this visit is to receive the Tika blessing, a dot of red paste placed upon the visitor's forehead by his elder's hand. Often the scarlet paste is taken from the Durga vessel in which it had earlier been presented as an offering – a mixture of vermilion powder, rice and milk curd. The Tika is an ancient emblem of victory and power worn by the Devi goddesses, often bestowed upon soldiers on their way to battle, and is now a blessing of good fortune upon one and all. Many wear it as a simple beauty mark as well.

Hundreds of Nepalese, dressed in their finest, rush from one end of the valley to the other to convey their respects, receive the Tika blessing, exchange pleasant greetings and partake of food and drink together. Those whose relatives are numerous may be occupied with this ritual for the next five days, until full moon day, for it is vital to overlook no one. *Tika Puja* is a time completely devoted to good fellowship, when all disputes, quarrels and feuds must be forgotten – when goodwill and good cheer must reign supreme.

When the King of Nepal receives the official Tika blessing at the palace from the royal Brahman priest as *prasad* or blessing from Goddess Durga – a thirty-one-gun salute reverberates round the valley. Thereafter he receives the blessing of the two Queen Mothers and traditionally spends the remainder of the day placing Tika benediction on the foreheads of royal family members, relatives, Nepalese dignitaries and the general populace.

During the afternoon of Vijaya Dasami curious parades are held simultaneously in several parts of old Kathmandu, known as *Kharga Jatra*, the Sword Processions. In ancient Tantric tradition Buddhist priests costumed to represent Kali, Bhairab, Kumari, Ajima, Ganesh and other deities march solemnly through excited, noisy crowds holding antiquated, sheathed swords before them, amid a fanfare of music, each beneath a twirling ceremonial umbrella. The sword, a symbol of Durga's power, trembles and vibrates in the hands of each priest, seemingly uncontrollable, indicating to one and all that he is possessed by the spirit of the deity he represents. Onlookers carrying umbrellas or wearing leather dare not approach the procession lest the sword-carrying deities attack the offender.

Occasionally a hypnotized, semi-conscious or entranced performer leaps out of control, escaping the guiding hands of attendants. Onlookers clap, whistle and cheer as though inviting danger, but they frantically scatter when he nears, surging back only when the sword-carrier becomes more tranquil. The parade moves single file around temples and Buddhist stupas while attendants fan smoking incense into their faces, musicians beat drums, and singers strain their voices in united high-pitched song.

People say the strange, prolonged shaking and trembling of such performers is not caused by liquors or drugs, since they have undergone the most severe fasting during the day, not being allowed even water or cigarettes. The only explanation given is simply that the god or goddess has entered his body and he is possessed by its spirit. Perhaps he is in a religious trance, either self-induced or brought on by day-long preparation amidst throbbing drums, smoking incense and priests chanting magic Tantric incantations, and his own intense faith in the mystic powers of the gods.

In homes, at the end of the Great Tenth Day of Dasain, the Dasain Ghar and Durga's sacred vessel are disassembled, the offerings disposed of in ritual ceremony, and the Brahman priest intones an ancient Vedic prayer: 'Give us peace, O Goddess, preserve peace, and give peace to the earth and the whole universe.'

On the day of the full moon or last day of Dasain fortnight, called Kartik Purnima, orthodox Hindu women begin a monthlong fast at Pashupatinath, at outlying temples or in their homes, taking very little food each day and drinking water in which the Shiva lingam is bathed. A month later, at next full moon, Pashupatinath temple is ablaze with lights, surrounded by singing and dancing devotees all through the night. Next morning the wan but triumphant women return to their homes and the acclaim of their families.

At the Dasain full moon Buddhists parade from early morning till dark past the hundreds of shrines, *chaityas* and Buddhist holy places of Patan scattering grains, foods and coins over each in a penance to bring peace to the souls of their dead, much as is done during the holy month of Gunla. This full moon day is also called Kojagrata, meaning 'who is awake', when the Hindu goddess of wealth, Laxmi, is worshipped again and private gambling games are played in the homes.

Now the nation settles back to normal, workers return to their jobs, travellers return to their homes, and the populace tightens its belt to repay loans and advances, strengthened by the knowledge that they have unstintingly given gifts and homage to Goddess Durga. For the holy texts promise that those who observe the ritual of Dasain will acquire virtue, power, wealth and many offspring, and they will surely escape the miseries of evil and sin.

18 PACHALI BHAIRAB JATRA
The God of Terror rides again

The fierce and terrifying Lord Bhairab, though known to represent the destructive power of Shiva, is more intimately concerned with day-to-day life than Shiva is, and stands independently as one of the most adored, feared and propitiated gods in Nepal. Bhairab's powerful name is evoked during every festival and for all the ceremonial rites concerned with the main events of one's life – like birth, the first rice-feeding, puberty, marriage and death. A new home cannot be constructed until Bhairab is propitiated, barren women petition him for fertility, and pregnant women are forbidden even to touch his picture or idol lest his wrath cause her to abort.

The estimated five million Bhairab images in Nepal are seen in sixty-four different manifestations and forms depicting his combined human, demonic and animal characteristics. His heavy, repulsively stunted body is garlanded with human skulls. He brandishes human heads and murderous weapons in his several hands and tramples on the prostrate bodies of his victims, the male counterpart of the terrifying Goddess Kali.

In thousands of clay, paper, metal and wooden masks Bhairab's malignant, bulging eyes glare above his open, snarling mouth, from which canine-like fangs protrude. As popularly represented by ceremonial dancers, he invariably wears a dark blue mask and robes below a great mop of unkempt, flowing hair. Often Bhairab is worshipped in the form of a sacred stone, perenially smothered with brilliant red powder, and he is frequently seen as an earthenware or metal water vase, a *kalash*, his awesome countenance engraved on its side.

Identified with Shiva, Bhairab is likewise considered the father of Ganesh. He is the husband of Ajima, that powerful grandmother goddess who controls disease – a holy terror in her own right. Bhairab has an insatiable appetite for meat, blood, and alcohol, and if hungry or unappeased he dances like a fiendish, drunken ogre, mad with rage, bringing death in a matter of minutes, by causing the negligent to haemorrhage from mouth and nose. Rare is the man who dares slight Lord Bhairab.

Like many deities in Nepal, each important Bhairab idol has a definitive name and is thought to possess peculiar traits and powers. Akash Bhairab is guardian deity of the Indrachowk locality, reigning from his second-story temple home in Kathmandu with eyes turned perpetually skyward, for his glance brings destruction wherever it falls. And whosoever dares to tell an untruth before the huge, black stone statue of Kal Bhairab that dominates Hanuman Dhoka's open square is sure to die vomiting blood. This accounts for the recently-abandoned custom of administering the oath of office to government officials and forcing accused criminals to swear before this awesome god.

Bhag or Tiger Bhairab in Kirtipur village, represented as a brass, tiger-faced mask, confirms the legend of boy cowherds in ancient times who playfully formed a toy tiger of clay. When they returned from the forest with a leaf for its tongue, they found their creation had taken life, and to this day Bhag Bhairab's gaping mouth is tongueless.

There are several Unmateswar Bhairabs in the valley – at Panauti village, inside the Shiva temple at Pashupatinath, and at Kumbeshwar Mahadev shrine in Patan. The last-mentioned is a decaying, life-size wooden statue in a latticed courtyard window. Its immense, erect penis is draped with flower offerings from women suffering from barrenness, frigidity and menstrual irregularity, and it is said that Unmateswar Bhairab's efficacy is so powerful that the mere sight of him causes women to be consumed with desire.

Of all the Bhairabs, one of the most popular, powerful and ancient is Pachali, whose outdoor temple site is near the Bagmati River between Tripureswar and Kalimati, just south of old Kathmandu. His shrine is in a square, sunken courtyard surrounded by stone gods and goddesses, open porches and three-storied, mud-brick dwellings and cloisters. In this courtyard, under a gnarled and spreading peepul tree, a canopy protects a most sacred hole, plated with sheets of brass. Here Pachali Bhairab is 'hiding'. Some say the smooth round stone visible in this six-inch-wide pit is the buried summit of five combined Shiva lingams – hence the name 'pacha-li' thought to refer to 'five lingams', affirming Bhairab's relationship to Lord Shiva and his phallic emblem.

Others, conforming with legends in which many Bhairabs are identified as various ancient Nepalese kings, say Pachali is the name of one such sovereign who ruled from Farping village near Chobar Gorge. They say this King Pachali tried to conceal his Bhairab identity by locking himself in a room each evening to consume the disgusting quantities of food required to satiate this deity – one full goat and tremendous mounds of rice. At last his young wife could not conceal her curiosity and insisted she be allowed inside his dining-room. In time, and unwillingly, Pachali succumbed to her persistence, warning her against becoming frightened at what she might see, and instructing her to throw rice over him once her curiosity was satisfied, for only this grain would restore his human form.

When Pachali sat down to his feast and assumed the monstrous shape of Bhairab, his wife completely forgot instructions and fled terrified into the night. He followed, searching everywhere, and at last near sunrise, fearing his subjects would see him in the form of a terrible ogre, hid himself near Pachali Bhairab's 'place' by the river, where he remains to this day. His wife fell, they say, some distance away and came to be known as Lumarhi, the dangerous goddess Bhadra Kali whose temple stands at the eastern edge of the Tundikhel parade ground.

A haunting and similar Newar story tells how a young girl of the Khasai caste used to herd her pigs daily in the vicinity of Pachali Bhairab's place. This monster god, who is thought to belong to the Newari Jyapu farmer caste, watched the girl and, contrary to all caste rules, determined to possess her. He changed his hideous form into that of a beautiful youth and before long was meeting the girl. Eventually she became pregnant. One evening, as the young couple lay talking, the girl asked her lover, belatedly it seems, just who he was and from whence he came. Pachali Bhairab begged her not to insist on an answer, but finally succumbed when she promised to throw the magic rice over him once she saw his true form.

When the young girl saw her lover as Bhairab with long fangs, bulging eyes, matted hair flowing around the gross body, she fled from the place in horror, with Bhairab in her wake pleading that she follow instructions. When the first cock crowed – a signal which still brings out the populace for morning ablutions and the calls of nature – Bhairab returned to his place by the river and hid in a hole. Today people say the rounded stone visible in the sacred pit is the buttocks of Pachali Bhairab.

As for the Khasai girl, the violent chase caused her baby to be born in the roadway, where she abandoned it and fled in panic, never to be heard of again. Some people of the Khasai caste found the child, reared him in their home, and when he grew to manhood they were astonished to find he was Ganesh, the Elephant God of Good Fortune, son of Shiva and thus of Pachali Bhairab. Today, in a certain Khasai household in Kathmandu, a gold-plated silver image of Ganesh, handed down through the generations, is worshipped by the Khasai people and brought out only once each year for the Pachali Bhairab festival.

While Pachali Bhairab is known to be hiding in the sacred hole, he is further manifested as an equally sacred four-foot gilded *kalash* or holy water vase on whose side is embossed a heavy mask of Bhairab. As customary with many important idols, this Bharab *kalash* is cared for by a different household each year, always by members of the Jyapu caste organization which is charged with the responsibility of Pachali Bhairab, his temple place and his annual festival. This same household maintains for a year an oval, silver bowl which is a most sacred representation of Bhairab's dangerous wife, Ajima.

Pachali Bhairab's festival begins on the fourth day of the waxing moon of September or early October, actually during the great Dasain holidays. On this night the ponderous Bhairab *kalash* is carried in triumphant procession from his 'home' in Kathmandu to his shrine near the river, where he is worshipped all through the night with music, religious ceremonies, and gifts of all kinds, including quantities of meat, rice-beer and the blood of countless goats and fowl, brought by crowds of fervent devotees. Towards daylight, when the astrologers calculate the stars and planets are correctly situated, a huge buffalo is sacrificed according to specific Tantric rules in a sacrificial fire glowing from a square pit in the sunken courtyard.

The animal's throat is slit and he dies as his blood is made to spurt high over the *kalash*, the sacred pit and the surrounding canopied area in a special offering to the bloodthirsty Pachali Bhairab. Next the head is severed and burned in the flames to honour Agni, the ancient Vedic God of Fire. An officiating priest cries, 'Thousands of gods – thousands of pieces of meat', as chunks of flesh and skin are hacked from the carcass and thrown high into the air to land in the fire. With each offering of raw flesh the priest calls out the name of a different god, as well as those of ghosts, evil spirits and unhappy, malignant souls of the dead who haunt the valley, whom Bhairab is thought to control.

The resultant ashes make a most powerful amulet when smeared on the body or forehead as a *prasad* blessing from Bhairab. People continue to come all through the second day to bring offerings, make blood sacrifices and carry away some sacred ash.

Starting in the early morning of this day, the fifth of the dark fortnight, a certain man of the Jyapu caste is kept in a building bordering the outdoor shrine of Bhairab being prepared to act as Ajima, the terrifying wife of Bhairab. He undergoes strict fasting, is 'purified' with a holy bath, has his finger and toe nails trimmed, hair and eyebrows shaved to remove all 'unclean' body growths. While the oval silver bowl itself is actually Ajima, when it is carried in this man's upturned palms and held close to his chest in a manner prescribed in the Tantric manuscripts, its spirit enters his

16. Flower and garland stalls, especially set up for Festival of Lights in preparation for Mha Puja and Bhai Tika   (Shridhar Manandhar)

17. Fruit, vital for Festival of Lights ceremonies, is sold in bazaars set up especially for this celebration   (Shridhar Manandhar)

Girl drawing sacred 'Tika' blessing mark on forehead of her brother during Bhai Tika—Brother Worship Day   (Teeka Simha)

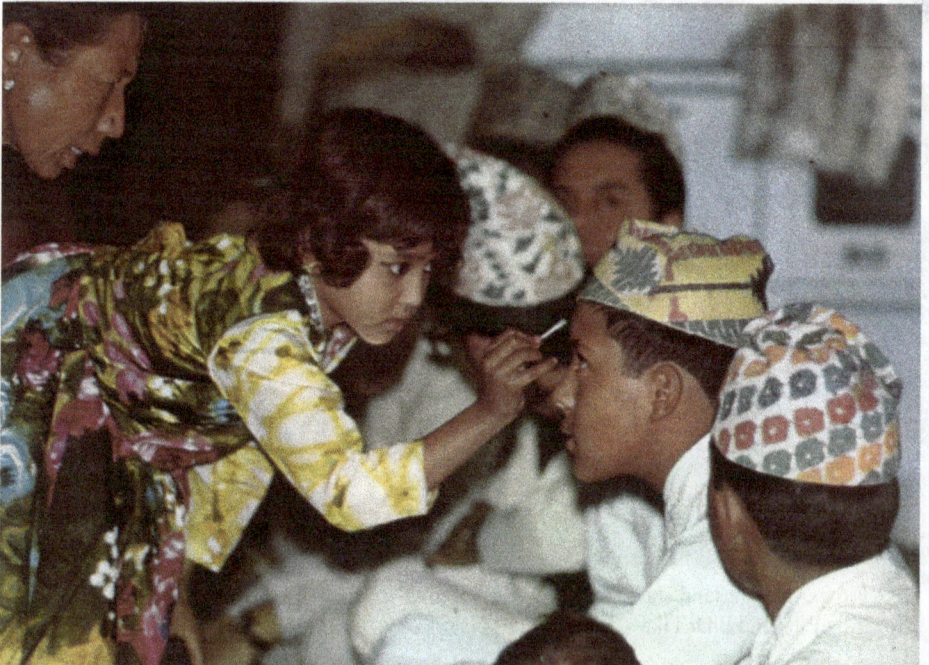

body and the man himself is worshipped as this powerful goddess.

By late evening both the Ajima bowl and the Pachali Bhairab *kalash* overflow with oblations of rice-beer in which float bits of meat, rice, red powder and flowers – a sacred liquid which people sprinkle into their mouths to assure themselves of Bhairab's protection.

A musical procession approaches from Bharmau Tole in old Kathmandu, with a Khasai man carrying the image of Ganesh almost buried in flowers and garlands as it sits atop the special Khasai caste drum. Since each Newari caste and blood-relation organization trains boys in singing and playing instruments, each is proud of his peculiar caste music. The paraders, happily under the influence of rice-beer, come shouting songs and clanging cymbals, bringing Ganesh 'to meet his father Bhairab and escort him back to his Kathmandu home'. They halt on the rough stone pathway in the light of flaming torches some distance away from Pachali Bhairab's shrine, awaiting the auspicious moment set by astrologers, when Bhairab is 'ready to receive his son'.

Ajima waits in a near-by building. Crowds wait in the courtyard, mostly men, milling about, gossiping, watching intoxicated neighbours good-naturedly jostling and rough-housing in the courtyard. Several dozen women huddle on the circular stone platform which rings a tree at the courtyard's edge, bundled in shawls. A band of Jyapu musicians play 'Bhairab music', parading about, crashing cymbals in a deafening, rhythmical din. Under Pachali Bhairab's canopy a crowd of men alternately pray, sing, read out instructions from a holy book and shout directions to others struggling to secure thick ropes about the shining, heavy Bhairab vessel in preparation for his homeward journey.

At last the signal is given, music blares forth and Bhairab's band walks up the path to usher the waiting Ganesh down to his father. Now both groups approach with crashing cymbals, pushing through the crowds and stumbling down the courtyard steps. The elephant god Ganesh is set beside the Bhairab vase and in a terrible clamour of cymbals and thumping drums, 'Bhairab greets his son, Ganesh'.

Now from the near-by building an unsteady group appears, leading Ajima dressed completely in white and holding the sacred bowl at his chest, obviously under a spell or trance, oblivious to the uproar around him. Eyes half closed, he is led, almost carried, down the steps. With another ear-splitting musical blast 'Bhairab greets his wife, Ajima', who, they say, is not Ganesh's real mother at all – only his stepmother.

There follows another long period of waiting while men shout discordant songs and enact religious rites under the canopy. The seated women break out in angry argument – someone wormed his way into their midst, they say – and the culprit is unceremoniously ousted.

Suddenly a path is pushed through the crowds and Ganesh is carried in a wild, noisy procession up the steps and made to circle the courtyard three times before leading off up the rock path toward Kathmandu town. Next the Ajima group, with the human 'goddess' held upright by surrounding helpers, his head lying back on the shoulder of an attendant, is guided – seemingly by Ajima's will, for they have difficulty in controlling her – round and round the courtyard and on up the path after the Ganesh parade.

Tension, excitement and noise mount to a fever pitch as the heavy, gleaming Pachali Bhairab vessel is hoisted by ropes and supported precariously by a dozen struggling men. They weave their way around the courtyard and up the path in the midst of a terrible din of music and singing. Holding flaming torches and blinding gas lanterns, hundreds of jubilant spectators follow in their wake to escort the gods back to their homes.

Suddenly there are excited shouts of 'Danger! Out of the way!' Crowds scatter from the path, jabbering, concernedly straining to see the cause of this reversal. Something has gone wrong, they say. Bhairab is angry or unhappy. Perhaps some Tantric rites have been omitted, some ceremony incorrectly performed which displeases the crotchety god.

Everyone looks worried as the Bhairab parade rushes back down the path and re-enters the sunken courtyard with those carrying Ganesh and Ajima hard on their heels, followed by attendants, musicians and the wondering crowd. The great *kalash* of Bhairab is re-installed in his canopied shrine, and after whispered speculations, long discussion and excited gesturing, the entire ceremony is begun again.

Long after midnight the procession once more heads for the city, staggering under an appeased Bhairab, to arrive in the small hours of morning at Hanuman Dhoka square in front of the old royal palace. Here a great *puja* is performed in which several goats and buffaloes are sacrificed and their blood drunk by performers costumed as Bhairab, Kumari and other bloodthirsty deities. The sacrificial animals are furnished by the Government in the name of the King of Nepal, complying with the ancient tradition by which Nepalese kings themselves formerly attended such ceremonies.

At last the revelling paraders deposit the Bhairab vessel and Ajima bowl back at their Jyapu home. Ganesh is returned to the Khasai household and the celebrating crowd vanishes, leaving the city strangely quiet. Perhaps it is because the dread Pachali Bhairab has been sufficiently fêted and gorged with enough meat, alcohol and blood to keep him tranquil all through the year.

OCTOBER-NOVEMBER

19 TIHAR OR DIWALI
Goddess Laxmi's Festival of Lights

The five days of Tihar are celebrated in October or early November, that glorious harvest moon season in Nepal when pathways, roadsides, courtyards and village squares are expanses of golden unhusked rice and brilliant red chilli peppers drying in the sunshine, when crisp, clear nights forestall the coming of winter. Tihar literally means 'a row of lamps', and lighting displays are traditional, but this festival is actually a succession of significant holidays celebrated for a variety of reasons.

Tihar brings the worship of Laxmi, Goddess of Wealth; and a day to worship one's own body or self. Worshipped in turn are the lowly dog and ill-omened crow, as well as the sacred cow, the family money box and the brothers of every home. The God of Death is propitiated; the ancient New Year starts; and throughout the land an avid and illicit five-day indulgence in that favourite Nepalese pastime – gambling with friends and family – takes place.

Through all five nights, especially during Laxmi Puja of the third day, every home, temple and building is graced by rows of lights – the traditional Nepalese lamp of twisted cotton wick in a small clay bowl of mustard oil – as well as candles and electric bulbs, burn at every window, verandah, doorway, courtyard wall and rooftop. Magnificent displays for those of means; simple ones in smaller homes where a lamp must glow at the roadway entrance as well as at every doorway, window and stairway, and always atop the baked-clay cooking stove. Friendly rivalry between neighbours results from this eagerness to please Laxmi, the goddess who loves light.

164

For she is wife of Lord Vishnu and Goddess of Wealth and Good Fortune, a deity of ethereal beauty who sprang from the froth of the sea when the gods churned the oceans. Laxmi wears a crown of jewels, garlands of flowers, arms decked with gems of heavenly brilliance – her 'treasures from the sea'. She holds a conch shell, lotus blossom and a sheaf of rice, and loves to play with sacred cowrie shells. Often she is pictured seated on a full-blown lotus with a steady stream of coins flowing into a money box.

Nepalese adore this beautiful goddess, make gifts and offerings to her, worship her idols and propitiate her, especially at Tihar festival, when she circles the earth on an owl, inspecting the homes to see that they have been scrupulously cleansed and a light left burning in her honour. For if she is pleased she will protect the money box and grain stores of each family, and grant prosperity throughout the coming year.

They remember the good fortune which came to the ancient King Bali, who had faithfully worshipped Laxmi through the years. Finally, by dint of his pious and charitable acts, Bali became more powerful than the gods and held them all in prison. It was through Laxmi's intercession with her husband Lord Vishnu that the gods were freed, and Bali was given the Kingdom of the Netherworld for his own.

And during Tihar they remember another king whose demise by a poisonous serpent had been foretold for midnight. A court astrologer advised the King he could escape death by placing lamps to Laxmi at his door and around his bed, but if the door light died out then death was near. In that event the Queen was to approach the snake and delay him with flattery and praise.

All happened as predicted, and the snake, blinded by the Queen's compliments, agreed to take the King's soul to Yama, God of Death, and plead that this life should be spared. Now when Yama Raj consulted his great ledger he found the King's age listed as 'zero', meaning his allotted time on earth had run out. But when the clever snake inserted a seven before the zero, Yama gave the King seventy more years to live, and for this miraculous gift of life the King instituted in his realm an annual Festival of Lamps in remembrance of the lights at his deathbed.

Thus Tihar Festival, starting on the thirteenth day of the waning moon, is often called *Panchak Yama*, The Five Days of Yama, when all due respect is paid to this God of Death. On the first day, called *Kag Bali*, the Day of the Crow, this messenger of Yama is worshipped. People set out small dishes made of green leaves sewn together, containing food, coins, burning incense and oil wicks to propitiate this black, predatory bird whose raucous scolding often foretells a death or impending disaster. The Nepalese say the crow leads a charmed existence, since one of his ancient forebears tasted the 'water of life', and in Nepal he is indeed quite free from harm at human hands. Infesting city, village and countryside, the crow fearlessly devours crops and fruit, steals food from the very hands of children, and brings his whole flock to swoop and scream if one member is endangered. Little does this bird of ill omen appreciate the ration of cooked rice set out for him every day by good Nepalese housewives before feeding their own families.

The second day of Tihar is for the worship of dogs, domestic pets as well as the scruffy pariahs that roam the streets. *Swan* or *Sho Puja* is a day when children are warned to treat dogs with kindness, for the dog is the guardian at Yama's gates, and also the steed of the fearful god Bhairab. To honour the dog on his special day means that the gate-keeper of Death's kingdom may ease the soul's passage into the Netherworld to receive Yama's judgment.

The red *tika*, a mark of blessing, is placed on dogs' foreheads, their necks are garlanded with flowers and they are fed like kings for a day. In general, dogs are regarded with disdain even though they provide an invaluable service in towns and villages lacking sewerage systems, for the pariah dogs live off refuse and human excrement. While relatively few Nepalese people keep dogs for pets, they do admire King Yudhishthira of the scriptures, who refused to join his four Pandava brothers and their mother in Heaven until his faithful dog had been admitted.

The third day of Tihar, Laxmi Puja, is of vital importance, for the sacred cow is worshipped in the morning and the Goddess of Wealth, together with the family treasures, at night.

Since time immemorial the cow has been sacred as the visible, earthly form of Goddess Laxmi, and as the 'Earth Mother' providing the essentials of life – milk, curds, butter and dung. In ancient days, and even today in some pastoral areas, wealth was reckoned in terms of cattle, and the offering of a cow to the Brahman priest during religious worship is the holiest of gifts. Thus when money is offered to priests on behalf of the gods it represents and actually takes on the embodiment of a sacred cow. So, for the devout, a sacred cow, a monetary offering and the Goddess of Wealth are one and the same.

During the morning the cows are bathed, vermilion is dabbed on their forehead, horns and tails are blest with red and yellow powders and paints, and garlands are hung from their necks. They are offered marigolds, sweets and fruits. Worshippers touch the cow's body with their foreheads, bow down to her feet, and humbly crawl under her stomach on hands and knees. It is on this day that the people remove the sacred yellow *raksha* thread from their wrists, bestowed upon them three months before, to tie on a sacred cow's tail, praying at the same time that when death comes this sacred animal will assist their souls into heaven.

Homes are thoroughly scrubbed with red mud and cowdung, lamps are made ready and the doorway is decorated with red powder, flowers and festoons, for on this night the Goddess of Wealth circles the globe at midnight, visiting only those homes that have prepared for her visit. Often a lacy white pathway is made on the floor with a blossom dipped in rice flour paste, from the front entrance to the place where the money box is kept, thereby sanctifying every spot whereon Laxmi treads. Flickering oil wick lamps are set near the roadway from which a pathway leads across the bare earth, moistened with holy water, to guide her into the door.

On this night the old people tell of the haughty king who banished his pious daughter because she declared, in all honesty, that her daily bread and sustenance was granted by Fate, and not through the beneficence of her father the King. So enraged was he that he married her off to a poverty-stricken Brahman and sent them to live in a meagre forest hut. Some time later this King, while bathing in his garden, removed his priceless pearl necklace and a kite bird flew away with it over the forests. When the bird spied a dead snake on the roof of a lonely hut, he dropped the pearls and flew away with the more digestible serpent. Now the Princess recognized the necklace on her roof, and when she heard that the King was offering a reward for its return, she sent her Brahman husband to ask only one boon from her father – that on this night during Tihar no lamp should burn in all the kingdom, not even the palace, except in one home – the Brahman's hut. This the King readily granted and redeemed his necklace.

When the midnight hour of Tihar came, the Goddess Laxmi, making her annual tour of inspection on her owl, found this kingdom in darkness except for one shack in the woods. When she entered the door she found the Princess sleeping, but was vastly pleased to see she had left her offerings and a special light burning. As time passed, ill fortune plagued the King. His wealth and power diminished and eventually his palace became a pauper's hut, while the Princess became fabulously wealthy, ending her days in a glittering mansion.

Small wonder that on this night a *puja* is performed for the Goddess of Wealth in every home, conducted by the man of the house. A flower-decked idol or picture of Laxmi is set before the family treasure box, which contains religious relics, jewels, money, deeds and that recent innovation – the cheque-book. Often the Goddess is represented by a gold coin, which is first bathed in milk or holy water from a sacred river. Smaller households use a silver coin, for worship of gold and silver is indispensable to *Laxmi Puja*. Accounts books are brought out and a row of lamps set before the image with invocations for the goddess's continued protection of this store of wealth and for increased prosperity during the coming year. A new supply of money is placed in the box, petitioning Laxmi to make it multiply – a 'nest egg' which is never touched except in dire emergency.

Throughout this sacred night a lamp must be kept burning in Laxmi's honour, and lamp-black accumulated thereby is especially efficacious when painted around the eyes in warding off disease and the dread influence of the 'evil eye'. On this evening, too, groups of women and children go from door to door singing the *Bhailo* song, asking for alms, receiving coins and sweetmeats from housewives in an old custom which is the perogative of men and boys on the following night. Towns and villages and rural shacks glow with rows of lights. Doors and windows are flung open to welcome Goddess Laxmi. Children run through the streets with glittering sparklers, and the crack of fireworks is heard all over town.

The fourth day of Tihar is celebrated in ways that vary with the different communities. Many families worship their bullocks in the morning, just as the sacred cow was honoured the day before in a rite called *Goru Puja*, in the hope that these valuable animals will be protected from disease and accident. On this day also household utensils, gardening tools and farming implements are worshipped and blessed.

For those who follow the cult of Lord Krishna, the morning ceremony called *Gobhardan Puja* reflects a kinship with the ancient cowherders and the scriptural story of Krishna supporting Mount Gobhardan on his little finger and so protecting the people, their cattle and land from rain and flood. For these rites the woman forms a miniature Mount Gobhardan from cowdung. On it is placed a clay figure of Krishna lying on his back surrounded with small cowdung cakes and sprigs of green grass, representing herd cows and trees. On this mountain is placed the butter churn staff, pieces of sugar cane, parched rice and lighted oil wicks. Worship is done before this idol and the menfolk file past, bowing reverently to the sacred mountain.

Cowdung is sacred throughout Nepal, a commodity essential for purifying the home and the individual, for enriching the fields and for burning as fuel when it has been dried into cakes. Farmers often prostrate themselves before the dung heap, presenting offerings of flowers, lighted wicks, boiled rice and fruits, asking that the land be well fertilized and the harvest abundant.

Of greatest importance on this fourth day of Tihar, the first of
the bright lunar fortnight, is the *Mha Puja*, Worship of One's Body
or Self. It reflects the mystical belief that the body is divine, that
the holy spirit dwells within not only each individual, but in every
object, inanimate as well as living. During the rites of *Mha Puja*,
Yama Raj, King of Death, and Yamadut his Messenger are worshipped for allowing life to exist, and petitioned to bestow longevity on each family member, as well as the implements used in
daily living. *Mha Puja* purifies the heart and soul for the coming
New Year and asks for enlightenment in sacred, ancient rites which
strengthen the perpetual bonds of kinship in families.

On this night members of the immediate family gather in an
empty room, where the mud floor has been washed with cowdung
and red earth, leaving the air sweet and clean. The father makes a
series of *mandals* all in a row, one for each person and one each
for the God of Death and his messenger. The *mandal* is a geometric
design made on the floor by rubbing white limestone over a paper
which has been perforated to leave a full-blown lotus pattern. It
is further decorated with sprinklings of red powder, concentric
circles of rice and dried beans, with a smaller inner circle traced
by an oil-covered finger. A large grapefruit represents purity of
heart.

Each person seats himself cross-legged before his *mandal* and a
long ceremony is first performed by the father to the *mandals* of
Death and his cohort; then by the mother to father and sons; next
by daughter to mother, and on down to the smallest infant. In this
ritual small pyramids of cooked rice, neck strings decorated with
pieces of satin, fruits, flowers, nuts, red tika for the forehead, an
eight-inch lighted wick representing human life and enlightenment, and the all-important good luck foods – fried hard-boiled
eggs, fried flat fish and country wine – are presented in turn to each
mandal and each person. When the *Mha Puja* is finished and the
mandals are aglow with burning wicks and incense, the family
partakes of a tremendous feast to celebrate the New Year.

For this day is the ending and beginning of the ancient year,
when families and merchants close their ledgers, balance their cash

and open account books, in accordance with the Newar calendar.

The oft-repeated legend of the New Year tells of an ancient king, Ananda Malla of Bhadgaon, east of Kathmandu, whose court astrologer ascertained that sand taken from Lakh Tirtha stream in Kathmandu at a certain hour would turn to gold. The King immediately dispatched four strong men. As they were leaving the stream with their burden of sand, they met a Kathmandu man, Sakhwal, who deemed it mighty suspicious that men from Bhadgaon should come this distance for sand.

Sakhwal invited the men to his home for food and rest, persuaded them to dump the sand there, pointing out that more was readily available. The Bhadgaon men complied, returned to the stream to reload, and headed for home, never realizing the bewitching hour had passed and the sand was worthless.

Now when Sakhwal's sand turned to gold and he found himself rich beyond belief, he performed a great *Mha Puja*, worshipping his own body and self in utmost thanksgiving. Next he went to the Kathmandu king, Jaya Deva Malla, with the proposition that, if a new calendar era could be started, he would pay off every debt in the kingdom. Thus every citizen, including the people from Bhadgaon, was freed from debt and the present Newari calendar era was begun. That was over a thousand years ago – in A.D. 880, to be exact, and although the Nepalese calendar was made official 200 years ago, the Newars still use their own calendar for all business transactions, religious festivals and traditional clan and family ceremonies.

The great last day of Tihar is a time when every boy and man in Nepal must be worshipped by his sisters and receive their blessings, thus being assured of increased prosperity for the coming year, and a long and healthy life. So important is *Bhai Tika*, or Brother Blessing, that if a man has no sisters a close female relative or friend is honoured to bestow this benediction. On this morning, when the King of Nepal receives the worship and *tika*-mark from his sisters, a thirty-one-gun salute from the royal palace resounds throughout the valley.

Some Hindu women perform preliminary ceremonies four days

earlier, on the first day of Tihar, visiting the brother, sprinkling sacred oil over his head with a bouquet made from peepul leaves, certain long-lasting grasses and purple flowers. According to tradition, she should provide him at this time with food for the five days of Tihar and extend to him a special invitation for *Bhai Tika* day.

In some families a Brahman priest is present to perform the rites, where Lord Ganesh is worshipped, as well as the sacred flame, the vessel containing holy water, and Yama the God of Death. Throughout the ceremony he chants prayers and blessings. In many Newar homes the sisters themselves perform these functions.

In all families the brother is seated on the floor with the offerings before him, much the same as on the preceding day's *Mha Puja mandal* ceremony. The sister pours around his body a circle of oil and holy water, casting a protecting spell or boundary over which Death and evil spirits cannot pass. Then, kneeling before him, she worships him with offerings of flowers, nuts, fruits and rice amidst flaming wicks and incense. The ceremony is climaxed by bestowing of the *Bhai Tika* upon his forehead – a vertical line of yellow paint drawn with her little finger on which is subsequently placed a series of different-coloured dots. Most important, too, is the exchange of presents between brother and sister, usually of money, cloth and clothing.

The invocation for *Bhai Tika* is, 'Thus do I mark my brother's forehead and thereby plant a thorn at the Door of Yama (making entrance into death impossible). As Jamuna streaked the forehead of her brother, so do I my brother's. As Yama is immortal, so may my brother be immortal also.' Another says, 'May your life be as long as the nut-flower remains unfading, your body hard as a walnut, and your heart as soft as butter.'

The tradition of brother worship originated from the scriptural story of the girl Jamuna, whose brother was mortally ill. When Yama himself came for the brother's soul, Jamuna pleaded with the God of Death to delay until she had finished worshipping her brother. This Yama granted. Then the girl underwent a long and complicated ceremony for her brother and performed the same for the God of Death. This so pleased Yama that he promised not to take her brother's soul so long as the offerings of grass and flowers should remain fresh and unwilted. All through the year Yama sent his messenger to inspect the flowers and grass, and when the next *Bhai Tika Puja* arrived, Yama admitted he had lost the boy's soul to his pious sister, and the boy was granted long life.

Now every man and boy is impelled to receive his sister's blessings on this day, after which the family celebrates with a sumptuous midday feast. Often the remainder of this final day of Tihar is spent in friendly family gambling games.

Before 1940 gambling was legal in Nepal during the five days of Tihar when, on the first day, troupes of musicians went around the towns announcing that games were now open to one and all. Streets and walks were crowded with canopied booths packed with happy gamblers, men crouching in tight circles on blankets or on the bare earth, shouting their bets, throwing the cowrie shells with a flourish of typical Nepalese exuberance. In the evening, when musicians announced that gambling was ended, men stuffed their winnings into their pockets and proprietors scrambled to close shop.

They say fortunes were won and lost in an hour in those good old days, and stories are retold of men who, having lost all, gambled away their surplus wives. One man is said to have cut off his hand, put it on the table as a wager before the one who had just taken his fortune. When he won, he demanded all his money back or the severed hand of his opponent.

Gambling seems to receive semi-religious sanction during Tihar in the belief that it is pleasing to Goddess Laxmi. Her favourite plaything, the cowrie shell, is often used in the games, and it was doubtless in ancient days a medium of exchange. Laxmi forbids all other monetary transactions during Tihar, such as making and repaying loans and the purchase of goods. Even today business is virtually at a standstill for from two to five days, when bazaar shops, business houses, schools and government agencies are closed. This leaves ample time for the ancient sport of gambling.

Now the law closes an eye upon these games in homes and among the groups of men and boys who squat along the streets and roadways throwing cowrie shells and stones. For who would not gamble when by refraining one might displease the Goddess of Wealth during Tihar and so appear in one's next life as a loathsome mole?

20 HARIBODHINI EKADASI
The Return of Lord Vishnu

The eleventh day of each lunar fortnight, totalling twenty-four throughout the year, are called Ekadasis, and each is observed as an auspicious holy day of religious fasting, especially by those thousands who look upon Lord Vishnu, rather than Shiva or Buddha as the Supreme God. Most observe a 'partial' fast, taking only one frugal meal of 'clean' food – fruits, sweets, milk – but many undergo complete abstinence, consuming not even a single drop of water during twenty-four hours, hoping thereby to attain forgiveness of sin. Rice is strictly taboo. No meat is consumed by the orthodox; Nepalese law forbids butchers to slaughter and sell; and the execution of a criminal is prohibited on all these 'meatless' Ekadasi days.

Before the world was created Lord Vishnu formulated a 'Man of Sin', whose snow-white mane and black, distorted face would strike terror into the hearts of evil-doers. This creature exemplifies and encompasses the whole sphere of sin, his head representing the crime of murdering a Brahman, and his evil eyes the drinking of alcohol. His face represents theft, particularly of gold, which is Vishnu's sacred metal; while the murder of a *guru* is represented by his ears, the murder of a woman by his nose, and the killing of a cow by his shoulders. His chest is the rape of another man's wife; his neck is the bringing about of an abortion; his belly, the oppression of the innocent and the just; his stomach, the mistreatment of those who seek protection. This monster's thighs and sexual organs represent the slander of a *guru*, the violation of a virgin and the betrayal of a secret or trust, while the body hairs represent a great host of lesser sins.

In time, when he beheld thousands of sinful people suffering

terrible agonies in the Underworld, Vishnu relented and transformed himself into the Ekadasi or eleventh day of each lunar
fortnight, when salvation is available to all mankind. That man
may prove worthy of this gift, Vishnu demanded he deny himself
certain foods on Ekadasi, especially rice, for on this day the Man
of Sin himself dwells in rice, and whosoever has the temerity to
eat this grain will absorb all this monster's evilness into his own
body, forfeiting all hope of redemption.

The most auspicious of these bi-monthly Ekadasis falls during
the waxing moon in November, four days before the full moon,
this one called Haribodhini Ekadasi, Hari being one of Vishnu's
thousand names, when this great god awakens from his annual
four-month rest far below the surface of the earth. During this
long vacation from his mighty, world-wide responsibilities, Vishnu
sleeps dreamlessly, reclining on the coiled body of an enormous
cobra, Shesha Naga, King of the Snake Gods who is often called
Ananta – Infinity. Over Vishnu's head spreads a graceful, protecting canopy of this serpent's thousand hoods.

Haribodhini Ekadasi ends a long summer of uneasiness for gods
and men, when Vishnu is welcomed back with a week of feverish
activity, involving long, penitent pilgrimages, lavish gifts and
offerings, solemn fasting and fervent prayers, for he is the Re-
deemer who grants absolution from sin and very many religious
rewards, even immortality, to those who adore him.

Narayan, as Vishnu is commonly known in Nepal, is more
benign than Shiva and much less awesome: a majestic, transcen-
dent protector, sustainer and preserver who inspires the most
loving and widespread adoration. Newari girls, before reaching
puberty, are solemnly united with Narayan in marriage, an
ancient, sacred and costly ceremony wherein her hand is given to
a *bel*-fruit which represents this god. For Narayan is immortal,
and if the girl's earthly husband dies, she is never a widow.
Theoretically her union with Narayan allows her to remarry if she
chooses, and to leave or divorce her human husband at any time.

Vishnu is adored in many forms, especially those taken during
his nine incarnations, when he appeared on earth nine times to

18. Devotees, with offerings arranged in readiness, await in the morning mists for the rising of Surya Narayan, the Sun God, at temple of Swa Bhagwati on Vishnumati River (Mary M. Anderson)

Bringing offerings to the Reclining Vishnu at Budha Nil Kantha, north of Kathmandu (Teeka Simha)

19. Close-up of the Reclining Vishnu called Budha Nil Kantha (Old Blue Throat), four miles north of Kathmandu
(D.D. Shrestha)

Leaving offerings at the feet of Reclining Vishnu
(D.D. Shrestha)

save the gods and mankind from demons and sin disguised in turn as a fish, tortoise, pig, man-lion, dwarf, Parasurama the young hero, Lords Rama, Krishna and, some say, Buddha himself. He is destined to come again, it is believed, as a flying white horse which will completely purge this world of sin and corruption. Narayan is further embodied in the sacred *tulsi* plant, *darbha* grass, the *peepul* tree, as well as the smooth fossilized *salagram* stones which are avidly collected and worshipped. Devotees drink the water in which the *salagram* is washed, praying, 'Narayan, you are the blessed ruler of the world; it is your pleasure to confer blessings on all created beings. I drink this water in which your sacred feet have been washed that I may be cleansed of sin. Vouchsafe to pardon me, who am the greatest of sinners.'

Vishnu is also identified with Surya, the ancient Sun God and Protector, who crosses the skies daily in a golden chariot drawn by seven white horses, a Nature deity brought from Central Asia by conquering Aryans two thousand years before Christ. Surya Narayan brings and sustains light and life, watches and governs the good and evil deeds of worldly creatures, bestows health and riches, and has the power to grant even the most fanciful of wishes and prayers.

Five days before Haribodhini Ekadasi, on the sixth of the waxing moon, hundreds of Surya Narayan's devotees gather at various riverside holy places, many at the shrine of Swa Bhagwati, on the west bank of the Vishnumati just below old Kathmandu. As the Sun God sinks in the west, a great *puja* is performed, after which worshippers, huddled in cloths and scarves, settle down for an all-night vigil to Surya Narayan, singing hymns in his praise, reading the sacred Vedic texts and concentrating on his image.

With the first light of the seventh day these people cleanse themselves in the river. Women from each family or clan-group arrange elaborate displays along the steps and river bank: plates and trays of colourful fruits, nuts, vegetables, sweets, grains and huge bouquets of brilliant flowers. Just as the first morning sun is sighted through the fogs and mist, strong men from each group enter the shallow water, holding copper pots heavy with offerings and overflowing with flowers. Traditionally each pot should contain an item of gold to honour Vishnu, the Sun God. They stand facing the sun, chanting prayers, offering the vessel to Surya Narayan by moving it first in a circle and lowering it five times into the water. This ceremony is repeated as the men turn to face each of the remaining directions.

Pious women from each party offer small plates of sweets and fruit to each gathering and to many spectators, though they may be strangers. Dishes made of leaves containing fruits, coins and lighted wicks are set afloat in the river current to be snatched downstream by devotees as a *prasad* from Surya Narayan, a gift which has the power to bestow fertility and many offspring.

On the evening of the eighth day of the waxing moon, three days before Ekadasi, Changu Narayan is honoured at his hilltop shrine two miles north of Bhadgaon, one of the four lovely Narayan temples which grace each side of the Valley. Oil wicks flicker everywhere while crowds again keep watch through the night fasting, praying, making offerings and chanting the names of Vishnu. Early next morning, on the ninth day of the fortnight called *Kushmand Nawami*, hundreds offer Vishnu green pumpkins in which coins or valuables are hidden, the most sacred *Gobhindo Dhan* ceremony of 'secret charity'. This day is also called *Akshaya Nawami*, an important landmark which tradition says was the beginning of an ancient calendar era. *Akshaya* means 'indestructible', signifying that good deeds, especially alms-giving, performed on this day continue to reap blessing for the donor for his next sixty thousand incarnations; that any project inaugurated is sure to meet with uncommon success; while the punishment for sin on this ninth day is multiplied infinitely, causing the offender to suffer the torments of Hell for ever.

At night on the tenth day, the eve of Haribodhini Ekadasi, hundreds of fasting devotees begin a long pilgrimage to glorify Narayan, visiting his four peripheral temples, each ten or more miles apart. Many, following ancient tradition, walk the entire distance, while others pile into overloaded trucks and buses and follow the roads as far as they reach. Singing, chanting the names of Narayan for hours on end, they circumambulate each shrine, make their offerings, receive back a 'gift' of *prasad* from their Lord, and proceed to the next. Many complete the circuit late the following evening, having gained great religious reward for staying awake throughout Narayan's sacred night.

With the dawn of Haribodhini Ekadasi, the great day when Lord Vishnu returns to look after the world, sacred baths are taken and Narayan is worshipped in sacred prescribed ritual, often in the home. One must be seated on a clean carpet before this god's image. Specific hand gestures are made, sacred hymns are sung, and his name is endlessly repeated, perferrably 1,008 times, while with each repetition his divine image must be visualized with fullest concentration. Before prostrating one's self to the ground before him, Vishnu's special ambrosia – a mixture of melted clarified butter, curds, milk, honey and sugar – is poured over his idol. *Tulsi* leaves are presented, a gift more precious to Vishnu than the offering of a thousand cows.

Many who have observed partial fasting for the past four months, and many who have not done so, now undergo twenty-four hours of complete abstinence, for he who fails to observe this Ekadasi may be reincarnated as a rooster; and he who neglects to contribute everything possible towards the pomp and ceremony of this occasion may be reborn dumb.

On the day following Haribodhini Ekadasi, and for the next three, through full moon day, thousands upon thousands of rejoicing devotees visit Sleeping Vishnu, the twelve-foot black stone idol which reclines on a bed of snake coils in a square cemented pond and outdoor shrine four miles north of Kathmandu. Here Narayan is called Budha Nil Kantha, 'Old Blue Throat', a name which causes confusion and speculation among foreigners, and not a little among Nepalese. For it was Lord Shiva, not Narayan, whose throat became blue from drinking poison that occurred with the 'churning of the oceans', a mythical episode wherein Shiva saved the lives of gods and men. To slake his burning thirst Shiva headed for the Himalayan snows, and some say that when he reached this sacred spot in the valley he assumed the form of a

Reclining or Sleeping Vishnu. Others maintain he merged himself with this image which was already there.

A convenient and perhaps foreseeable result is that the famous, ever-popular 'Old Blue Throat' is worshipped as Lord Vishnu by most, as Lord Shiva by some, as Brahma the Creator by a few, while a minority look to him as a Buddha, the deified Lokeswar.

It is generally agreed that this great stone idol was once buried under monsoon landslides from near-by Shivapuri hill. Ages passed, until one day a farmer discovered that the grain harvested from this spot continued to multiply endlessly, a miracle he reported to the King. Soon thereafter a goddess appeared to the ruler in a dream, advising him to excavate the site. As the image of Vishnu reclining on a bed of snake coils was unearthed, a workman's spade severed part of its nose. When the King and his distraught people saw blood gushing from the wound, they fell before Lord Narayan with offerings and sacrifices. A voice from the idol commanded, 'O Raja, have a pond built around me', a request immediately fulfilled, together with the establishing of an annual festival during the week of Haribodhini Ekadasi, when thousands of pilgrims come to see Narayan reclining in the water.

Legends abound concerning this idol. Newari farmers take credit for accidentally discovering it as they tilled the soil in ancient times. Some say it was Vishnu's lovely consort, Laxmi, the Goddess of Wealth – herself created from the 'churning of the oceans' – who caused the miraculous multiplying of grain harvest, thereby pointing out her buried spouse. As for the broken nose, still much in evidence, rumour has it that the idol was defaced by invading Moghuls, who seem to be blamed for most of the damage seen on Nepalese idols and monuments, though they occupied the valley briefly in A.D. 1349. Another belief is that this Narayan idol was installed by an old Brahman man, Nil Kantha, by whose name it has since been known.

One of the Malla kings had water channelled from this pond for his own use and on the night the water reached its destination in Kathmandu, the ruler dreamed that the 'Old Blue Throat' came to him, proclaiming that he and his descendants or future rulers would die if they went to see the Reclining Vishnu idol. Consequently, a smaller replica of 'Old Blue Throat' was installed in a pond in Balaju, where the kings of Nepal worship. Possibly they believe, as do their subjects, that the ruler would die of bleeding and that great calamity would befall the nation if he cast his eyes upon Budha Nil Kantha.

For the four days following Narayan's Ekadasi the four-mile road leading north from Kathmandu to the Reclining Vishnu is thronged with humanity – packed buses, trucks, cars and taxis inching their way through clouds of dust and gaily dressed pedestrians, many with huge marigold bouquets for Narayan and scarlet poinsettias bouncing in their hair. They carry picnic baskets, garlands of blossoms and cloth-wrapped offerings. After climbing the steps leading to the shrine, all circle a near-by idol of Ganesh, the sage elephant god who sanctions all prayer and ceremony, before crowding around the sunken pond. There they gaze in adoration upon the immense black stone Vishnu, reclining in the murky water all but buried in flowers, rice, fruits and red powder, offerings from the worshipping multitudes.

Some people light oil wicks on the wall around the pond. Others toss in coins and flowers after touching them to their foreheads. They whisper prayers and chant Vishnu's sacred names. Thousands, in a never-ending line, guided by solicitous policemen, make their barefoot way through the arch and down steps to the water, slipping, balancing and clinging to others in the crowd at Narayan's huge black feet. They strew offerings over him and take back a sprig of flowers for the hair or a smear of red paste for the forehead, a mark of Narayan's blessing.

All ages, country peasant and nylon-saried city matrons, men and women together crowd about in a spirit of carnival, yet displaying deep, almost frantic, religious devotion. One village woman tosses a banana to Narayan, misses her mark and laughs aloud. Now she prays over touching palms, stoops to touch Narayan's feet with her forehead, and an attendant retrieves the banana in Vishnu's name. An old crone carries a vessel of water dipped from the pond up to surrounding crowds. A dozen eager hands scoop up the sacred liquid to sprinkle into their mouths and over their heads. Barefoot temple attendants crawl back and forth over the slippery idol, scraping litter from Narayan's impassive face, setting aside coins and worthwhile scraps of food.

Near the edge of the pond huge bells in wooden arches are rung periodically to invite Lord Vishnu's attention. In surrounding porches and patios seated women listen enthralled to scriptural stories of Vishnu read by *gurus* bundled up in soiled sweaters and baggy trousers who, though they may be gaunt and unshaven, have proud and knowing faces. Musicians sit in groups or parade around blowing wooden flutes in sheer joy of thanksgiving. Side-walk merchants, peddling flowers, rice and vermilion powder, and seated holy men, beggars and cripples all do a flourishing business. Many devotees walk round and round the pond, for to circumambulate Narayan's idol, to give alms to Brahmans and the destitute, to play or listen to Narayan's music – all these things bring untold reward and forgiveness of sins during his special Ekadasi week.

Having completed their worship, hundreds of family groups leave the temple to purchase sticky sweets, pounded rice, curried goat meat, spicy vegetables and pancake-like loaves cooked on open fires and served on green leaves at temporary vending stalls. Now they make their way to the hillside trees, huge flat boulders and dry rice terraces to picnic in the warm sunshine and bracing air, where many enjoy their first complete meal since Lord Vishnu began his annual vacation four months earlier.

Among the lively picnic groups children, with their eyes turned skywards and clutching balls of string, run over the countryside following their air-borne kites, for this marks the end of the traditional one-month kite-flying season. Elderly people believe this pastime will bring prosperity to the family, that it is a means of contacting and honouring dead ancestors, and of guiding recently-released souls into Heaven. But for children the last day of kite-flying means an outdoor picnic and a chance to see once more the enormous black figure of Reclining Narayan – The One Who Abides Upon the Waters.

21 MAHALAXMI VILLAGE PUJA
For the Goddess of Wealth and Harvest

With the storing of the autumn harvest in Kathmandu Valley the
country folk rejoice, inviting friends and kindred from miles
around to their villages for celebrations which honour, propitiate
and give thanks to the beneficent goddesses who protect the
stored grain and, hopefully, will cause it to multiply in the bins.

Mahalaxmi is the Great Goddess of Wealth, wife of Lord
Vishnu, exemplifying riches of the sea from whence she sprang –
pearls, coral and shells. But to country people wealth means rice
and grain, gifts from Mahalaxmi, whom they identify with the
Mother Earth goddesses, Basundhara and Annapurna, bestowers
and protectors of agricultural produce.

Many rural inhabitants associate Mahalaxmi also with Bhairabi,
the female counterpart of the terrifying and powerful Bhairab,
who represents the destructive aspect of Lord Shiva, or Pashupatinath the Protector of Cattle. Conceived in this fearsome aspect,
Goddess Mahalaxmi, herself an embodiment of the sacred cow,
must be assuaged with tumultuous celebrations, blood sacrifices
and the offering and imbibing of native spirits distilled from the
harvest – rice, grains, fruits and vegetables – brewed in immense
clay pots in a dark corner of the top-floor cooking area of every
home.

In many villages Mahalaxmi is the presiding patron deity, and
at the tiny hillside hamlet of Tikhanpur near Thankot, a few miles
south-west of Kathmandu, she is fêted for three days after harvest,
starting on the day before the November full moon at the close of
Haribodhini Ekadasi festivities. On this evening her small brass
idol is carried from the home of the village headman in a religious
procession, made gay with music and singing, to a hilltop outdoor

shrine under the trees. Male inhabitants of Tikhanpur bring gifts and offerings, sacrifice goats and fowl, and receive *prasad* blessings from Mahalaxmi by eating the cooked flesh of the decapitated sacrifices in a great ceremonial feast enlivened with rice-beer, music and dancing all through the night. With the morning of full moon the women are invited to another outdoor feast, cooked and served by the men, a courtesy unthinkable at any other time. Now the brass idol of Mahalaxmi is carried back in lively parade to the headman's home, where she remains 'hidden' for another year, worshipped only by the village *thakuri* or chief.

Late on full moon night, and on the following night as well, the males of Tikhanpur – musicians, dancers, singers and actors trained since childhood – stage an amazing programme of native dances to honour and entertain Goddess Mahalaxmi. While the performers are being painted and garbed in ancient, ornate costumes – village treasures carefully kept stored in the headman's home – the inhabitants congregate on the hillside at 'Narayan's Place' near a Buddhist stone *chaitya* monument in which is enshrined an image of Lord Vishnu.

Flaming torches light the faces of women and babies, huddled on rice-straw mats. Barefoot men and boys crowd into an open covered porch – the village meeting-place – and around a grassy arena. Two dozen musicians and singers, all men in Nepalese *topi* caps, sit cross-legged on a raised stone platform, some holding ancient, many-toned drums, while others clasp plate-shaped brass cymbals in either hand. The head drummer, noted for his artistry, controls the show wherein no performer, young or old, displays the slightest shyness or self-consciousness.

The opening number depicts a royal jungle hunt led by a man costumed as a palace servant, who mimes the organizing of a greating hunting camp with the procurement of vast quantities of food and supplies from the surrounding countryside, performed with stylized but graceful movement and posturing. Next comes a red-coated royal guard, darting here and there, jabbing his old musket into the 'thicket' to drive out lurking enemies. Now enter two haughty princes prancing as if on horseback, wearing jewelled head-gear and ornate velvet coats. Huge metal hoops are suspended at hip level, over which are draped full white skirts with protruding carved wooden horses' heads. These noble, handsome princes whirl and gallop through an exciting 'chase', delighting their village neighbours.

Throughout this performance one seated woman, consoled by her companions, weeps openly, remembering that her dead father for many years enacted the part of the red-coated guard. As the dancers leave the arena, a tipsy spectator, blinded by the flaming torches, lurches about centre-stage to be rescued by a friend and led good-naturedly to his seat.

Blaring music announces the next performance, in which two men re-enact a rigorous boat trip down the Trisuli River to the west of the Kathmandu Valley, rowing gracefully as they forge through the rapids in a realistic adventure which greatly excites the audience.

Now a tall bony man, supported by a trembling cane, shuffles in, his face and near-naked body strewn with ashes, loins swathed in rags, head and shoulders shrouded in a mangy and matted wig. He carries a rolled, moth-eaten deerskin, typical of the mats used by Hindu *sadhus* and holy mendicants who worship Lord Shiva. The crowd snickers at this familiar, travel-weary pilgrim, representing one of the hundreds who trek over the hills from India to the Shiva Ratri festival each year. And they roar with laughter when the sacrilegious performer, tossing rice upon imaginary holy places along the journey, periodically casts sacred grain at his own genital area and backside as well. When he meets up with two fellow travellers, the three seat themselves on the deerskin mat to hold a seance, rocking to the beat of the music, miming the rolling of marijuana leaves and the smoking of drugged cigarettes by drawing through the clenched fist. Soon one traveller loses all control, becomes violently ill and passes out completely. Frantic, clumsy and exaggerated first-aid is administered by his two staggering comrades, and at his revival, all shuffle off-stage to continue their pilgrimage.

Now two fishermen glide in, casting ragged, ancient fishnets.

Their imaginary catch is peddled to the spectators with loud mock arguments and violent haggling over price. After an exchange of ribald comments, the spectators laughingly dig for coins which the fishermen thrust into their pockets. This is continued all through the encircling crowd until the head musician thumps his drum in quiet cadence, indicating that the fishermen's time on the stage is up.

Now a peasant from Tibet enters with his wife, *Bhotes* as they are called, wearing the conical cane hats of the field worker, carrying heavy back-packs of goods for Kathmandu markets. During their dance the man discovers his wife has missed the trail. Shading his eyes, calling her name over imaginary mountain-tops and vast expanses, the Tibetan searches for his wife, much to the amusement of the audience. At last, when he comes upon her the man, though obviously relieved, beats his wife soundly none the less.

When the laughter dies down a burst of music introduces a tall, handsome youth wearing heavily jewelled crown and lavish, silken robes, who dances with obvious pride, for he portrays the ancient 'king' who once ruled over this village. He is followed by two lovely queens, faces modestly lowered, wearing tiaras and brocaded gowns, one from Tibet and the other from the south. King and consorts, all wearing huge home-made dark glasses – ever a symbol of royalty – dance in unison with delicate posturing of hands and bare feet, their every movement wistfully watched by the country girls and women.

The head drummer cradles his drum while his nimble, expressive fingers fly over the leather. His face is turned to the immense full moon; his eyes are closed. He is completely absorbed in the complicated rhythms. Now a younger drummer loses the beat and the head man stops the music, his lips pursed in silent displeasure. Others scold the offender and the rhythm is taken up anew. Again the head drummer drops his hands and all is still. Gradually his body commences to tremble, knees spasmodically bouncing and jerking, his face pale as in deep trance. 'Ah,' whisper the spectators, 'the Goddess Mahalaxmi is angry because the boy keeps

"spoiling" her music. Now her spirit has entered the head drummer's body.' The offending youth hangs his head before the excited
gesticulations and threats of fellow musicians and interrupted
performers.

Now the head drummer's brother, seated directly behind him,
tightly embraces the afflicted leader, holding him firmly that the
spirit of the angry goddess may pass from this body into his own.
Gradually he, too, goes into trance and begins the epileptic-like
shaking, as the leader regains his senses and starts the music and
show once more. These villagers say that the spirit of Mahalaxmi
will possess only those she 'likes and finds pleasing', and that this
head drummer's father, when he lived, was village leader, the
only man in the settlement whose body Mahalaxmi would enter.
When he died the goddess transferred her favours to the two sons,
both drummers endowed with this remarkable gift whereby her
displeasures are made known when she possesses and enters their
bodies.

Gradually, as the close of the performance nears, women and
children drift away to their homes, but many stay wakeful through
the night, listening to the music. Before dawn on the day of the
full moon the village is stirring again and most of the inhabitants
are making their way through the fields and footpaths to nearby
Thankot town, where another festival for Mahalaxmi is being held.

In Thankot Mahalaxmi is attended throughout her celebration
by Lord Ganesh, the elephant-headed god who brings success to
all ceremonies. Both brass images are installed in heavy 'portable
temples' under ornate, garlanded brass canopies affixed to two
bamboo poles. These palanquins or *khats* are hoisted by the bamboos which rest upon the shoulders of eight men and are then
carried to a large sunken courtyard just before Mahalaxmi's great
tiered temple in the centre of the village.

Some two dozen men, dressed in their finest, wait with handfuls
of scarlet powder on the porch bordering the courtyard; groups of
women holding oil lamps and offerings wait in the opposite corner;
musicians stand in readiness at one side, while hundreds of villagers
crowd the edge of the square. The music commences with a

deafening, incessant throbbing of drums – 'Bong, bong, BOOM!
Bong, bong, BOOM!' while clashing cymbals shatter the air –
'Cling, cling, CLANG! Cling, cling, CLANG!' – in an overpowering rhythm that rings and reverberates, hypnotic and
compelling. Now the eight-foot trumpets are raised, giving forth a
series of deep, mournful blasts. Then the *jatra*, or procession,
commences. The eight bearers of Mahalaxmi's *khat* move down
the steps into the courtyard and around an immense tree at its
centre, proceeding ponderously at first, but gathering speed as
their feet stamp out the rhythm. This is followed by the *khat* of
Ganesh, only slightly less lavishly decorated.

Soon both *khats* are gyrating, zigzagging round and round, up
and down the courtyard and around the sacred tree. They appear
to move with a will of their own (or Mahalaxmi's, as the people
say) as they are rushed to one corner while women surge out to
place lights and offerings around the idols. Now they careen off to
the opposite porch, where waiting men shower them with handful
after handful of brilliant red powder which clouds over the *khats*,
the idols and the sweating, celebrating *khat* bearers. Off they go
again, sometimes gyrating in complete circles, missing each other
by inches in a breathless, hair-raising ride, the like of which
Mahalaxmi should never forget.

One strong lad, obviously jubilant with the honoured task of
bearing Mahalaxmi, struts under the heavy load in gay abandon,
vaguely distracted now and then by his sliding, baggy-seated
trousers, the drawstring having loosened; and as the *khat* circles
the tree at dizzy speed, the trousers drop to his ankles. A replace-
ment rushes in, shoulders the heavy bamboo and takes up the beat,
but once the trousers are secure again the wearer dashes back into
the fray to be whisked across the courtyard once more. Attendants
dart in to thrust short, Nepali cigarettes into the hands of the
carriers, while others tip their home-brew into their open mouths
from jugs, without which refreshment they may never be able to
maintain the gruelling pace. Periodically one of the *khats* leaves
the courtyard and makes a swift circle around steep, rock-paved
lanes and near-by temples to return with a heightened din of music.

By the end of a strenuous hour the sixteen carriers, Mahalaxmi, Ganesh and most of the spectators are scarlet with the powder that clogs their hair, eyes, ears and clothing. At last both *khats* are made to circumambulate Mahalaxmi's temple and are carried on to a narrow side-street, where they are lowered to the ground. Immediately they are surrounded with a crush of humanity frantic to leave offerings and to snatch back a scrap of red paste or a blossom as Mahalaxmi's blessing. Chickens and goats are sacrificed before both images, the blood spurting from their slit throats over the interior of the *khats*, the idols and on to the ground, where it is lapped up by waiting pariah dogs along with scattered food offerings.

Now groups of noisy singers and vividly dressed laughing women carrying flaming *sukundas*, brass ceremonial lamps, parade through the streets and around the many temples to the opposite end of the village, where they surround a huge earthen vase filled with rice-beer. This pot represents and is worshipped as the powerful Lord Bhairab whose brass mask with flowing black hair is affixed to the side, for he is the God of Terror whom few village people would dare overlook even on Mahalaxmi's day. They strew the pot and the mask with offerings and garlands while an attendant scoops up handfuls of the sacred liquid for worshippers to drink as a blessing from Bhairab.

The country people return to their homes and villages confident that an appeased Mahalaxmi will bless and protect their store of food-grains and keep watch over the next year's harvest. The ensuing weeks of leisure will be devoted to gathering grass and fodder to winter the few animals they keep tethered in the ground floor of their homes; to collecting wood for the firepots above; to weaving rice-straw mats and rugs for smooth mud floors; with ample time left over to attend the harvest festivals of all the neighbouring villages.

NOVEMBER-DECEMBER

22 GUJESWARI JATRA
Worship of the Secret Goddess

Gujeswari is an enigmatic, mystifying goddess whose inscrutable ways and terrifying powers are beyond human understanding. According to mythological history she has held sway over Kathmandu Valley ever since it was a lake in remotest antiquity. Gujeswari is considered by many to be on a par with Adi Buddha, the Self-Existent One who appeared as a blinding flame emanating from a lotus which bloomed upon the waters. Her temple, located a mile up the Bagmati River from Pashupatinath temple, enshrines a small bottomless pit where the full-blown lotus is said to have taken root.

It is believed that the *kunda* or sacred water hole of Gujeswari was discovered ages ago by a religious ascetic, one uncommonly well versed in Tantric rites and magic spells. A shrine was erected to protect it and the small six-inch opening of the *kunda* itself, covered by a stone slab carved with an eight-petalled lotus blossom. Later a pagoda temple was built on the walls of which are images of the eight powerful Mother or Shakti goddesses, with a golden lion, mythical carrier or vehicle of Gujeswari, standing near by. Eventually the area was fenced with an iron railing and high wall which deny entrance and view to all who are not Hindus or Buddhists.

Through the years kings, maharajas and ruling prime ministers have donated monuments and wealth to decorate and beautify the temple, to promote the worship of Gujeswari, to keep her pacified, and to seek her powerful and protective blessings. The present ruler's image and that of his queen stand on a stone pillar beside the golden lion. It is said that the last of the old Malla kings in Kathmandu, Jaya Prakash, was once deposed by his ministers and took shelter in Gujeswari's temple to pray and meditate before her image. Evidently the goddess was pleased, for an enlightened *yogi* or ascetic emerged miraculously from the sacred pit and presented a sword as reward for the King's devotion. With this divine and powerful weapon in hand the King defeated his ministers and regained his throne.

Gujeswari is a form of Kali, Durga and Taleju, the Universal-Mother Goddesses who represent Shakti, that awesome supreme power embodied in all that is female. Although animal sacrifices are made to other mother goddesses, blood is never offered directly to Gujeswari. Instead, the animals are sacrificed to Bhairab, who stands in her temple courtyard, for he is her male counterpart, representing the wrathful, destructive, blood-craving aspect of Shiva. This Bhairab at Gujeswari only receives blood sacrifices three times a year – on the eighth day of the bright lunar fortnight during the Buddhist summer month of Gunla; on the eighth day of the great autumn festival of Dasain; and again for Chait or 'Little' Dasain on the eighth day of the waxing moon during the last month of the year.

However, hundreds come daily to this mystic female divinity, supplicants from all walks of life, men and women, Buddhist and Hindu alike, seeking her blessing of fertility, relief from sickness, the fulfilment of needs and desires, and for power to overcome threatening difficulty and danger.

The wife or consort of Shiva is worshipped under several different names – Durga, Kali, Uma, Sati Devi, Parbati and others, whose lives and experiences with the Great Lord are related as if they were individual goddesses. All Nepalese know, however, that they are one and the same. The site of Gujeswari's temple in Slesmantak Ban, the forested hill beyond Shiva's Pashupatinath temple, became sanctified, most believe, during the mythological period when Shiva's consort was called Sati Devi.

It seems that Himalaya, Sati Devi's father, disapproved of his divine son-in-law, regarding Shiva as an ash-strewn, long-haired vagabond who played with serpents and decked himself in scanty animal skins and necklaces of human skulls. Once, when the father was holding a great sacrificial fire ceremony to which all the gods were invited, Shiva was purposely omitted. Goddess Sati was so consumed with sorrow at this slight to her beloved husband that she went alone to the assembly and took her own life by leaping into the flames. The spectators trembled in awed silence when the mighty Lord Shiva appeared, consumed with a profound and terrible grief, taking the corpse of his divine goddess upon his shoulders and striding blindly away across the face of the earth over rivers, mountains and valleys. All Nature shuddered under the impact of his terrible sorrow. Volcanoes erupted, storm and flood engulfed the land, plants and harvests withered and the gods themselves trembled with fear.

At last Lord Vishnu, foreseeing the annihilation of mankind and of the whole world unless Sati Devi's corpse could be removed from Shiva's shoulders, caused the body to decompose and scatter in pieces over the land, unnoticed by Shiva in his madness. At last the Great Lord, vaguely conscious that the weight of his beloved wife had been lifted, retired to Kailas, his abode among the Himalayan snowpeaks, to lose himself in meditation.

Each of the sacred sites, in India, Nepal, Assam and Kashmir, where the fifty-two sections of Sati Devi's rotting corpse fell have become holy places called *pithas*, where temples were built to honour the goddess, before which stand images of Shiva keeping eternal vigilance. The ancient religious texts list the areas where each part of her body fell: her finger bones, for example, are enshrined at the great Kali temple in Calcutta. Which part of Sati Devi fell into Kathmandu Valley at Gujeswari shrine is a matter of confusion. The name Gujeswari is a commonly used, corrupted form of 'Guheswari', which refers to the word 'secret', indicating to some that it was her *yoni* or female sexual organs, as the Swastani text seems to indicate. However, almost all the Nepalese worship Gujeswari as the place where Sati Devi's anus or buttocks fell, and this site is without question one of the holiest in the valley.

Water always stands in the *kunda* at Gujeswari shrine, indi-eating that this sacred pit opens on to a spring. A red clay water vessel or *kalash* filled with home-made liquors, which mother goddesses are thought to relish, is removed from the pit when devotees, hundreds daily, come to strew offerings in and about the *kunda* – eggs, fish, liquors, flowers, rice, red powder and coins. The supplicant scoops out a handful of this holy liquid and floating offerings to sprinkle over their heads and into their mouths as a powerful *prasad* gift or blessing, thought to come directly from Goddess Gujeswari.

Her annual festival or *jatra* is held on the tenth day of the waning moon in November or early December, when worshippers bring offerings and gifts throughout the day, each bowing before her sacred *kalash* to receive her *prasad*. This vessel is never removed from the temple. Another which represents Gujeswari is kept throughout the year at the temple of Goddess Taleju in Kathmandu and is carried to Gujeswari on the previous evening, where it remains throughout the eve and the day of her festival, worshipped as the goddess herself. That evening the duplicate *kalash* of Gujeswari is placed in a temple-like palanquin and carried on the shoulders of a group of men around and about the locality of Pashupatinath and eventually back into Taleju temple, accompanied all the while by musicians and a worshipping crowd of devotees.

It seems fitting that Gujeswari's duplicate idol or sacred *kalash* should be enshrined in the temple of Taleju at the ancient royal palace of Kathmandu, for both goddesses are a form of Kali and Durga; both have since ancient times bestowed power upon rulers of the valley, and both have always protected and blessed the local inhabitants.

23 INDRIANI PUJA AND NHAYA GAYA JATRA

Festival of Goddess Indriani and the Seven Villages

Deeply pervading the Hindu and Buddhist faith in Nepal is the worship of Shakti as the Supreme Energy, always represented in powerful female deities known as Devis – goddesses – such as Kali the Terrifying Black One and Durga the awesome Divine Mother of the Universe. To these the Nepalese have added a whole pantheon of Mais and Ajimas, mother and grandmother goddesses who, though widely worshipped, are not necessarily adored. Even though their wrath can bring illness, affliction, epidemics, death and calamity to individuals and entire communities, they need not be feared so long as their might is respected, so long as they are kept tranquil with mystic Tantric rites, sated with an abundance of food, blood and rice beer, and entertained with festivals and gay palanquin rides.

Each city community, each village and rural hamlet is protected by its own patron goddess, whose annual harvest festival, usually celebrated for two or three days, is the most important, and often the only, public event in the year. Dignitaries, relatives, friends and neighbours come from miles around, especially married daughters and their broods, who are always invited back to their parental homes for auspicious occasions.

Such a festival is held each year at the ageing temple of Goddess Indriani which flanks the Vishnumati River just below old Kathmandu town. Here Indriani is known also as Luti Ajima, the grandmother goddess whose popularity may be attributed in part to her divine powers in curbing dysentery.

No doubt Indriani's empathy with common people derives also from the well-known story that she was once a wretched, poverty-stricken widow who struggled against discouraging difficulties to keep her many children clothed and fed. It happens that Indriani has several affluent sisters, all important goddesses around Kathmandu – Bhadrakali, Kankeswari Kali, Neta Ajima and others – who once in ages past decided it was beneath their dignity to invite their unfortunate sister and her ever-hungry brood to their Pasachare festival. Instead, they asked Indriani on the following day, provided the children with stale food and bread left by their festival guests, and offered Indriani thinly veiled excuses. Indriani, proud but broken-hearted, refused the food, gathered up her offspring and returned weeping to her hut, vowing never again to see her sisters.

One day soon thereafter, while Indriani was cooking a large green pumpkin, a gift from a kindly neighbour, she lifted the lid and was stunned to find the pieces of vegetable had turned to gold and the steam to diamonds and pearls. This miracle made her so fabulously wealthy that her proud sisters were most contrite. The people, sympathizing with Indriani, instituted an annual festival in her honour, now held every year three months before the Pasachare celebration of her sisters.

In the evening of the thirteenth day of the waning moon in late November or early December, devotees start gathering at Indriani's temple to present her with offerings, lighted ceremonial lamps and cotton wicks, to sing her praises all through the night. Local musicians, squatting in an adjacent verandah, wrapped in homespun shawls and warmed by home-brewed spirits, are reflected in the glow of a sacrificial fire kept burning in a shallow square pit just before the temple archway. The thumping of their drums and ringing of their cymbals is periodically drowned when they raise their voices in plaintive song.

Sometime between midnight and dawn a water buffalo is led inside the crowded temple, his throat is slashed and his blood, spurting from the wound over Indriani's small bronze idol, is offered as a gift to keep this goddess tranquil. Then the animal's head is completely severed and tossed into the sacrificial fire for Agni, the God of Fire.

Next a strange Tantric ceremony is performed in which a male and female snake are thrown high into the air and allowed to escape, while another pair is burned alive in the fire. The same rites are again performed, using pairs of insects and pairs of sparrows. The freeing of male and female of these species is performed, allegedly, that they may breed, making a new pair for the coming year. It is said that if no snakes can be procurred – for they are rare in the valley – they may be found beneath the stone lions which guard either side of Indriani's temple door. Those burned alive in the sacrificial fire are meant, again, to propitiate Agni, the God of Fire.

Throughout the following day people come in droves with trays of flowers and fruits to scatter over Indriani. Raw eggs are broken over her idol by those who cannot afford a chicken, duck, lamb or goat. Many wait outside the small shrine room, holding their tethered animals. Holy water is sprinkled over the beasts, and when the beast shakes his body and head it is deemed acceptable to Indriani. Later the headless body is carried three times around the fire before being taken home for family feasts, when it is consumed and regarded as a *prasad* or blessing from the goddess. Many smear the sanctified ashes from the fire on their foreheads and carry ashes home in small packets that family members may benefit from the goddess's protection.

During this fourteenth night of the fortnight, decorated temple-like palanquins containing patron goddesses of other Kathmandu localities are carried in procession to Indriani's temple. She herself is placed in a *khat* from which hangs a blood-red cloth painting of Indriani holding a great bowl of blood. Shortly before daylight all the decorated palanquins are hoisted upon men's shoulders and carried in gay, noisy parade to Tahiti Tole in Kathmandu – an open area where several streets meet at a Buddhist stupa shrine. From its dome, four pairs of all-seeing Buddha eyes seem to brood over the proceedings. Here the canopied goddesses are lowered and set in a row, where each is immediately surrounded by worshippers who decorate the roofs with garlands, flowers, large fruits and vegetables and sprinkle the deities with red powder, rice and coins. All through this day – the last of the dark fortnight called *Aunsi* – musicians, seated crosslegged on mats at the foot of Lord Buddha's shrine, blow horns and thump small drums. After sundown the *khats* are raised again and carried triumphantly through the lanes and around the temples in a grand parade before each is returned to her 'home'.

This Kathmandu festival for Indriani seems to bear some relationship to a festival held nine days later for their own Goddess Indriani by the inhabitants of Kirtipur village, two miles to the south-west. In former days, they say, during the sacrificial burning of male and female species in Kathmandu, pigeons were always included. One year a pair of pigeons tossed into the air took roost in Kirtipur nine days later, an omen which prompted the people of that village to inaugurate their own festival, which they had been longing to do. It is the practice, also, that certain people of Kirtipur come secretly to the Kathmandu Indriani festival every year and carry away coals from the ceremonial fire to ignite their own sacrificial blaze nine days later.

The Kirtipur celebration is called *Bakhu Mara Asthami*, the Pigeon Festival of the Eighth Day, which comes during the waxing moon in December, when this ancient hilltop village, with its jumble of houses, bazaar stalls and temples teems with unaccustomed activity. The ascending road, steep rock pathways and stone steps are filled with colourfully dressed festival-goers. They come to present Indriani with gifts and to watch her taken from her shrine near the famous Tiger Bhairab temple and placed in a decorated palanquin. They follow in tumultuous procession as she is carried through the sloping streets and installed in her 'outdoor temple', a shrine under a great gnarled tree beyond the old city walls.

Many village deities, besides their main temple or dwelling place in the town, have an open-air shrine where they are represented only by stones. In this aboriginal form the goddess is often worshipped and propitiated with greater fervour than as the fine golden or brass idol. These outdoor shrines are often near cremation grounds where it is hoped the goddess will control the witches and evil spirits who haunt these unclean places.

Goddess Indriani of Kirtipur visits her outdoor temple all through the night, surrounded by jubilant worshippers, entertained by troops of musicians and singing devotees. Nowadays she is closely guarded, for all remember the night in 1968 when she was stolen. The people of Kirtipur, desolate at the loss of their holiest idol, lived under a cloud of foreboding for a month, when the thieves were finally apprehended in Kathmandu. When Indriani was returned to Kirtipur the people went wild with joy. Every able-bodied citizen – man, woman and child – gathered in a long procession to welcome her return. Her festival began anew, though belatedly, and through the night musicians played while people danced in the streets and rejoiced in their homes with feasting, drinking and merrymaking.

Now on the tenth day of the fortnight the palanquin of Indriani, accompanied by Ganesh in his own *khat*, is carried back to the village square where throngs gather to offer gifts and blood sacrifices. Young men, surrounded by musicians and eager, sometimes inebriated spectators, dance for hours at a time. Long ropes of pine-needle sprays are wrapped round and round the gilded roof of Indriani's *khat* by men balanced precariously on its supporting bamboos, obviously conscious of the importance of their duties. Great bouquets of blood-red poinsettias, melons, pumpkins and the typical two-foot Nepali radishes are handed up as offerings to be placed among the greenery. Women and girls offer lavishly decorated trays of sweetmeats made in the shape of large lacy discs in many brilliant colours. These are spun high into the air, to be caught by mobs of screaming, scrambling children.

In early afternoon a flurry of activity and blare of trumpets announces the arrival of the King's sword from old Hanuman Dhoka palace in Kathmandu, which symbolically represents the ruler's presence and sanction. The group carries a great banner of multi-coloured paper with pomp and ceremony through the mobs and carefully arranges it over the roof of Indriani's palanquin. Now the procession of some fifty men moves single file, led by the village chief carrying the ancient royal sword, always draped in cloth to indicate that it comes in peace. This ceremony is watched with great excitement, obviously the highlight of the festival. Two centuries have softened the memory of the day when Prithvi Narayan Shah, ancestor of the present ruling family, conquered the valley and amputated the noses of every man and boy in Kirtipur in revenge for this village's brave resistance.

Each man in the official procession carries a great tray of offerings over his head and places it on the earth before Indriani. After the sword is presented to the goddess, mobs press in once more with offerings and blood sacrifices. Then the *khats* are carried down the crooked, narrow streets to be lowered periodically at intersections which have been swept and cleansed with cowdung. At each stop householders swarm about with offerings. Then the *khats* are raised once more and whirled dizzily about in a circle before moving on to the next halt. When Indriani is at last installed in her temple, the whole town celebrates with great family feasts, with great quantities of rice beer, sure that for another year the fêted and pacified goddess will protect the people of Kirtipur.

Simultaneously, dozens of smaller surrounding villages are honouring their own patron goddesses. Many hamlets, in order that their festivals may be more spectacular, bring their deities together for a common celebration. Such a celebration is Nhaya Gaya Jatra, Festival of Seven Villages, on the tenth day of the waxing moon at Bakhu Besin Devi, two miles west of Kathmandu, off the Tribhuvan Rajpat, the sole highway leading over the hills to India. Here the guardian goddesses of seven villages, carried in festive *khats*, meet in the morning while crowds of villagers in their most colourful finery jostle to present brass and copper plates to each goddess, all carefully arranged with rice, red and yellow powder, flowers and tiny oil lamps. An essential offering is a mixture of pounded rice, pieces of ginger, scraps of fire-roasted meat and fried soya beans. Countless animals and fowls are sacrificed. Rice beer is offered to the goddesses and a goodly quantity is consumed by the donors.

In the evening there is a communal feast at which people from the seven villages – friends, relatives and guests – drink together, a time when all feuds and enmities are traditionally forgotten. One time-honoured ceremony of this evening feast, at which the men sit cross-legged according to seniority and rank, is that a Newari man of the untouchable Pode caste occupies the honoured seat. The remainder of the year he is in general avoided, a scavenger who clears away the night soil. Once each year at this gathering he reigns as king for a day.

And so it continues from harvest until the coldest weather in village after village around the valley. Many fall into the hands of money-lenders in order to provide lavish feasts, new clothing, offerings for the gods and animals for sacrifice. Such is the importance of preserving family status and reputation, the clan's prestige and the goodwill of one's guardian goddess.

24 BALA CHATURDASI
In Remembrance of Bala and the Dead

For one year after death the wandering soul hovers about, awaiting entrance into the Underworld, and it is the inescapable duty
of living relatives to provide it with sustenance, comfort and peace
until it passes on into the Judgment Gates which are opened only
once or twice each year. During this waiting period, and at
certain times throughout their lives, the kinfolk are required to
perform *puja* ceremonies and lamp-lighting rituals; penances
and pilgrimages must be undertaken and sizeable offerings
of food, money and clothing must be made in the name of the
dead.

Thus the gods are propitiated and besought to facilitate the soul
along its difficult and hazardous journey, while at the same time
the mourners enhance their own chances of easier access to
heaven. Great care is taken to atone for all sins and slights committed against the deceased while he lived, and to avoid incurring
his dead soul's displeasure through neglect, thereby bringing
punishment or calamity down upon one's own head.

One of the most vital death duties is the observance of Bala
Chaturdasi festival on the fourteenth day of the dark half of the
moon in November or early December – Chaturdasi being the
fourteenth day of every lunar fortnight, and Bala a most unfortunate Nepali man who, through no fault of his own, was transformed into a demon. These ceremonies take place at the famous
Pashupatinath temple of Lord Shiva on the western outskirts of
Kathmandu, the shrine where the devout are brought when near-
ing death, since to die with one's feet in the sacred Bagmati River
fulfils a lifelong desire. And to be cremated at Pashupatinath's
riverside ghats and have one's ashes scattered into these holy

waters, which eventually flow into the sacred Ganges, brings one many steps nearer to Eternal Release.

On the day before Bala Chaturdasi all roads and footpaths leading to Pashupatinath for miles around are crowded with pilgrims from distant hill villages, dressed in their brightest finery, carrying bundles and baskets of supplies for an all-night vigil to honour the souls of their dead. Their naïveté and inexperience of city traffic – rickshas, bicycles, bullock carts, buses and automobiles – creates a hazard not only for themselves. By dusk the environs of the great temple are packed with people, pushing among the pedlars and stalls where *puja* supplies and offerings are sold, crowding into the temple gate, around the massive 'golden bull' to the inner shrine for a *darshan* or meeting with Shiva, who is represented as a most sacred lingam. There the pilgrims make their offerings, receive in return a *prasad* from Shiva, and emerge to search for a spot to keep their all-night vigil.

When darkness falls hundreds of family groups sit and squat in circles around their camp and worship area lighting wicks in small, oil-filled clay bowls or in dishes of hand-sewn green leaves, or igniting two-foot bamboo torches, which are inserted in the ground in small mounds of mud and cowdung. The flames light up thousands of faces, turbaned and wrapped in shawls and cloths against the chill night air. Soon the entire area is ablaze with lights on every level of the hills flanking each side of the river, the porches of every pilgrimage inn and sanctuary, and the steps and recesses of every temple.

Most are fasting in special penance for their dead, and many fortify themselves for the long night with spirits. Vigilant women replenish the oil lights, and as the night wears on the thumping of little hand drums is heard here and there in the turbulent sea of humanity. Troupes of singers and musicians stroll through the mourners shouting hymns, and soon the fun-loving, energetic hill girls are dancing, surrounded by circles of eager watchers.

It is during this night, they say, that an enamoured youth from the hills may coax a lively girl away from her heavy-lidded mother and dozing granny to some secluded spot on the river bank, the wooded hillsides or a dark corner of some dilapidated inn for a romantic encounter. And it appears that the young men from Kathmandu, in their fine Western clothes, who strut about eyeing the unsophisticated and unwary lassies from the villages, have not come to the festival to mourn for their dead.

Long before daylight the ceremonies begin. The lamps and flaming ceremonial torches are carried down to the river and cast into the sacred waters. Shivering with cold, the devotees take a holy bath, hurry to the temple once more to pay respects to Lord Shiva, and start an arduous, two-and-a-half-mile barefoot pilgrimage over and around the sacred hill, through the woods and temples, along a dusty path laid out with brambles, down rough stone steps and along a rocky trail. At three-foot intervals along the way are stones splashed with white paint to represent gods and goddesses. On each of these and on each of the countless holy places and idols along the route the single-file devotees toss a scattering of *satbhiu*, a mixture of seven seeds and other offerings – rice, barley, wheat, lentils, corn, bits of radish, fruits, marigold blossoms mixed with red powder to please the gods and succour the souls of the dead.

By sun-up many have completed this ritual pilgrimage, packed their belongings and started on the long trek back to their villages, while new arrivals flock in throughout the day from hamlets and cities of the valley, rich and poor together of every caste and creed, to scatter *satbhiu* for their dead. Most flock back into the main Pashupatinath temple to do *Chaun Sathi* – a ceremonial walk around the sixty-four Shiva lingams therein, making their offerings and receiving Shiva's blessing. To overlook one of these lingams, which represent Lord Shiva himself, is to commit a sin which erases any merit gained.

This all-night vigil and the scattering of grains on Bala Chaturdasi completes one more of the year's obligatory duties for the dead, and it also honours the memory of a most unfortunate ancestor called Bala.

It seems that in olden days it was the duty of Bala Nanda to sweep and clean the inner sanctum of Lord Shiva's temple at

Pashupatinath. Bala often took his meals down near the burning grounds at the riverside, while corpses were being cremated. One day one of the heated bodies exploded and a piece of charred flesh fell into Bala's plate, which he unwittingly consumed, only noticing that his food was especially palatable. From that moment Bala became addicted to human flesh. His appearance gradually changed to that of a fiendish ogre, who snatched corpses brought for cremation, terrifying the people, who soon found it impossible to perform the last rites for their dead. They began to call him Balasur – the demon Bala.

Finally, word of this monstrous creature reached the King, who, deeming it futile to combat a giant, decided to outwit Balasur by entering into a solemn, sacred oath of friendship with him. This done, the King gave a great feast for Balasur, and as soon as the demon became drunk, the King led him to a well, shoved him in and ended the menace then and there. Now to compensate for the terrible crime of betraying a friendship, the King burned ceremonial torches for two years continuously at Pashupatinath and scattered grains about the vicinity to feed the wandering soul of the betrayed Balasur.

Some say it was not the King who plotted Balasur's end, but a Newari farmer carrying quantities of food and drink to his traditional ancestor-clan celebration. The farmer, waylaid by the demon Balasur, placated him with his entire supply of liquor, and finally killed the giant when he became totally intoxicated. Others say it was a witch who lived in the near-by forest, ever in fear of the demon Balasur, and that she took matters into her own hands at last, hypnotized the demon and induced him to lay his head in her lap, that she might pick the lice from his hair – a common sight in Nepal. As the witch deloused him in the warm sunshine, Balasur became drowsy and she calmly knifed him to death. Most stories agree that Balasur met his end through the chicanery of those he trusted.

A popular version says that Bala Nanda was a common citizen who inadvertently consumed a morsel of the remains of a kinsman's corpse which he was dutifully burning. Immediately after, they say, Bala's head became a solid ball of silver. In this form he became a recluse in Pashupatinath forest, frequenting the burning ghats, terrorizing the people who came to cremate their dead, hopelessly addicted to cannibalism. Finally the King called upon Brika Singh, a man who was known to have been a former friend of Bala, and ordered Singh to kill the demon. Singh and twelve men carried into the forest a cask of home-made wine on a funeral litter, just as corpses are still taken to cremation grounds, and induced Balasur to consume the contents. When the demon was drunk, Singh threw him to his death in a well. Then Singh cut off the demon's silver head, had a special ornament fashioned from this precious metal and presented to Lord Shiva as an offering. When Shiva in return promised Singh any boon he desired, this man begged only for atonement for the murder of a friend. Shiva complied by saying, 'In memory of Balasur, this day shall hence-forth be known as Bala Chaturdasi. On this day each year I shall wear the ornament made from Balasur's silver head, and all those who come to my temple and scatter grains for their dead shall gain heaven, and even the sin of manslaughter by such a person shall be expiated. And, Brika Singh, you must do likewise.'

Others say that Bala was in reality a poor man who earned a living supervising the burning of corpses at Pashupatinath. One day, while eating his meal and tending a cremation, the heated skull burst and cooked brains fell into his plate, which he consumed unknowingly. Thereafter he was powerless to resist breaking the skulls and eating the brains of the corpses. He haunted the pyres, a fiend with long shaggy hair, monstrous claws and a gross and filthy body. He took up residence in a near-by forest den, and when he began attacking innocent passers-by the King offered a reward for his death. It was a barber, they say, a former devout friend, who came to the den to deceive the demon with food and drink. When the monster became drunk, his barber friend begged him to improve his hideous appearance, thereby regaining his former beauty. At last Balasur agreed and allowed the barber to cut his claws and shave his mangy beard, during which process the barber slit Balasur's throat and killed him. The King's reward made the barber wealthy, but he was ever haunted with the memory of a friend betrayed. At last a learned pundit advised the barber to take a pilgrimage to Pashupatinath and scatter grain seeds to the gods on Bala Chaturdasi day, thereby absolving himself of sin and securing peace for the soul of the slain Balasur, ceremonies which the Nepalese people observe to this day.

On Bala Chaturdasi people remember Ranjit Singh, last of the old Malla kings of Bhadgaon, who 200 years ago was involved in a feud with his relative, Jaya Prakash Malla, King of Kathmandu. When a group of gay young men from Kathmandu journeyed to Bhadgaon to celebrate the annual Bisket festival at New Year, the foolish King of Bhadgaon had them imprisoned on the improbable charge that they were offensively vain in their jaunty, big-city clothes. When the King of Kathmandu protested, his subjects were finally released, but he never forgot this affront. Some seven months later King Jaya Prakash of Kathmandu retaliated by imprisoning visitors from Bhadgaon who came to Pashupatinath to scatter grains in the name of their dead on Bala Chaturdasi day. These innocent victims were released only after the ruler of Bhadgaon had paid a heavy ransom, but he was so incensed that he severed all diplomatic relations with the kingdom of Kathmandu and extravagantly encouraged Prithvi Narayan Shah, King of Gorkha, forty-three miles to the north-west, to invade Kathmandu and punish Jaya Prakash. This the Gorkha Shah king proceeded to do and in the process conquered Patan, Bhadgaon and the entire valley. Thus ended the feuding, as well as the reign, of the Malla kings and to this day the Shah kings from Gorkha rule Nepal.

The ritual grain scattering on Bala Chaturdasi day ends with the blowing of a horn. The people return to their homes satisfied that they have atoned for any sins committed against the deceased, that they have properly appeased the gods, as well as mollified the wandering souls of their dead.

Most touching is it on this day to see the barefoot, grain-scattering women stop at an ancient stone idol of Ganesh, the Elephant God who brings success to all undertakings, located on

Mrigasthali hill. They give the image a violent shake to command his attention and shout in his ear, 'Convey to my deceased father that I have come to scatter grains in his honour!' For, as all know, this particular Ganesh, though he be stone deaf, has a direct line from the living to the souls of the dead.

25 SITA BIBAHA PANCHAMI
The Wedding of Goddess Sita and Lord Rama

During one distant period of Hindu life, depicted in the lengthy and beloved Ramayana texts, evil ruled the world in the form of a fiendish demon king, Ravana, and his horde of devilish followers. Their realm was Lanka, a mythical country now believed to have been Ceylon. With the spread of Ravana's wickedness the sinful prospered; those who honoured neither parents nor the gods enjoyed the best of fortune; and those who knew not right from wrong triumphed over those of virtue.

The gods, themselves helpless against this demon king, finally appealed to Lord Brahma, the great Creator. They pointed out that Brahma himself had bestowed this terrible power on Ravana as a reward for the demon's having performed years of meditation, penance, prayer and arduous fasting. This Brahma readily admitted, but assured the gods that, while he had granted Ravana immunity from death at the hands of gods and other demons, he had promised nothing to protect him from mankind. At this the gods rejoiced and made arrangements whereby Lord Vishnu would again reincarnate himself on earth in human form, together with a host of monkeys – brave, wise and swift, who could change in form, making their destruction all but impossible. The faithful monkey-god Hanuman was their leader.

Now it happened that a wise and kindly king, Dasaratha, ruled the fabulously wealthy city of Ayodhya in northern India. His one unhappiness was that his three queens bore him no sons. Now Lord Vishnu appeared and saw to it that the King's wives each drank a certain nectar containing Vishnu's own essence, and soon the eldest produced Rama Chandra, the next gave birth to Bharat and the third had twins, Lakshman and Satrughna, for this last queen had taken two sips of the sacred liquid. All four, then, emanated from Lord Vishnu, but it was Rama, the eldest, who grew in grace and virile beauty. His strength, courage, purity of heart, compassion, sweetness of speech, serenity and abiding wisdom made him the favourite of his father, idol of the people and the adored elder brother of Lakshman, who would stay for ever by his side.

Another king, Janak, whose very name is synonymous with wisdom and goodness, ruled the kingdom of Mithila in southern Nepal, where his city of Janakpur, now called Janakpurdhan, is still a place of pilgrimage. One day, when the childless Janak was tilling and sanctifying the land, preparing it for a religious ceremony, he discovered a beautiful baby girl lying in a furrow. He carried her to the palace, where she grew into a princess of breathtaking loveliness. When she was about sixteen Janak held a great tournament wherein the one who could bend the divine bow of Shiva – which had been presented to Janak as a gift – would win fair Sita's hand. Princes and kings came from far and wide, but each failed to bend the tremendous and powerful bow.

It so happened that Rama and his brother Lakshman were in the vicinity of Janakpur, having just finished off a horde of demons. With great ease Rama not only curved the bow, but snapped it in two. Its rending sounded like an earthquake and thousands of onlookers fell to the ground in awe. When the lovely Sita put the wedding garland about Rama's neck there was universal applause, and the throng cheered to see this meeting of Eternal Lovers. It is said their hearts communed without speech, such was their divine love.

A sumptuous wedding ceremony was held wherein Rama's three brothers were also united with neighbouring princesses. When these gorgeously arrayed couples held hands and thrice circumambulated the sacrificial fire, the marriage dais, the King and all the hermits, flowers rained down from heaven and celestial music was heard. Then Rama and Lakshman took their brides, with mountains of costly gifts, in a wedding procession that stretched for miles across the plains. When they reached the city of Ayodhya, Rama's home, they found it festive with flowers and shining like an abode of the gods.

Some years later when King Dasaratha prepared to have Rama, his eldest son, crowned ruler, the youngest queen, incited by an evil hunch-backed servant named Manthara, forced the king to send Rama into the forests for fourteen years of exile. The distraught King was powerless to deny her wish, since years before he had promised this queen any reward she wished for saving his life. Today, after thousands of generations, Hindu men, women and children remember and detest the hunchback Manthara as the cause of Rama's long banishment, the King's broken health and death, and the sorrows which befell the royal family of Ayodhya. Thousands have come to adore Rama and his noble, gracious acceptance of fate, and to admire his faithful wife Sita and loyal brother Lakshman, who stayed by his side throughout all his years of wandering.

It was during this period of exile that the hideous sister of the demon king Ravana tried to seduce first Rama and then Lakshman, and in repulsing her Lakshman found it necessary to cut off her nose and ears. When she fled bleeding to her fiendish brother, Ravana was mad with rage, and returned to kidnap Sita, a sacrilege which caused the jackals to howl and the birds to cry in the forests. He carried her off to his palace in Lanka, where Sita pined away and resolutely resisted the demon king's advances.

It was the loyal monkey, Hanuman, son of the Wind God, endowed with his father's energy, swiftness and ability to penetrate every place on earth and sky, who discovered Sita's whereabouts. Eventually, with his and the monkey horde's assistance, Rama and Lakshman slew the evil Ravana and eradicated the whole dynasty of demons from the earth.

Later, when Rama was crowned King of Ayodhya, the prevailing code of honour and his own royal blood prompted Rama to place duty above love. As an example to his people, he renounced the beautiful Sita, for no righteous Hindu man will keep a wife who has been touched by another. Her fair cheeks bathed in tears, Sita accepted her husband's verdict, knowing his heart was broken.

However, the gods themselves intervened, advising Rama that he was an incarnation of Lord Vishnu and that Sita was Laxmi, Goddess of Wealth. They assured Rama that his wife had remained unblemished throughout her ordeal in Lanka. It seems, however, that a citizen later questioned her chastity, and Rama the king, knowing in his heart that Sita was guilty of no transgression, allowed her to repair to the forests, where she lived with the hermit's wives.

Just before his death Rama bestowed great gifts upon his loyal followers, and to the monkey god Hanuman he said, 'It is determined already that thou shalt live for ever: do thou be glad on earth so long as this story of me endures.' Thus immortality was assured to the most selfless and loyal of servants.

As for Rama, to this day no name is more on Hindu lips, repeated at the beginning of all undertakings and again at completion in pious thanksgiving. Every child hears his story from birth and it becomes a part of his life. Youths are enthralled by his noble exploits; men ponder the great truth revealed in his legends. The aged derive spiritual consolation by telling the name of Rama on their beads, and it is whispered again into their ears at death, chanted in chorus as the body is carried to the river bank for cremation.

Sita is ever exalted as the highest example of womanhood – beautiful, pious, courteous, loyal and unassuming. To her birthplace in Janakpur in southern Nepal thousands upon thousands come from all over India and Nepal to celebrate her marriage to Lord Rama each year on the fifth day of the waxing moon in late November or early December. Cultural, agrarian and commercial exhibitions are held at a great *mela* or fair, which lasts for a week. Hundreds of booths and bazaar shops do a resounding business. Dust flies, loud speakers blare, and the roar of the crowd can be heard for miles around. Pilgrims who have walked for days dry their laundry as they travel, stretching yards of colourful sari lengths between them on the sun-baked roads, carrying bundles of cloth-wrapped provisions on their heads.

On the first day a great procession starts from Rama's temple.

His idol, dressed as the bridegroom, is placed under a lavishly decorated *khat* on the back of a caparisoned elephant. A fringed, gold-tipped ceremonial umbrella is made to whirl constantly over his head while musicians play and a cheering mob swarms along his route to the Janaki temple of Sita a short distance away. The next day, her idol is carried amidst a great fanfare to Rama's side in a re-enactment of Hindu wedding ceremonies, including rituals before the sacrificial fire.

Again on Lord Rama's birthday on the ninth day of the bright lunar fortnight in March, a similar procession is held in Janakpur, when elephants, horses, bullock carts and sometimes 10,000 pilgrims follow in their wake. In Kathmandu many people, including the royal family, go to the temples to pay homage to Rama, while symposiums are held to exalt the ideal life he represents.

In Bhadgaon town, on the bank of the Hanumante River, named after the monkey-god Hanuman, are burning ghats which bear the name of Rama and his faithful servant, and a great temple to enshrine their idols. Legend has it that Hanuman, during the great battle with the demons in Lanka, flew to the Himalayan mountains to procure a life-giving plant which was to revive the dying brother Lakshamn. On his return journey, they say, Hanuman carried a hill containing this medicinal herb and stopped to rest at this river just north of Bhadgaon.

Most Nepalese know the life-story of Rama well, and the myriad characters who shared his adventures, for in conclusion this epic masterpiece says:

'Thus ends Ramayana, revered by Brahma and made by Valmiki. He that hath no sons shall attain a son by reading even a single verse of Rama's lay. All sin is washed away from those who read or hear it. He who recites the Ramayana should have rich gifts of cows and gold. Long shall he live who reads the Ramayana, and he shall be honoured, with his sons and grandsons, in this world and in heaven.'

26 YOMARHI PUNHI OR DHANYA PURNIMA

Rice Cakes for the Harvest Moon

Yomarhi Punhi, on the full moon day of December, is a very old celebration originating no doubt with Newari farmers. Today it is observed in almost every home in the valley by both city and rural dwellers as a time when the heavy labour of rice harvest is over, the storage bins are full, the crisp nights are bright with moonlight, and all men's minds turn once more to pleasure.

Indispensable to the many ceremonies and festivals of this agrarian valley people is food: food to offer to the gods and food for the great family and community feasts. To Newars – who speak the dialect of their ancestors as well as the official Nepali language – fig is *yo*, and bread is *marhi*; hence *yomarhi*, a sweet-meat as traditional to Yomarhi full moon as plum pudding is to Christmas. This fist-size confection of rice flour dough is moulded to resemble a fig fruit, filled with molasses-like brown sugar and sesame seed, and steamed over the opening of a *chulo*, the Nepalese cooking stove. Nepalese housewives pride themselves on the dexterity with which they manipulate this pastry, creating, besides the fig, amazing likenesses of animals, fruits, nuts, ceremonial lamp stands, together with figurines of Ganesh, the good-luck god, and Laxmi, the Goddess of Wealth.

All Newars in the valley, regardless of their station in life, observe Yomarhi Punhi or full moon, for all Newars are farmers at heart, each clinging to a small piece of ancestral land from which he collects a share of harvest. An ageing widow's fourth-acre plot is bequeathed to her by parents as marriage dowry; a poor priest tills his meagre share of old family holdings; craftsmen, government servants, teachers, bankers and merchants are all landlords of at least a few acres once farmed by their great-great-grand-fathers. Larger acreages are owned by the ancient Newari *guthis*, social organizations based on caste, kin and religion of the members and their ancestors. Each member earns a small share of the harvest by cultivating the land in rotation, or having a tenant till it for him on behalf of the *guthi* society, whose main purpose and profit is to maintain the group's guardian or patron deities, their temples, festivals and related community feasts.

Thus sundown on harvest full moon finds every family gathered together as the housewife places a small selection of yomarhi cakes in a bucket, including two rice-dough figurines of a peasant farmer and wife. A simple religious ceremony blesses the cakes and gives thanks to the gods for the harvest. Now the bucket of sweetmeats is placed amidst the heaps of unhusked rice in the family storage room to be left 'hidden' for a four-day period. Women are strictly forbidden to look upon the consecrated cakes or grain during this time, and nothing will induce farmers to unlock the bins, not even a vastly profitable offer of purchase, for it is generally believed that some miracle may cause this unseen rice store to multiply in the bins, a long-standing dream of Nepalese people.

At night, when the yomarhi cakes are securely locked away, the traditional family feast is celebrated, when they all sit in long rows about the room where the surplus cakes are eaten. Four days later, when the bucket is removed from the granary, the cakes are distributed and consumed by family members. Only with the completion of these ceremonies do city landlords expect their share of the harvest.

Festivities break out all over the valley during the harvest full moon. The tiny village of Thecho, four miles south of Kathmandu, long famous as the home of one of the finest Newari dance troupes, stages spectacular performances where people come from miles around to watch the well-trained, ornately-costumed dancers and musicians. Their most lavish performance is held the day before full moon, when the proud troupe dances all afternoon to commemorate the harvest's completion.

Non-Newars call this full moon day *Dhanya Purnima, dhan* meaning either wealth or unhusked rice, synonymous terms in Nepal. These Parbate people, as Newaris call all non-Newars, will not use the new crop of rice for food until it has been blessed in the store-room on this full moon day. Many place yomarhi cakes in their treasure boxes with cash and valuables, praying to the Goddess of Wealth for continued and multiplying prosperity. Hundreds go to Lord Shiva's shrine in Panauti village near Banepa, where this deity is called Dhaneswar Mahadev, signifying his relationship with wealth and rice. Devotees present him with offerings and yomarhi cakes, receiving in return his blessing for prosperity. This gift from the deity, or *prasad*, may be a smearing of red paste transferred from the idol to the devotee's forehead by the temple priest, or a taste of the food and drink which others have offered to Shiva.

It was during this festival in 1969 that an entire family of eight, members of the priestly caste, lost consciousness soon after consuming a little *prasad* which had been left by a middle-aged woman. All were hospitalized and eventually recovered, but it was whispered that perhaps the woman was a witch, afflicted with the 'evil eye', who had laced her offerings with some magic ingredient or drug. Others say it was simple food-poisoning, a logical deduction considering the distance people carry their food offerings and the insanitary mixture which results when they are strewn about the idol.

A legend relating to the harvest full moon tells of Kuber, one of the Gods of Wealth, who disguised himself as a beggar and appeared at the door of a wealthy merchant in Panauti village. Completely unaware that the god was testing his character, the merchant, with unfailing Nepalese hospitality, invited the stranger in, offering refreshments and yomarhi cakes. This so pleased Kuber that he revealed his true identity to the merchant and presented him in turn with gifts of figs. Thereafter, the fig-shaped yomarhi became the traditional food of harvest full moon, when every housewife makes an extra supply for distribution to neighbours.

YOMARHI PUNHI OR DHANYA PURNIMA

Children look forward to the evening of the yomarhi full moon as Western children anticipate Hallowe'en, a time when they troop from house to house mischievously demanding yomarhi cakes. The traditional song, however, which these candid urchins sing, would no doubt startle Western housewives:

> 'The fig (*yomarhi*) has a tip,
> It is dark within.
>
> It will taste sweet if you give;
> If not, it is tasteless.
>
> She is young who gives,
> She is a miserly old hag who does not.
>
> If you do not hurry and present us with *yomarhi*,
> We will relieve ourselves in your rice-grinding machine.'

DECEMBER-JANUARY

27 SETO MACHHENDRANATH SNAN
The Public Bath of Lord White Machhendra

Just as Nepalese religions require the people to cleanse themselves periodically with ritual holy baths, so the gods themselves must be washed on occasions, drenched as they are with daily offerings of red powder, holy water, milk, honey, liquors, blood and eggs, and blackened with smoke from ceremonial lamps, flaming oil wicks and smouldering incense. Thus the god's annual holy bath is a multiple blessing, providing an opportunity to deck his idol in splendid new robes and, most important perhaps, a chance to celebrate once more.

Of the many Machhendra idols in the Valley, White Machhendra of old Kathmandu ranks second in popularity only to the famous Red Machhendra in Patan. Some believe these two idols represent the same god, but most consider them sisters endowed with both male and female aspects, even though they be male in appearance and Buddhist scripture. Each is paraded annually through the streets in majestic festival chariots, and each is identified as the Buddhist saint, Aryavalokiteswar, who attained the stature of Buddha in ages past.

Though his idol, temple and festival are the responsibility of Buddhist Newars of the priestly caste, White Machhendra is also widely worshipped by devotees of Shiva and Vishnu, for he bestows the priceless gift of longevity, especially upon children, and removes the cause of sterility in women – a merciful God of Pity, known as the 'Ocean of Compassion'.

Legend relates that in ancient times White Machhendra was stolen from Kathmandu by an invading king from Magala to the west, who neglected the idol, eventually discarding it in the

Gandaki River. Thereafter the King developed a strange malady, suffering abnormally from cold and from painful body swellings. He had the statue hastily retrieved and, as instructed in a dream, returned to Kathmandu, where it was thrown in a pit, eventually becoming buried under rubbish and earth. Years later, when a Newari porter, digging for clay at Jamal near Rani Pokhari, unearthed the image, the valley people rejoiced. Their king installed Lord Machhendra in a fine temple and on the advice of learned pundits inaugurated both a bathing festival and annual chariot procession in his honour.

A similar folk-tale says that long ago a Newar of the soil-tiller caste – among whom Machhendra is still exceedingly popular – unearthed the White Machhendra idol while cultivating his field, carried it home and kept it in his rice-storage bins. As time went by the farmer was astounded to find, though he used the rice, his supply never decreased. The King, advised of this miracle, decreed that since the idol was discovered in common soil, all must benefit. Thereafter White Machhendra was enshrined near the public granaries, which remained for ever filled.

News of this good fortune travelled north. The King of Tibet had White Machhendra stolen and carried to his own country, where the unknowing Tibetans worshipped him with improper rituals – even animal sacrifices. As a result an epidemic swept the country, whereby people suffered terrible body-swellings. The King returned the image to Kathmandu forthwith and dropped it in a well at Jamal. In time, a man drawing water found the idol and dreamed that it should be enshrined at its present site, called variously Machhendra Bahal, Ja Bahal or Jamaleswar in remembrance of the place of its discovery. He was further instructed that animal sacrifices are displeasing to Lord Machhendra, as they are to this day.

Now Lord Machhendra's week-long bathing festival is celebrated every year in the courtyard of his gilded, double-tiered temple off the crowded bazaar street between Asantole and Indrachowk in the heart of old Kathmandu.

Starting on the eighth day of the waxing moon in early January, sometimes late December, people arrive with plates of offerings and crowd to Machhendra's open archway, around the ancient Buddhist *chaitya* shrine alleged to have been built over two thousand years ago by the Indian Emperor Ashoka. Devotees amass their flowers and leaf-decorated trays, touch Lord Machhendra's feet with their foreheads, or toss coins over the heads of waiting worshippers to this beneficent Lord. In their midst a cow munches greenery that has fallen from the offerings, pariah dogs eat scraps of sweets, while pigeons peck at scattered grains of rice.

At dusk the crowd swells rapidly. Musical groups stroll around the courtyard and through the maze of surrounding Buddhist *chaityas* tooting horns and thumping drums. Small boys play under the roof of a twelve-foot-square platform where the sacred 'bathing throne', backed by a canopy of carved brass snakes, is being prepared. An old lady, chanting softly, places oil and flaming wicks in metal cups which line the platform's railing. Very soon the entire courtyard is packed with people, men, boys, women and children, crowding on temple steps and over the stone *chaityas*. Excitement mounts when a blast of horns announces the beginning of activity.

From the temple archway a solemn priest, wearing ornate robes and jewelled crown, emerges, followed by young, shaven-headed attendants carrying the idol of Lord Machhendra. The crowd gasps in unison, drinking in the sight of this four-foot idol with its stark white Buddha-like face, gleaming tiara, ornate earrings, necklaces and silk brocaded robes. With slow dignity the procession moves through a narrow opening in the throng to mount the bathing platform. Here White Machhendra is placed on the throne to stare benignly over a sea of adoring faces. Doll-size images of Machhendra's attendant goddesses are placed at his feet – Green Tara on one side, White Tara on the other – seen only during this annual ceremony, hidden as they are throughout the year by Machhendra's spreading robes.

Men of the priestly caste, impressive in red caps and sashes, sit before the idol amongst a gorgeous array of flowers and offerings. After lengthy discussion on correct procedure, with gesturing and good-natured shouting, a blare of music brings the chief priest before Machhendra. An attendant carries a great copper bowl of offerings, over which the priest performs ancient Tantric rituals, halting at each of the four sides and again at each corner of the platform. Ringing a hand bell, gracefully posturing hands and bare brown feet, rolling and flashing his eyes weirdly about, the priest chants the magic phrases and incoherent incantations required by the mystic rites of Tantrism.

Another fanfare of music at the temple gate announces the arrival of the Living Goddess Kumari, wrapped in scarlet, carried in the arms of an attendant. This deified child of two or three has only recently been chosen to replace a girl who has reached puberty, whose story has already been told. Preceded by torch-bearers, she is taken through the crowd to a vantage-point on the temple verandah to witness the bathing of Lord White Machhendra, a ceremony which cannot begin until she arrives.

Now all eyes return expectantly to the bathing platform. With a blast of trumpets, two priests quickly and methodically disrobe the idol, layer after layer of gold-brocaded silks, embroidered satins, necklaces and garlands and finally undergarments. Now the chalk-white image stands bare to the waist, his lower portion being painted red. Attendants on each side hold large vases of water over his head and the mob rumbles with excitement. Suddenly with a fresh blare of music the water is poured over Machhendra's head, on to the Tara goddesses and over his feet, bringing roars of approval from the crowds. Verging on hysteria, they push frantically toward the platform, ecstatically waving their hands while priests toss the bathwater, now consecrated and collected near the idol's feet, high into the air and over their heads – the wondrous gift of White Machhendra's blessing.

Now the mobs parade jubilantly around the courtyard and platform, fêting Machhendra by circumambulating his idol. Others clamour for bits of flowers, leaves and rice for their hair, while many catch Machhendra's bathwater in open palms, sprinkling it into their mouths and over their children.

Though this week is by tradition the coldest time of year, during the succeeding days Machhendra is laved in milk, oil, hot water and, hopefully, sunshine, for without fail his bathing festival brings clouds and rain in a winter season otherwise blessed throughout with daily sunshine. People say that when Machhendra's naked figure is exposed for ritual sunbath, his seemingly spiteful stepmother, the cloud goddess, purposely hides the sun, sending chilling drizzle as added penance for her son.

Crowds come each day to leave offerings and watch Machhendra being rubbed, anointed and transformed. An idol-painter, himself prohibited from touching the sacred idol, squats before it giving two youthful priests explicit instructions from a tattered manuscript. Under his guidance the body is whitewashed, fingernails retraced, eyes and placid features outlined, and even the Green and White Tara goddesses are given a fresh coat of colour. The most important day of painting is the day before full moon, when Machhendra's benevolent, merciful eyes are painted before hundreds of spectators. On the twelfth day of the fortnight Machhendra is taken to the sacrificial fire, where his sacred Hindu thread is changed in the same holy rituals required when all high-caste Hindu men undergo this ancient, annual ceremony.

All through the last day, full moon, women sit before the temple fashioning *yomarhi* cakes and figurines of rice-flour paste – flowers, animals, birds; small likenesses of Ganesh, the ever-present Bestower of Success; lacy, miniature temples complete with spires and tiers. These are set before Machhendra; the greater the quantity and intricacy of design, the greater the blessing bestowed by this deity. In the evening crowds gather once more for the ritual re-enshrinement of Machhendra in his temple archway, resplendent now in dazzling crown, jewels, fresh flower garlands and bulky silken robes. The time of day for these ceremonies varies considerably from year to year in compliance with astrologer's positioning of the planets.

At night the high priest holds a ritual feast for householders who occupy the several-storied buildings bordering the temple courtyard, perhaps to compensate for a week of bedlam which often prevents access to their homes.

Now White Machhendra awaits his next outing, a festival held three months later when he is carried from his temple in joyful parade to a towering temple-like chariot waiting at Jamal near Rani Pokhari where he was discovered so long before. Starting on the eighth day of the waxing moon in late March or early April, his chariot is pushed through the streets of Kathmandu in riotous celebration, traditionally for four days ending at full moon, unless the huge wooden wheels break down or some ill omen occurs, in which case the festival is easily, and frequently, prolonged.

28 THE HOLY MONTH OF MAGH

The unholy month of Poush, which begins on the currently-used Nepalese solar calendar in mid-December, is so ill-omened that most religious ceremonies are forbidden, no weddings take place, and wary Nepalese refuse to shift from one abode to another during these unlucky thirty days. However, with Magh Sankranti, the first day of the following month, usually in mid-January, everyone rejoices that the threat of misfortune is behind and better days have come at last.

Magh Sankranti then is one of the few holy days which does not follow the old religious lunar calendar. It marks the changing of the winter sun's course toward the northern hemisphere, which eventually brings the long-awaited warmer weather, a decided blessing in Nepal where most homes, whether mansion or hut, are inadequately heated. Every day of winter finds city matrons, peasant women and village housewives sitting in their gardens or sidewalk doorways soaking up the sun, their only source of warmth.

Although Magh Sankranti may be the coldest day in the year, it is none the less one of the most important for holy bathing, especially at the confluences of sacred rivers and streams. Sankha-mole, on the Bagmati River below Patan town, is one of the holiest of bathing spots to which, on this day, people bundled in shawls come hurrying through the pre-dawn fog, past groups of intrepid musicians and singers muffled in scarves and blankets, who perform on the open porches along the river's edge. Some strip to loincloth or tubular cotton bathing garment to shiver and splash in the shallow water, while others merely stoop at the cement steps, rinsing hands and face or flicking droplets over their heads.

Hundreds proceed up the rough cobbled street through Patan

to circumambulate the tiered temple of Red Machhendranath, pushing their way through crowds of worshippers to leave offerings for this powerful deity. Most visit Agima Ta temple, where a sacred fire is kept eternally burning to light the firepots carried in funeral processions, a flame used to ignite the pyre of the dead at the riverside.

Vital for good health and fortune are certain auspicious foods on this holy day – sesame seeds, sweet potatoes, green leaf spinach, *khichari*, a mixture of rice and lentils, great quantities of meat and often home-brewed wines and beer, all shared with friends and family. As on most holy days, a married daughter, her husband and children are invited back to the parental home, where on Magh Sankranti the mother blesses all family members with a patting of mustard oil on the head, with a few drops in the ear for a lengthy, fortunate life. Everywhere – in cities, villages and countryside – old and young, peasant and aristocrat alike sit in doorways, porches, courtyards or along the streets in varying states of un-dress, taking the sun and mustard-oil massage, a common sight throughout the year, but thought absolutely essential on this first day of Magh.

Priests call at homes or sit in roofed, community meeting plat-forms reading aloud from holy books to receive alms and gifts of the season's auspicious foods. A traditional offering to the Brah-man priests on this day is a clay fire pot and a small bundle of wood.

Legend has it that once on the first day of Magh in Bhadgaon town a bazaar merchant, seated before his pile of *til*, or sesame seed, noticed that, although he had done a thriving business, his supply of seeds had not diminished. On searching he discovered the cause of this miracle – the idol of Narayan or Lord Vishnu hidden within the sesame. Ever since, on Magh Sankranti the Til Madhav idol, as it is now called, is massaged with clarified butter and worshipped with offerings of sweetened sesame balls in the expectation that this god will continue to bring an ever increasing supply of food and wealth to the people of Bhadgaon.

Magh Sankranti also commemorates that ancient day during

o. Chariot carrying Lord Machhendra
rrives for exhibition of 'sacred Bhoto' or
arment during his Patan festival
  D. D. Shrestha)

Decorated image of White Machhendra
vaits for his annual ceremonial bath in his
emple archway, Kathmandu, behind men of
  certain caste who will officiate
Shridhar Manadhar)

an khamole shrine, on the sacred Bagmati
River below Patan town, an important site
or holy bathing, especially on the first day of
he Holy Month of Magh
Betty Woodsend)

21. Image of Kal Bhairab, the Black Bhairab of Hanuman Dhoka Square in Kathmandu, before which nobody dares tell a lie   (Betty Woodsend)

Brahman (note sacred Hindu thread over his chest) leaves offerings for Hanuman, the Monkey God who befriended Lord Rama, at Gauri-Shankar near Pashupatinath (Betty Woodsend)

Animal sacrifices by Nepalese military units in Kathmandu near Hanuman Dhoka. A man has a sword raised in readiness while goats and buffalo are lined up for slaughter in the name of Goddess Durga during Dasain festival   (Betty Woodsend)

the much-fabled Mahabharata war between related families, when Bishma the elderly grandfather of both sides laid himself on a bed of arrows, determined not to die until the sun entered its northern path, opening the way to the region of the gods. Thus he lay discoursing to his young kinsfolk on the duties and mysteries of life and death. When finished, through his own will, Bishma succumbed, freeing his soul from the bonds of his body and life on earth – an accomplishment possible only for the extremely pious, who have devoted their lives to communion with the gods. Thus it is believed that the souls of those who die on this day go straight to heaven, as did Bishma's, forever released from the burden of endless rebirth.

The full moon day of Magh always just precedes or soon follows Magh Sankranti day of the Nepalese solar calendar. Full moon is actually the beginning of the sacred month of Magh as calculated by the old religious lunar calendar. It falls in January and ends with the following full moon thirty days later.

Swastani Purnima, as this full moon day is called, marks the first day of a month devoted to religious fasting, holy bathing and the study of the Swastani religious text, a chapter or story of which is read each evening by priests or householders to the gathered family. The book, worshipped each day with offerings of sweetmeats, glorifies the Goddess Swastani and the merits of a month-long religious fast held in her honour. It is the Hindu 'bible' and explains the Creation, propounding Shiva as Mahadev and Vishnu as Narayan, paramount deities whose miraculous feats invariably resulted in peace, prosperity and spiritual bliss for the suffering, lifting them from the morass of pain and poverty which is the lot of many a Hindu hero or heroine. The Swastani shows how the wrath of neglected gods spells ruin for the sinful, and points out hope of redemption if he repents and devotes himself to righteousness.

Exemplified in the Swastani is the month-long fast during Magh, performed by Goddess Parbati, whereby she attained the love of Mahadev and gained everlasting happiness and spiritual bliss. It was Parbati, through her divine messengers, who taught the strict, fastidious rites required for Magh fasting and holy bathing to people on earth – especially women – that they too might attain their heart's desire.

Many observe the fast of Magh in their homes, while others retire for thirty days to temples where they take the vow of Swastani Brata, fasting for Swastani.

Hundreds go to the Salinadi River at Sankhu, an ancient village of great sanctity, eight miles north-east of Kathmandu. Here at the hillside temple of Mahadev-Narayan, where the two deities are represented in one figure, women garbed in simplest robes, often of plain red cotton, take ritual holy baths thrice daily, eating only a few bites of 'clean' vegetarian food, most of which is bestowed as alms by visiting devotees. Combing the hair is strictly forbidden. Sleeping on hard mats, chanting the names of the gods for hours on end, listening to the long Swastani stories recited by the priests, the women concentrate solely on spiritual matters, for they must be scrupulously clean in thought, word and deed. If by chance they come into contact with a person wearing leather, or one from the untouchable caste, they must purify themselves at once in the sacred Salinadi River, returning to their day-long vigil, seated before the idol of Mahadev-Narayan.

Groups of men fast at another level of the temple area, observing the same regimentation and strictest continence.

Great crowds come to Sankhu's Salinadi River each day of Magh, usually in early morning, when the first sunrays stream through trees to light the near-naked bathers splashing, immersing and sprinkling themselves in the sacred, chilly waters. Women pray over gracefully cupped hands through which water slowly flows. Men bend double with foreheads at water level, facing the rising sun.

Next the bathers throng about the low ten-foot boulder at the river's edge, a most holy representation of Mahadev-Narayan known here as Hari-Har, which they smother with offerings of flowers, burning incense and flaming wicks. As this sacred rock's thick coating of red powder becomes damp with countless sprinklings of holy water, people place a dot of this sacred paste on their foreheads or set flowers atop their heads as a blessing from Hari-Har.

All climb the stone steps to the finely-carved image of Mahadev-Narayan, while a crush of worshippers push to and fro amongst them, for in Nepal queuing up in orderly fashion is not the rule, and nobody resents the resultant delay and confusion. They make their way past rows of fasting women, placing food offerings at their knees, and move on to worship Mahadev-Narayan before ascending the hill to Shiva lingams, idols of Vishnu Bhagawan, Sita-Rama, Saraswati the Goddess of Learning and countless others.

Crowds cross the river on stepping stones to follow a foot-wide raised path bordering the rice fields, balancing precariously as they meet returning devotees. There they worship before three ver-milion- and flower-covered rocks representing characters from a story told in the Swastani Purana texts.

It seems that Navaraj, a poor but devout Brahman boy, left his pious, trouble-beset mother and young wife Chandravati to search for his father whom he had never seen. When he found his dead father's bones, Navaraj carried them to a riverside and performed the last rites and cremation, as all true Hindu sons would do. Then he set out once more in search of work and food for his loved ones.

His mother, alone and penniless, was advised by Goddess Par-bati's messenger to undergo the Swastani fast on her son's behalf, and on the final day, as she prayed for his safe return, Navaraj appeared. Next morning, as the pious boy bathed in the river, the God Hari-Har appeared before him, gave him a blessing and ordained that Navaraj would become a king if he went to a certain village. On reaching this place Navaraj was struck with wonder when he was proclaimed ruler of the land, for an elephant gar-landed him and lifted the boy on his back – an ancient means of choosing a king from the populace. Navaraj sent for his mother, who spent the rest of her days in the splendour of the palace. Such is the good fortune which comes to those who observe the Swastani fast.

Now when Navaraj dispatched two porters with a litter to carry his wife Chandravati to his palace, the foolish girl's head was completely turned at the realization that she was now a queen. Along the way she made arrogant demands of the porters, insisting that they travel with haste. When they reached the Salinadi River near Sankhu, the porters begged for water, and Chandravati begrudgingly granted their request. Now at the river's edge the porters found the people worshipping Goddess Swastani, and carried back to their mistress a piece of the offerings as a *prasad*, or blessing from the goddess, but the impatient girl spat upon this sacred gift and ground it into the earth with her foot.

As the party crossed the Salinadi River, however, Chandravati was repaid for her sinful behaviour when the porters lost their footing and all three crashed into the rocks and water. The two men were killed and their souls went straight to Lord Shiva, but Chandravati was left very near to death. During the following days, as the people came to do their Swastani bathing, they found the river has ceased to flow. King Navaraj ordered nets thrown to remove the obstructions, and Chandravati emerged with flesh falling from her body, more dead than alive. At last she found strength to pray to the goddess for help, and was advised to undergo the fasting and bathing rituals set down in the Swastani. When this was done, Chandravati gradually regained her strength and beauty and lived with her husband for the rest of her life as Queen.

Now during the holy month of Magh people worship the three large rocks on the opposite bank of the Salinadi as manifestations of Chandravati and the two porters who lost their lives.

Throughout the thirty holy days devout men perform special penance by walking through the streets or around the temples carrying on their heads earthen jars which have been pierced with holes through which countless hollow straws protrude. Devotees pour holy water into the pots, which then pours down over their faces and naked chests while they endlessly chant, 'Mahadev-Narayan, Mahadev-Narayan.' Sins are thereby washed away.

Some people pilgrimage from temple to temple, prostrating themselves every few steps, marking off the distance with their own dusty bodies, a severe penance which ensures the granting of any boon they may ask of Mahadev-Narayan, be it prosperity, a good and beautiful wife, a son from a barren spouse, or the freedom of a jailed relative.

The beginning full moon day of Magh is also known as *Mila Punhi* to followers of Lord Vishnu. During the Mila Punhi festival, Vishnu as Narayan is carried from his famous hilltop temple at Changu, two miles north of Bhadgaon and a short distance from Sankhu village. Narayan is represented as a carved silver water-vase, a *kalash*, with Narayan's image engraved on four sides. This heavy, sanctified *kalash*, thought to contain the spirit of Changu Narayan, is filled with holy water and suspended in a cloth tied about the neck of his bearer.

The procession passes through the narrow crowded streets of Kathmandu at Asantole and Indrachowk just at dusk, led by elderly soldiers and musicians in rumpled blue uniforms, carrying antiquated swords and flags. Accompanied by a fanfare of drums, bagpipes and fifes, this is the military contingent of the old royal priest at Hanuman Dhoka. Spectators dart out to scoop holy water from the garlanded *kalash*, while others snatch flowers from its decorations to place in the hair as a blessing from Changu Narayan.

The parade stops before the closed gate of Taleju temple at Hanuman Dhoka, waiting to be greeted by Kumari the Living Goddess whose house is near by. People press about, fervently whispering, 'Narayan, Narayan, Narayan', while certain religious ceremonies are conducted in the light of flaming torches. Soon a small band of musicians arrives with Kumari in its midst, carried in the arms of an attendant. He seats her on a low bench near the Narayan image, whence she gazes with round, exotic eyes at the crowd of worshipping onlookers.

Finally, the Taleju temple gate is opened, Narayan is carried quickly inside, guns crack in salute, Kumari is whisked back to her home and the priestly military band marches through the Hanuman Dhoka gate. Nobody is certain what ceremonies are performed inside, and most feel it unwise to probe too closely into the secrets of the gods, but it is said that the King, who is considered an incarnation of Narayan, receives the image with utmost respect and presents it with a golden coin. They say the King looks into the mouth of the sacred vessel, where he sees his image reflected in the holy water and asks, 'May I know the pleasure of your visit?' Narayan replies, 'I am going away to Benares and have come to bid you farewell.' At this the King entreats Narayan not to leave the valley, but the deity departs on his journey none the less.

Now when Narayan leaves through the city streets he sees great piles of blackened earthen pots and hears a series of explosions which he considers such a bad omen that he cancels his journey and returns to Changu Narayan temple.

As for the earthen pots, children look forward to collecting for this occasion cracked and useless clay vessels from neighbouring housewives. They are gathered in tall stacks at various open squares near Changu Narayan's route through the old city, and small fires are built to heat them. When the charred pots are pelted with stones and bricks they explode like gun shots, to the delight of screaming urchins. According to legend Narayan should actually hear these explosions as he leaves Kathmandu, but most children are too impatient to await his passing. Perhaps for Narayan it is enough just to see the carnage of broken blackened pots, for he invariably returns to his hilltop temple every year, whence he continues to protect the people of the valley.

Always on the fifth day of the waxing moon during Magh, ten days before full moon day in late January or early February, Basant Panchami, the Advent of Spring, is officially heralded, even though only few buds and blossoms have made an appearance. Despite the chill in the air, Nepalese know the valley will soon bask in balmy weather.

The ancient royal palace at Basantpur, Place of Springtime, was first inaugurated in Kathmandu on Basant Panchami day with rites still officially commemorated at Hanuman Dhoka by the mid-morning gathering of hundreds of government officials, resplendent in black and white formal dress, and military officers laden with ribbons and medals. The King of Nepal arrives in motorcade, escorted by mounted cavalry officers and military band. Inside the old palace they all stand to attention through the strains of the traditional Song of Spring. Then the season is inaugurated with gun salutes, while the royal priest conducts elaborate ceremonies in honour of Saraswati, the Goddess of Learning.

Most believe that Goddess Saraswati actually visits Kathmandu Valley on this, her birthday, which coincides with the Advent of Spring, when she is lavishly fêted by students, scholars, writers, poets, artists and musicians, even spinners and weavers. She reigns over the realm of speech, letters, arts and sciences, and all her tools are worshipped accordingly – pens, ink, books, pencils and spinning wheels.

Saraswati is the lily-white daughter of Shiva and Durga, Lord Brahma's wife, a maid of peerless beauty in spotless white robes, seated on a full-blown white lotus. Her carrier is a snow-white swan. She is also one of the Devi goddesses, having sprung from Durga, but does not wear the red robes symbolic of her blood-thirsty counterparts. Her brother Ganesh, the elephant god, is invariably close at her side, and he receives animal sacrifices in her stead. In her hands Saraswati holds a book, *vina* harp, and sometimes a great sword, the one wielded by the Buddhist god, Manjusri.

For some believe that Manjusri and Saraswati are one and the same. It is not clear how these two deities came to be thought identical. Some people worship the idol enshrined behind Swayambhunath hill as Saraswati the Goddess of Learning; while others make offerings to it for Manjusri the God of Knowledge, the Buddhist saint who walked from China in remotest times to drain the water from this valley. It is interesting that in the evening before this first day of spring country girls, following the belief that Goddess Saraswati has just arrived for her annual visit after a strenuous trek across the high Himalayas, worship her idol and massage it with sesame oil to ease her weary limbs.

Basant, or Shri Panchami day, brings people of all ages, castes and creeds, both rich and poor, to temples of the Divinity of Knowledge, especially to the idol behind Swayambhunath, recessed in the wall of a small Buddhist *chaitya* shrine. The image is inundated with gifts, sweets, fruits, flowers and items of food, so that she may break her fast, for it is believed that Saraswati, like her worshippers, abstains from food on this holy day. Many offer small garlands of white cottonwool puffs, one ball of which is taken back home to use on the shuttle in the hope that Saraswati will increase the skill of the spinner. Villagers bring a large roll of cloth on a temple-like litter to represent, some say, the carpet Saraswati laid out for Lord Buddha's footsteps.

Close by Saraswati's idol ceremonies are performed to please the crude stone image of Ganesh. Women come with small school-age children, followed by bearers with trays of offerings, leading a bleating goat or squawking chicken. The creature's throat is slit and blood made to spurt over Ganesh and the surrounding mass of broken eggs, flowers, vegetables, holy leaves, grains, flames and incense. Milling devotees pray, gossip and shout instructions for the correct sacrificial procedure. Then the goat's head is completely severed, topped by a lighted wick in a small clay dish, and placed before Ganesh, who bestows success in all undertakings – even petitions to Saraswati for blessings on one's school career.

This is the day when children of five to seven years – many consider six to be unlucky – are taught their first alphabet, which is repeated after the teacher or parent and traced on wooden or stone slates. And around the city are seen numerous wedding processions, with the young groom in a palanquin, or a bride swathed in scarlet accompanied by musicians and marching relatives, for Basant Panchami is the most auspicious and most popular day in the year for marriages, when they are blessed personally by Goddess Saraswati.

With the arrival of full moon day ending the month of Magh, usually in February, the auspicious season for reading the sacred Swastani is over. Thousands consider it essential on this day to visit the temples and bathe in the rivers. In Kathmandu, after taking a chilly morning holy dip, men and boys in groups from each city division parade round the temples singing devotional songs in a procession which often swells to a happy, rejoicing throng.

Many pilgrimage to the shrines around Pashupatinath and bathe in the sacred Bagmati, where women form miniature Shiva lingams of sand, which they worship with lights and offerings. A mile up the river at Gauri Ghat, under the bridge leading to Gujeswari shrine, hundreds crowd in and out over slippery rocks to smother the beloved idol of Gauri-Shankar with offerings, for this crude, riverside boulder represents Goddess Parbati and her divine lover Shiva – the ideal union of supreme conjugal bliss, as related in the Swastani. Others splash and dip in the shallow water, oblivious to all except their own prayers and rituals.

At midday, from the great Shiva temple of Pashupatinath, ringing bells, blasting horns, throbbing drums and ear-shattering cymbals announce the *Maha Snan* ceremony – the Magh holy bath of the famous Shiva lingam. Hundreds swarm to the shrine to join the frenzied mob watching the phallic idol bathed in cow's milk, then yogurt, honey, sugar and clarified butter, alternating with a dousing of holy water. Finally, a cleansed Lord Shiva is anointed with sandalwood paste, 'dressed' in new and costly robes and garlanded with fresh flowers and glittering necklaces.

At night, at the sacred Salinadi River in Sankhu, throngs assemble to close the holy month by worshipping a tremendous bonfire. Women continue their month-long fast and keep vigil through the night. Next morning, weakened bodily but strengthened spiritually, the penitents are carried home to their admiring friends and family, confident that the troubles and grief which prompted their vows of abstinence will now be banished by the satisfied gods and goddesses.

29 BHIMSEN PUJA

A Deified War Hero becomes Patron Saint of Merchants

Fascinating to Nepalese are the mythological Mahabharata stories of the famous Pandava brothers, five Hindu princes whose heroic feats of strength and valour in epic struggles against a clan of one hundred cousins culminated in the catastrophic war at Kurukshetra, near the present site of New Delhi.

Although Arjun is glorified for unfailing virtue and mighty military prowess, it is Bhimsen, the second brother, who attained divinity.

Bhimsen was a youth of Herculean strength and matching appetite, always chided as a glutton who consumed more than his four brothers together. His youthful pranks and rowdy good humour early aroused the enmity of his cousin clan, for the boys of both families were trained together in the arts of war. Bhimsen was straightforward, boisterous and perhaps a bully, known to grasp several of his cousins in his arms, dive into a pool and hold them under until they all but drowned. If his cousins climbed a tree, Bhimsen kicked it until they tumbled down like ripe fruit; their bodies were perennially bruised as a result of Bhimsen's practical and painful jokes.

At last the cousins, driven to desperation, poisoned Bhimsen and threw him into the Ganges, the only result being that river snakes attacked him, their venom counteracted the poison in his body, and he became stronger than ever. Although Bhimsen's temper was not always under control, he is idolized as one who used his power and will for the protection of others. To this day Nepalese people invoke his name when lifting a heavy weight, believing him second in strength only to his brother Hanuman, the monkey god, for both were fathered by the Wind God, evidently on different mothers.

234

Eventually the hundred scheming cousins, in a gambling game rigged secretly against the Pandava boys, succeeded in winning their wealth, kingdom and even their lovely wife Draupadi, to whom all five brothers were married. Drunk with victory and hatred for Bhimsen, the evil cousin Dushana dragged Draupadi by the hair into an audience hall, stripped off her sari and vilified her before her husbands and gathered clansmen. The prevailing code of honour rendered the brothers helpless to defend her, but just before all was lost, Lord Krishna, their lifelong friend, came to Draupadi's rescue. They say Bhimsen's blood boiled, actually, in his powerful frame, smoke issued from his ears and he vowed never to rest until he had sucked the blood of Dushana. Draupadi, unspeakably dishonoured, ordained that she would not tie up her dishevelled hair until it was dipped in the villain's blood.

Revenge came during the titanic eighteen-day battle between the forces of the Pandavas and their cousins when, with one shattering blow of his mace, Bhimsen decapitated Dushana. Two spouts of blood shot forth from the headless trunk. Bhimsen drank from one, while Draupadi washed her hair in the other. Now the gentle Arjun, alarmed at his brother's demonic behaviour, called Lord Krishna, who recognized at once that Bhimsen had taken the form of the wrathful Bhairab, the God of Terror who sips blood from a skull cap and shares it with Goddess Bhairabi, his female counterpart, now seen as the Pandavas' wife Draupadi. At this revelation, both Arjun and Lord Krishna fell down before the divine couple in adoration.

To atone for the heinous sin of cannibalism, Bhimsen underwent austere religious fasting on Ekadasi day, the eleventh of the bright fortnight in January or early February, a severe sacrifice, considering his penchant for food. This day is now called Bhimsen's Ekadasi, when Nepalese people, especially those of the merchant classes, abstain from nourishment for twenty-four hours, as they believe Bhimsen himself is doing. On one occasion Draupadi and his four brothers became amused when this man of strength and mighty appetite grew faint and irritable from fasting. To test his will and determination they loosed wild animals – lion, snake and tiger – to test his power. When the creatures approached, the surly Bhimsen easily pinned them under his arms and legs, proving to his wife and brothers once more that he was the great Bhimsen.

Nepalese tradition has it that Bhimsen is the guardian deity of all merchants and tradesmen, a bestower, controller and protector of wealth and prosperity. People of Kathmandu Valley thank Bhimsen for the brisk commerce which developed in ages past with Tibet and India, and today with countries across the sea. Throughout Nepal, wherever the merchant classes have settled, usually in villages along the old trade routes, temples of Bhimsen are found where his festivals are the greatest event in the year. Bhimpedi village, just over the foothills on the old route to India, bears his name. Countless shopkeepers have enshrined this God of Wealth's image in wall niches at their stores, daily invoking his blessing.

Legend says that Bhimsen, his idol and cult, were brought into the valley in ancient times by a princess from Dolka village, some fifty miles to the east – a daughter of the old Thakuri kings who married a prince from Kathmandu. In her retinue was a farm worker of unusual height and massive build who sported an aggressively long moustache. His brawn proved of little worth, however, for he idled his days away at the inn. Finally a Prince upbraided him, pointed out his enormous food consumption and lack of productivity. With a wave of his hand the farmer informed the Prince that he could finish all the field work in a single day, provided he were furnished with an ample basket of food.

Next evening, when the servant-farmer reported his work complete, the Prince upon investigation found the entire field tilled, flooded, hoed and planted with rice seedlings – the work of a thousand hands. Then and there the Prince realized no mortal was capable of such a miracle; that the farmer was the mighty God Bhimsen. As the Prince fell at the large man's feet, the farmer turned to stone, a statue of Bhimsen. Around him the Prince erected a temple which still stands at Bhimsenthan near the Vishnumati River, on the south-western edge of old Kathmandu town. Thereafter the Prince was the farmer's keeper and worshipped him as Bhimsen, and the people believe their offerings to this idol actually go to the Prince, who shares his wealth with the farmer.

It seems in the old days that when people went before this towering, moustached image of the fierce Bhimsen, many died soon thereafter, a phenomenon which, incidentally, is today attributed to idols of the God of Wrath, Bhairab. To pacify Bhimsen and avert further calamity, the people installed at his side an image of his beloved wife Draupadi. And when her presence failed to lessen the number of deaths, an idol of the noble warrior brother, Arjun of benign and gentle nature, was set beside Draupadi.

Bhimsen is one of the few Nepalese gods whose idol is always found in the second level of his temples. An oddity in the Kathmandu Bhimsen shrine is the stooped and shrouded figures which flank the two brothers and their wife. Some say these are the two youngest Pandava brothers, while others believe they represent the parents. Curiously, women call them both Dhushi Ajima, who, despite their perpetually crouched posture, will cure backache. Women who bring them offerings must never bend to touch Dhushi Ajima's feet with their foreheads in the usual manner, but must always stand upright if they expect their ailment to be cured.

On the twelfth day of the waxing moon in January or early February, after the merchant classes have completed their Bhimsen Ekadasi fast of the preceding day, lavish offerings are distributed between the two idols of the Pandava brothers, but with careful discrimination. Great trays of flowers, fruits, sweetmeats, eggs, coins and lengths of cloth are offered to the gentle Arjun in accordance with ancient Vedic worship. But the fiercely moustached, scarlet-faced Bhimsen, who towers to the low ceiling, is drenched in blood from sacrifices of innumerable buffaloes, goats, ducks and chickens as required in Tantric rites, the same as those needed to pacify the bloodthirsty Bhairab.

In villages all over the valley, and outside, where Newar merchants have made their homes, Bhimsen's annual festivals, held at various times throughout the year, are occasions of tumultuous merrymaking. In Patan town, near Kathmandu, on the ninth day of the dark half of September, two days after Lord Krishna's birthday, Bhimsen is taken from his silver-encrusted temple near the old palace square, placed in a temple-like litter and carried triumphantly through the streets with a fanfare of music and a parade of celebrating devotees. No merchant neglects Bhimsen, especially on his festival and Ekadasi day.

On the first day of the waning moon in January, the day after full moon, Bhimsen and his wife Draupadi, each in a decorated, canopied palanquin, are honoured with a chaotic ride around the lanes of Bhadgaon, eight miles to the east. In many of Bhimsen's festivals, following ancient tradition, ceremonies are delayed until the arrival of a headman of the Newari Thanko-juju clan whose patron deity is Bhimsen, for these people are considered to be descendants of the old Thakuri kings of Dolka from whence Bhimsen originated.

For centuries the tradesmen of Kathmandu have believed that Bhimsen every twelfth year makes a journey to Lhasa, where he visits and gives his blessings to Newar merchants who have long maintained residence in this capital city of Tibet, conducting trade with their counterparts from Nepal. For this journey, a farmer is chosen to represent Bhimsen and sent on his way by a great gathering of rejoicing devotees. When he reaches his destination, they say, he is warmly and reverently received by the Nepalese of Lhasa, who return him to their countrymen laden with riches and presents.

This practice may be an enactment of the ancient story when the five Pandava brothers were suffering drastic reversals in their struggles against the cousins. Goddess Bhagwati – also known as Bhairabi – advised them to 'disappear' for one year, during which time they worked in a far-away household in the mountains disguised as servants. Now with the closing of the Nepalese-Tibetan border, perhaps this traditional twelfth-year journey of Bhimsen will be no more.

30   A THOUSAND AND ONE LIGHTS
The Buddhist Procession at Bodhnath

The final full moon of Magh in February is celebrated also as the 'Festival of a Thousand and One Lights' at the tremendous, white-domed Buddhist stupa of Bodhnath, a few miles north-east of Kathmandu.

For centuries the Bhote people, as the Nepalese call the Buddhists from Tibetan and Nepalese Himalayas to the north, have trekked each year through icy mountains, seeking the mild winters of Kathmandu Valley, to conduct trade, and to worship again at the valley's ancient and sacred shrines to Lord Buddha. Most make their winter headquarters at Bodhnath stupa, in its encircling several-storied homes, shops and monasteries.

These amazing and often odorous trekkers, some having walked for weeks, pass through the streets of Kathmandu swathed in heavy layers of clothing, huge leather fur-lined boots, thick ornate head-gear, the women in traditional multi-coloured woollen aprons. Robust Bhotes from the north consider valley winters excessively warm, many striding along with one bare arm free of the heavy wine-coloured robes and dark wool coats, leaving the sleeve to hang empty. The men pile their matted hair in a top-knot, or let it hang in braids like their cheerful womenfolk. Both sexes are laden with heavy turquoise and coral necklaces, earrings, trinkets and amulets against evil spirits, and both possess a remarkable openness of face, seemingly never ill at ease nor self-conscious of their colourful and bizarre appearance.

Their numbers swell during February for the celebration of the Tibetan New Year, which usually falls in this month, and for the annual Festival of Lights commemorating the completion of Bodhnath shrine on this full moon day hundreds of years ago.

239

According to Nepalese legend there was once a King in Kathmandu who built an aqueduct and pond at Narayan Hiti, near the present site of the new royal palace, and was greatly distressed to find that no water came from the three stone-carved dragon spouts. After pondering this mystery, the King decided that water would be forthcoming only with the sacrifice of a man of extraordinary characteristics, such as he himself possessed. He then summoned his son and instructed him to go to the newly-constructed water tap next morning and sever the head of a man whom he would find lying there completely covered with white cloth.

Never questioning the King's command, the son accomplished the deed, and water gushed from the taps immediately. So horrified was one of the dragon-headed water spouts at the sight of patricide that it turned its face to the sky, a position it maintains to this day. Now the Prince, on recognizing the severed head of his father, was stricken with grief. The burden of this awful sin drove him into retirement and solitary meditation at the temple of Bajra Jogini, high on a hill near Sankhu village. After a lengthy period of abstinence and prayer to this goddess, she ordained that the Prince could redeem his sin only by building a great temple to Buddha, the site to be chosen by the landing of a white crane sent by Bajra Jogini herself.

The Prince, in his determination to construct the largest Buddhist shrine in the land, encountered a series of plaguing difficulties, the worst of which was a twelve-year drought which parched the entire countryside. Water needed for mudbricks and masonry was secured by spreading sheets of cloth in the fields each night, wringing out the collected dew next morning. Years later, when the splendid hemispheric temple was completed and four pairs of All-Knowing Buddha Eyes were affixed to its spire, Khasti, the Temple of Dewdrops, brought Buddhist pilgrims from far and wide.

Thus the sin of patricide was expiated, and to this day the Bhote people hold this shrine in highest veneration, since it was built, according to old Tibetan tradition, by a Raja of Nepal who in a former incarnation was a high lama of Tibet. Now it is called Bodhnath in honour of Lord Buddha and ranks with the hilltop

22. Erotic woodcarving on a temple strut in Hanuman Dhoka Square, Kathmandu
(Betty Woodsend)
Carved stone lingam, male phallic symbol of Lord Shiva, based in circular yoni, symbol of
the female, Bhadgaon town   (Betty Woodsend)
Sadhus, or Hindu holy men, pilgrimage from India to Pashupatinath temple for Sacred
Night of Lord Shiva   (Betty Woodsend)

23. Taking holy baths for April full-moon festival at Baisedhara, near Balaju, where sacred water flows from twenty-two dragon spouts   (Shridhar Manadhar)

Swayambhunath as the most famous Buddhist shrine in Nepal.

Starting at dusk, chanting pilgrims and monks circumambulate the white dome, shaped like an inverted rice-bowl with 'lotus-bud' cupola reported to contain gems of untold worth. They spin hundreds of prayer wheels mounted in its base, each turn of which is equivalent to reciting all the paper prayers rolled up within. Some prostrate themselves full length in the dust every few feet, hands stretched over their heads, circling the shrine in special penance. At dark the air hums with the steady drone of their voices chanting a united prayer of thanksgiving.

When the Chinai Lama, resplendent in golden robes and tiara, descends from his quarters and raises his hand in benediction, devotees bow before him as the spiritual head of Nepalese Buddhists and direct representation of the famous, now deposed, Dalai Lama of Tibet. He stands before an idol of the Tibetan goddess Tasca Muni, ensconced in the stupa's outer wall, a deity who to all appearances is a replica of the terrifying Tantric Nepalese goddess, Kali. Here the Chinai Lama conducts elaborate religious rites and prayerful rituals, periodically ringing a melodic hand bell. When he distributes hundreds of scarlet strips of cloth to tie around the necks of devotees, a riotous scene develops as thousands of hands reach for this powerful blessing, youths from the valley jostling with their northern neighbours.

Usually, near midnight, the great parade of 'a thousand and one lights' begins, when Buddhists from Tibet, Sikkim, Bhutan and Nepal carry flaming wicks and lamps around the stupa of Bodhnath, white in the rays of the full moon, while droning voices chant a prayer of thanksgiving for the completion of this sacred shrine in centuries past.

FEBRUARY-MARCH

31   SHIVA RATRI
The Sacred Night of Lord Shiva

One can almost literally feel the presence of Lord Shiva in Kathmandu Valley. His spirit is everywhere, dwelling in the thousands
of idols and monuments which glorify his holy name, and pervading the hearts, minds and lives of the Nepalese people.

For Shiva is the Great God, Mahadev, whose Paradise on
Mount Kailas in the Himalayas and whose famous Pashupatinath
temple on the outskirts of Kathmandu – one of the most sacrosanct
of all Hindu shrines – have made Nepal for ever hallowed ground.
Here he is called Lord Pashupati, the protector of animals. Here
Shiva appeared in remotest antiquity disguised as a forest deer,
and again as a flame over which legend says the shrine was first
built. On this temple's wooded hill, just across the holy Bagmati
River, Shiva, this time portrayed as a huntsman, once made sport
with Parbati, his lovely goddess consort. This is the arcadia, some
believe, where the famous warrior Arjun pilgrimaged to receive
from Shiva the divine and all-powerful bow with which to slay the
enemy in the great Mahabharata war which resulted in a triumph
for righteousness.

Just as Shiva embraced Nepal, so have her millions of Hindus
and Buddhists accepted this Lord as their guardian deity.

It is not sufficient to describe Shiva as the Destroyer, one of the
Hindu Triad of which Brahma is the Creator and Vishnu the
Preserver, for he is a multifarious deity exalted in Sanskrit literature under 1,008 names, adulated in countless manifestations, each
famed for certain attributes, deeds and powers. His supremacy in
the Hindu pantheon was aptly revealed in one of his endless wars
with the giants, when Lord Shiva split the earth into two equal

242

parts and used one half as his weapon, made Brahma the general of his army, the four holy Veda texts his horses, Vishnu his arrow, a Himalayan mountain his bow, and a monstrous serpent his bow-string. Against this sort of power, the giants were invariably annihilated.

Shiva as Mahadev is the majestic, gracious Supreme Lord, infinite and eternal, whose ways are so inscrutable as to defy comprehension. Yet he is the kindly husband of Parbati, father of Ganesh the elephant god, and of Kumar-Kartik the warrior-hero, Laxmi the Goddess of Wealth, and Saraswati the Goddess of Learning. In this serene aspect, Shiva is capable of bestowing unlimited prosperity in this world and a blissful life in the next.

Widely is Shiva adored as the brooding, long-haired ascetic, his body smeared with ashes, his loins girded with animal skins, his neck garlanded with snakes and rosaries of nuts, carrying the familiar three-pronged iron trident. This mendicant Shiva renoun-ces the world and is completely emancipated from the bondage of sensual passion. Once, when Kamadev tempted him during pro-found meditation, Shiva reduced this God of Love to ashes by a flame shot from the 'third eye' which sits vertically in his forehead. The three eyes of Shiva are symbolic of his omniscient knowledge of the past, present and future.

Shiva is Nateswara or Nataraj, who dances in the sheer joy of creation, the god and very essence of classical Hindu dance and music.

But Shiva can dance also in a mad frenzy of destruction as Bhairab, God of Terror, who haunts burning ghats and cremation grounds, playing with the skulls and bones of the dead. As Bhairab, Shiva represents the disintegrating powers of Nature – disrup-tion, decay and death – and can be pacified only with liquor, meat and the fresh blood of sacrificed animals. Here Bhairab's or Shiva's female counterparts, including Durga, Kali and Bhairabi, are a host of terrifying goddesses who portray Shakti, the Supreme Energy centred in the female. Many of these Mother Goddesses, or Devis, are represented as holy rivers, such as the waters which originate with Goddess Ganga, emptying on to the matted locks of Shiva's head and on down to earth as India's Mother Ganges.

Shiva is widely worshipped as the god of reproduction, represented in the lingam, Shiva's sexual organ of heavenly grandeur. Most ancient civilizations have worshipped the phallus, and how Shiva came to be identified with it is lost in antiquity. Hindu scriptures say, that once, when Vishnu and Brahma were quarrelling over which was supreme, there arose before them a glorious, fiery lingam, blazing like a hundred universe-consuming fires, without beginning, middle or end, incomparable and indescribable. Vishnu, determined to locate the source of this blinding column, became a giant boar and plunged down below, but though he travelled a thousand years no base could be found. Brahma meanwhile became a swan, white and fiery-eyed, swift as thought, and travelled upward, seeking the pillar's end, but was equally unsuccessful. When both returned amazed and weary, Shiva appeared before them. As they bowed to this great Lord there arose on every side that sacred, mysterious monosyllable, 'Om', clear and lasting.

Then Shiva announced, 'Vishnu, you are the creator, preserver and destroyer of the worlds; do thou maintain them. For I, the undivided Overlord, am Three: I am Brahma, Vishnu and Rudra (Shiva) who create, maintain, destroy. Cherish Brahma, for he shall be born of thee in a coming age. Then you both will behold me again.' Thereafter Shiva's symbol of the lingam was established in the Three Worlds, and so was his supremacy.

The Linga-Purana text has more to say about the Shiva lingam. It seems that one day Brahma, Vishnu and other illustrious personages went to Shiva's mountain Paradise, Kailas, to pay him a visit. There they found the great Lord in the act of love with his wife, here called Durga. But Shiva, far from being disconcerted, continued to gratify his sensual desires, a shamelessness prompted not only by passion but by intoxicating liquor previously consumed.

Now it seems that some of the gods, especially Vishnu, roared with laughter, while the rest of the dignitaries were indignant and hurled insults and curses upon Shiva and retired to fume in mortified silence.

When at last Shiva recovered his senses and asked his guards who the visitors were and what had taken place, they disclosed the sordid truth, including the outrage of some of the illustrious guests. These words fell upon Shiva and Durga like a clap of thunder and both died of grief in the very position the visitors had found them.

Now Shiva, who in reality is immortal, decided that the act which brought him shame and death should ever be celebrated among mankind. This was his pronouncement:

'My shame has killed me, but it has also given me new life and new shape, which is that of the lingam. You, evil spirits, my subjects, regard it as my double self. Yes, the lingam is I, myself, and I ordain that men shall offer to it henceforth their sacrifices and worship. Those who honour me under the symbol of the lingam shall obtain without fail the object of all their desires, and a place in Kailas. I am the Supreme Being, and so is my lingam.

'The margosa tree of all trees is the one I love best. If anyone wishes to obtain my favours, he must offer me the leaves, flowers and fruit thereof. Hear once more, evil spirits, my subjects. Those who fast on the fourteenth day of the moon in February (Shiva Ratri) in honour of my lingam, and those who that night do *puja* and present me with leaves of the margosa shall be certain of a place in Kailas.

'Hear again, evil spirits, my subjects. If you desire to become virtuous, learn what are the benefits derived from honour rendered to my lingam. Those who make images of it with earth or cowdung, or do *puja* to it under this form, shall be rewarded; those who make it in stone shall receive seven times more reward and shall never behold the Prince of Darkness; those who make it in silver shall receive seven times more reward than the last named; and those who make it in gold shall be seven times more meritorious still.

'Let my priests go and teach these truths to men and compel them to embrace the worship of my lingam! The lingam is Shiva himself; it is white; it has three eyes and five faces; it is arrayed on a tiger's skin. It existed before the world, and it is the origin and beginning of all things. It disperses our terrors and our fears and grants us the object of all our desires.'

Thus the worship of the Shiva lingam is very old and it is by far the most common idol in the valley, found in untold numbers as stone-carved, rounded pillars enshrined in temples large and small, or standing uncovered on hillsides, in fields and forests, along city streets and village pathways, and often as a crude oblong rock which some pious person has placed at the base of a tree. Holy water is poured over them daily and they are sprinkled with flower petals and vermilion powder, worshipped as Lord Shiva himself.

But the Pashupatinath lingam, enshrined at the great temple of the same name near Kathmandu, is the holiest of them all. Here on the banks of the Bagmati are the royal and public burning ghats. Here people come to die with their feet in the sacred waters, that their released souls may eventually be washed into the Ganges and on to Heaven. Their bodies are cremated on the round, cemented burning ghats at the river's edge and their ashes strewn upon the holy waters. Pashupatinath is one of the most sacred of bathing places, an important pilgrimage centre where sadhus, yogis, ascetics and holy men came in ancient times and still come today to sit in meditation and penance in the ancient quest for divinity.

The main temple, with double-tiered, gilded roof and high surrounding walls, is closed to non-believers, foreigners and tourists lest they desecrate the sacred precincts. It is encircled by a maze of temples, monuments, idols, rest houses for pilgrims, homes for the indigent and dying, and hermitage retreats. On the hills and tiered, cemented embankments rising either side of the river are hundreds of stone Shiva lingams based in the circular stone discs, the *yoni* symbol of the female. Some stand in open areas, others are enshrined in small temples established through the ages by kings, wealthy devotees and pious saints.

Shiva Ratri, literally meaning 'the night consecrated to Shiva', falls on the fourteenth day of the waning moon in February, or in some years early March, when often 100,000 worshippers pass through the temple gates during the twenty-four hours dedicated to the exaltation of his holy name. Thousands and thousands of pilgrims stream into the valley from all over Nepal, and especially India, arriving days in advance by airplane, bus, truck and automobile. Hundreds walk the entire distance and arrive weary, footsore and dusty. They trudge through the Kathmandu streets on the way to Shiva's shrine, bundles balanced atop their heads, men's *dhoti* skirts and women's cotton saris flapping about bare brown feet, many sacrificing their life-savings to bow before the holy lingam of Shiva on this sacred night. They camp in the woods around the temple, sleeping on mats or in huts provided by Nepalese welfare organizations, apparently oblivious to discomfort, for the merits earned by such a pilgrimage are enhanced in direct proportion to sufferings undergone.

The Skanda Purana texts tell of a man from Benares in ages past who belonged to the huntsman caste, long dimly regarded as takers-of-life, but this man was of especially violent and destructive nature. One day he killed such an enormous quantity of birds in the forest that he was unable to carry them home. Night overtook him in the thick jungle, forcing him to hang his bag on a limb and climb a margosa tree to await the dawn. Although the hunter did not realize it, this happened to be Shiva Ratri in late February, when nights are chilly and dew falls heavily. Soon he was benumbed with cold and fatigue, filled with terror of prowling animals, beset with worry for his waiting family and tormented by hunger, for he had passed the entire day without food.

Some say it was his own tears of woe, others that it was the dew which fell from the tree, together with withered margosa leaves, onto a Shiva lingam which happened to stand at the base of the tree. Lord Shiva, to whose worship this night is specifically consecrated, was deeply gratified at this offering, even though made to his lingam unwittingly. He ordained that the hunter who made this sacred offering should be rewarded, and added that the man's long abstinence from food and his attendant discomforts and anxiety should reckon greatly in his favour, completely absolving him from *pap* or sin.

247

This all came true a few days later, when the fortunate man died. Yama, God of Death and King of Hell, immediately sent his emissaries to secure the man's soul, but Shiva dispatched his own messengers to oppose them and claim the hunter's spirit. A violent quarrel ensued between the rival parties, but those of Shiva, being more powerful, put the agents of Death to flight. When they returned to their leader wounded and ashamed, Yama, beside himself with indignation, went at once to Kailas in the Himalayas to complain directly to Shiva. At the palace gates Yama was met by Nandi, the great white bull who has ever been the trusted minister and vehicle of Lord Shiva and whose idols crouch before every Shiva temple. Yama explained his visit, expressing disapproval that Shiva should protect a common huntsman whose trade necessitated the slaughter of living creatures.

'King of Hell,' replied Nandi, 'it is true this man has been a great sinner with no scruples regarding bloodshed; but before he died, fortunately for his own salvation, he fasted, kept a sleepless all-night vigil, and made offerings to the lingam during the night of Shiva Ratri. This meritorious action has obtained for him remission of all his sins, the protection of Shiva, and an honourable place in his Paradise at Kailas.'

When Yama heard Nandi's words, he became very thoughtful and finally withdrew without a word. The hunter's soul lived in Kailas and other abodes of the gods through thousands of blissful years, and finally was reborn on earth as a Hindu king, Chitra Bhanu, who in the Mahabharata texts was blessed with the memory of all his former lives. Now the mere listening to this story brings enormous rewards from Shiva and prompts millions of Hindus, and many Buddhists in Nepal, to celebrate his Shiva Ratri festival every spring.

At Pashupatinath many commence their twenty-four-hour fast before dawn on Shiva Ratri day, when the temple is already crowded with devotees. The poor bring holy water to splash over the sacred three-foot black stone lingam, the holiest of holies, and over the five faces of Shiva carved at its head. The wealthy undergo elaborate rites, offering costly gifts to the lingam and substantial alms to the Brahman priests. Many give bitter margosa leaves, as did the hunter who became a king, and receive back a small portion, which is eaten as a gift or *prasad* blessing from the Great Lord.

City men in Western suits, their wives in gorgeous silk saris, hillmen in homespun baggy trousers, their women in vivid blouses and sarongs, holy men wrapped in saffron robes, naked *sadhus* smeared from head to foot with ashes, form a tidal wave of humanity flowing in and out the temple. During the day a prolonged cracking of military guns from the Tundikhel parade ground in Kathmandu salutes Lord Shiva. In the evening the King and the royal family pay homage to Lord Pashupatinath and offer him gifts.

When darkness falls, religious fervour is intensified. The temple yard is aglow with burning tapers and oil-fed lamps whose yellow light reflects from the mammoth gilded image of Nandi, Shiva's loyal bull, who crouches on a pedestal with head raised in adoration to the sacred lingam in the shrine. There is a pulsing of drums and a wail of flutes in the smoky incense-filled atmosphere, while the multitudes, transported in ecstasy, move and surge in and out as one living entity.

The surrounding slopes, lit by camp-fires, echo with singing and chanting of Shiva's many names. Fasting devotees remain awake through the entire sacred night, many taking holy baths in the river and returning to the temple every three hours with offerings and prayer. The maze of lingams around the temple are showered with holy water and flowers, which fall on to the courtyard floor and are trampled in the mud by thousands of bare brown feet.

Around the valley, in city and village courtyards and at crossroads, bonfires are built and family groups keep all-night vigil to glorify the Supreme Lord of Creation. Boys go round the town begging for firewood from neighbourhood housewives, chanting an ancient phrase:

'Two sticks of firewood we beg of you,
For Mahadev (Shiva) is feeling cold.'
Was ever there a god so adored as Lord Shiva?

32 HOLI
Red Powder, Romance and Haunting Demons

The ancient Hindu festival of Holi, named allegedly after the mythical demoness Holika, brings eight rowdy days in March, sometimes late February, when men, women and children – foreigners as well as Nepalese – may find themselves doused with sacred red powder or splashed with scarlet liquid. The religious significance of this springtime celebration is all but lost in an outburst of youthful exuberance in which the throwing of 'colour' on all passers-by should, according to tradition, be accepted by the victim with the same good humour with which the prank is performed.

Rung Khelna, the playing with colour, is given sanction beginning on the eighth day of the waxing moon in March with the installation of a twenty-five-foot bamboo ceremonial pole, topped with three umbrella-like tiers, each fringed with colourful strips of cloth. This *chir* pole is erected with pomp and ceremony amidst a crowd of revellers in the street at Basantpur, near Kathmandu's old royal palace. Guns crack in salute, flutes and drums echo round the square, while red ceremonial powder is sprinkled about the pole and into the outstretched hands of surrounding spectators, and the week of Holi commences. Throughout the week the *chir* pole is considered sacred and people come to place at its base small lighted wicks, flowers and red powder.

Most believe the *chir* during Holi, with its fluttering strips of cloth, is symbolic of the tree on which Lord Krishna hung the garments of milkmaids who bathed and sported naked, and unseen they thought, in the Jamuna River of northern India. When the maidens, all of whom were consumed with love for Krishna, heard the familiar notes of his magic flute they blanched in shame, submerged their bodies in the sacred water and entreated their Lord to return the clothes. Calmly Krishna informed them that nude bathing in holy rivers is a sacrilege; that they must atone for their sin by standing knee-deep in the river and offering libations to the Sun God by allowing the liquid to flow slowly from their hands, cupped in the shape of the sacred conch shell. Until this ceremony be performed, their garments would remain in the tree.

When the maidens, 'their cheeks dyed crimson', arose from the water and performed the ritual as instructed, Lord Krishna, ever the Great Lover, watched with relish. Now he returned their saris with a warning never to bathe and frolic naked in the holy river, and to this day Nepalese women, when taking a holy bath, wrap themselves in a cotton garment and stoop gracefully over cupped palms, allowing the water to flow back into the river as they pray.

Perhaps it is Krishna's adventures which prompt Nepalese youths to harry young ladies with unaccustomed boldness during Holi, smearing their cheeks with red powder if they venture out, regaling them with romantic and risqué songs if they show their faces in upstairs windows. They say Lord Krishna himself once held a Festival of Colour to entertain the 16,000 adoring milk-maids of Brindaban where they played with crimson powder made from red fruit which hung from the tree. Although Krishna taught that life's true purpose is single-minded devotion to duty, he himself led a joyous, playful existence surrounded by beautiful women, for all who cast their eyes upon him fell hopelessly in love.

The erection of the *chir* pole gives eight-day licence to one and all to drench almost anyone he meets, including cows and dogs, with powder of the most brilliant vermilion. Handful after handful is thrown into the air, over clothing and into the hair and faces of strangers and friends in gay abandon. 'Lolas', miniature balls of shellac filled with vermilion, and balloons of scarlet liquid are tossed everywhere, including into upstairs windows where laughing girls are watching. Rowdy youths troop from home to home of relatives and friends, challenging everyone within range to share their fun. Girls excused from school, and women who keep to their homes, indulge in this seasonal sport amongst themselves.

Each afternoon the groups of boys swell into crowds, tossing scarlet clouds in the streets and narrow alleys. According to tradition, no one should take offence, 'for it is the king's festival', but occasionally tempers flare and fisticuffs result. The custom is abused when packets of powder are hurled at busses and automobiles and startled passengers find themselves and their clothing covered with powder. Expensive cleaning bills result – if the garment is not totally ruined – a real calamity for the increasing numbers of Nepalese men who are forsaking washable Nepalese costume for Western suits and shirts.

Thus the indiscriminate throwing of colour during Holi is losing favour. Many sniff at these unsophisticated antics, especially those who can afford 'modern' entertainment in movie theatres and coffee-houses. In recent years it has become illegal to throw colour at any citizen who objects, or at unsuspecting foreigners and tourists, despite the insistence of some that the dousing of passers-by with red colour during this week is a mark of respect and honour.

Not too many years ago 'playing with colour' was popular in the courtyards and gardens of even the wealthy, when men, women and children drenched each other in vermilion or were gaily tossed into huge pots of brilliantly coloured water. It is said that civil servants were required at one time to attend the palaces of prime ministers during Holi, where they were soaked in vivid colour in a gay free-for-all and went home, pockets bulging with scarlet powder. This custom has long been discontinued, but it reveals a past when wholesale colour throwing was not confined to youths in the streets.

The story told during Holi has it that a fiendish demon named Holika was sister of a wicked, irreligious king whose son, the saintly Prince Pralhad, had since boyhood been an ardent devotee of Lord Krishna, despite the threats of his aunt and angry interdiction of his father. At last, when all methods of punishment failed to shake Pralhad's faith, the King ordered his son trampled to death by an elephant, but when the Prince advanced upon it chanting the sacred names of Krishna, the great beast humbly knelt before him. Next the Prince was hurled from a rocky precipice, and again into a swollen river, but each time he was saved – for Lord Krishna protects those who love him.

At last the wicked aunt Holika, believing herself immune to death by fire, snatched the boy and leaped into a blazing furnace built especially for his destruction. The King rejoiced that his son had met his end, and that Holika had performed self-immolation on his behalf. But Lord Krishna interceded again, for when the flames died, Holika had perished and the unscathed Prince was sitting among the embers as if they were flowers in the forest. Now the antics of Holi festival are thought to celebrate her extermination.

During the last three days of Holi the fervour of 'playing with colour' increases when bands of young men wander through the powder-stained streets and winding lanes singing at the tops of their lungs. The traditional songs of Holi often praise lovely maidens and glorify romance, perhaps in remembrance of Krishna's amorous escapades. Many of the old ditties are deemed indecent, stemming from the time when use of obscene terms during Holi was considered a most auspicious practice, since they were supposedly addressed to the demon Holika. For another version of the legend says that Holika held such sway in the land that mothers were forced to provide in turn one child each day for the demon to devour. A learned *sadhu* finally advised the women to collect all the children together where they should accost the fiend with a volley of filthy abuse. When this was done, Holika died on the spot.

The indiscriminate use of vile language has all but disappeared, but youths still sing with unusual boldness during Holi to lovely, sloe-eyed Nepalese maidens whose laughing faces in balcony windows have tantalized young men in the streets for ages. Since Nepalese mothers keep their daughters well protected, this may be all they ever see of their hearts' desire. During Holi the most reticent youth is emboldened to sing, 'This is the king's Holi. You are angry, young lady? But this is the king's Holi! All I see are mustard plants in the window. O, without you I cannot live.'

Girlish Nepalese laughter follows the traditional refrain, 'I love the young lady in the window. I vow I will not take my rice until she is mine.' And mothers must frown when they hear from the street, 'I'll have a basketful of parched rice ready, and two duck eggs fried for us; and when your brother-in-law comes, I'll have him beaten with a bamboo cane.'

With the arrival of the final day called Holi Purnima, or full moon of Holi, men and boys indulge in a last orgy of colour-throwing in the streets, their merry faces completely obscured with vivid scarlet powder. Hair and hands caked with red, white clothing stained as with blood, they await the lowering of the *chir* pole, which may take place any time during the day or evening, depending upon the calculations of astrologer-priests. When the sacred *chir* finally rests on the ground before Goddess Kumari House, guns boom and countless hands wildly grab for pieces of the colourful fringe, for such an amulet when worn on the person will discourage evil spirits and disease. Now the heavy pole is borne by a swarm of men past Hanuman Dhoka and on to the Tundikhel parade ground a few blocks away.

The crowd which gathers on this vast, moonlit field includes many Indians of the Marwari class, merchants who for centuries have made their homes and livelihood in Kathmandu. Their women in brilliant saris and glittering shawls toss coconut shells into the bonfire, while men heap on leafy branches. Many carry lighted oil wicks and squat before the smoking flames for a pinch of sacred ash to smear their foreheads as charms, especially for children, to ward off the 'evil eye'. Musicians play, the old colour guard stands at attention, while exuberant youths dash around the field in a last burst of playful energy. The pole is shoved into the fire, and after the umbrella tiers have burned, it is carried by a long line of men and boys in a gay turn about the area. Many carry away pots of glowing coals from the Holi fire to purify their homes with sanctified smoke and ash.

Some believe the traditional bonfires at Holi commemorate the fiery death of Holika, while to others it symbolizes the burning of the mythological 'old year', since Lord Brahma created the world on the day following Holi full moon. Many prepare special sweets from milk and curd, refusing meat on this holy day. Others believe that a hearty meal at Holi will assure plentiful food for the coming 'new year', even though this mythological day coincides not with the Nepali, Newari nor old religious lunar calendar's New Year Day.

Now the burning of the *chir* pole indicates to most Nepalese that further tossing of red powder is forbidden and the festival of Holi is over. On the following day, however, large Indian communities in Kathmandu continue to 'play with colour'.

Late in the night of Holi full moon a weird ceremony is conducted on the Tundikhel, which appears to have little relation to Holi.

In ancient times a young boy, Keschandra, was King of Itum Bahal area – a great open square and Buddhist monastery cloister deep in the crowded bazaars of old Kathmandu. Keschandra was a compulsive gambler, and when at last he lost all his possessions and property he went to live with his sister, wife of a merchant Chakandeo who was later deified and whose idol is enshrined in Thamal monastery-temple a few blocks away. The good sister brought food to her brother on golden plates, but the next day, when she discovered he had gambled even these away, she served him his rice on the earthen floor. Now Keschandra, completely despondent, gathered up the rice in a cloth and retired to a country place. There he opened the rice and found it cold and full of maggots. Carefully he spread it in the hot sunshine and fell asleep, waiting for it to be cleansed and dried. When he awoke, Keschandra cried out in despair to find the pigeons had eaten all his food. Hearing his wailing, Lord Bhairab, the ogre-like God of Terror and Wrath, caused the pigeons to return and replace the rice with great piles of droppings, which turned into glittering gold.

As Keschandra gathered up this windfall, a hungry demon Guru Mapa appeared, threatening to devour him. Keschandra mollified Guru Mapa with flattering words, not knowing he was the terrible Bhairab in disguise, promising that if the ogre would help to carry the gold to Itum Bahal, Keschandra would give him a home where he would always be well fed. Now in time Guru Mapa became a menace, for when he heard parents of Itum Bahal threatening unruly children that they would be given to Guru Mapa, the ogre, took them at their word and started stealing and eating the youngsters. Some say he even devoured dead bodies. Eventually, neighbours' complaints forced Keschandra to find the demon a permanent abode in a great open field which is now the Tundikhel, promising to provide a half-bushel of rice and the meat of one buffalo annually if he mended his ways. As an added measure to keep the ogre out of mischief, Keschandra instructed Guru Mapa that he should busy himself dispersing stones or bricks whenever such objects were found, three or more, in one spot.

To this day Guru Mapa gets his food. Each year, on Holi full moon night, the people of Itum Bahal sacrifice a water buffalo near the Vishnumati River, where Guru Mapa is said to have stopped to rest when carrying the heavy sacks of gold. Following ancient Tantric rites, the living animal must be hacked into quarters. This meat and specified amounts of rice are later cooked at Itum Bahal while religious rites are held and the inhabitants continue to play with red colour, even though other sections of Kathmandu have finished Holi.

Toward midnight the cooked rice and meat, in great caldrons suspended from shoulder-carrying poles, is carried slowly through the darkness by the people of Itum Bahal. Some hold small, dim oil wicks, while others quietly beat a drum and occasionally clang their cymbals. They proceed to the centre of the Tundikhel, where a certain amount of the food is poured on the ground for Guru Mapa's yearly ration, and the remainder is distributed and consumed by the crowd. Many living outside Itum Bahal will not go near this ghostly ceremony, insisting that each year on Holi Purnima a man or boy disappears – a victim to Guru Mapa.

They say to this day that when necessity forces an individual to traverse the Tundikhel at night, he often becomes hopelessly confused and loses his way, harassed by the demon's spirit. And a few years ago, when the great, spreading tree was removed from the centre of this parade ground, the workmen proceeded to the eastern side to fell Guru Mapa's tree also. But at the first stroke of the axe blood ran from its trunk, and the axeman fell dead on the spot. As a result, Guru Mapa's tree was left standing.

Many remember a certain hole in Itum Bahal where Guru Mapa was supposed to have lived, now obliterated as a result of the 1934 earthquake. In the Buddhist monastery nearby, the priestly caste will not eat pigeon meat nor tread on jute bags in which the golden droppings were carried. And each day during the four summer months called Hindu Chaturmas, rice is fed to flocks of pigeons that inhabit Itum Bahal, while on Bahi Deo Boyegu day, during the holy Buddhist month of Gunla, the birds are given over 200 pounds of rice.

Recessed in the walls of this monastery a great, glaring mask of Guru Mapa, looking remarkably like Lord Bhairab, serves as a constant reminder to children whose parents still threaten to give them to this demon if they misbehave.

Many, especially youths, regret this festival's passing, but others hail the final ceremonies of Holi as a blessing which terminates the most unholy time of year.

33 CHAKANDEO JATRA
A Travelling Merchant becomes a God

The people of Kathmandu Valley have since remotest times relied upon their merchant classes and castes to obtain from far-away places vital goods, such as salt, which they themselves do not produce. These travelling traders have long been revered as affluent and influential citizens, for only stout-hearted men of uncommon valour and ingenuity could negotiate the malaria-infested flatlands which once barred the route to India, and the narrow trails over treacherous gorges and glacial mountain passes on the long trek into Tibet. In former times these heroes, returning from foreign lands, were fêted in tumultuous celebrations, carried about the streets in fancy palanquins or on the backs of caparisoned elephants.

Such a merchant was Singha Saratha Bahu, who once set out with a party of a hundred assistants for Lhasa, then considered a remote city inhabited by demons and devils. When the party neared the Tibetan border, Singha, ever a devout and pious man, decided to remain for a time at a beautiful golden temple of Buddha on the Brahmaputra River, sending his men ahead to Lhasa to arrange lodging. When Singha joined his companions in the Tibetan capital, he found them splendidly housed with the most beautiful women in the city, which had captured the heart of every Nepalese travelling man.

It seems Singha himself succumbed eventually to the charms of the city, for one night, as he said his evening prayers, Karunamaya, the God of Mercy, called Machhendranath, appeared before him, pointing at Singha's bed. There, instead of his lovely mistress, the stunned merchant beheld a sleeping but fanged ogress. When the

God Karunamaya informed Singha that each man's mistress was just such a demoness, each planning to devour her lover once he was sufficiently fattened, the merchant implored Karunamaya to save them.

In response to his plea the God of Mercy ordained that a giant white horse would be waiting at the riverside to fly the entire party back to Kathmandu, but, he warned, once started, no man must dare look back. Singha hurried to his men who, far from ready to leave their delightful companions, refused to listen or believe. However, when Singha led them outside the city, pointing out a mountain of human skeletons which Karunamaya had described, the travelling men, now thoroughly terrified, were well ready to depart. And when they rushed to the river and beheld the great white steed, each bowed down in obeisance before mounting, recognizing it as Karunamaya himself.

Now as the steed soared off over mountain and valley, female cries were heard at their rear, so compelling and beguiling that the men were powerless to resist a last look at their ladies. Then one by one they fell from the horse into the hands of the long-haired she-demons and were devoured, but Singha, who kept his eyes fixed straight ahead, was flown alone into Kathmandu, arriving on the full moon day of the Holi celebration. When people heard his incredible story, they installed Singha in a decorated palanquin and carried him around the streets for hours, for here they knew was a man 'whose sun was on his right-hand side', or, as Westerners would say, 'born under a lucky star'.

From then on he was revered as a leading citizen of Thamal area, a north-western sector of Kathmandu; but one day misfortune appeared at his door in the form of his Tibetan mistress, lovely as ever, begging to be taken in. When Singha unceremoniously sent her away, she went to the topmost man of Thamal, a learned sage on whom the entire community depended for guidance. Since by tradition Nepalese men have always provided well for their concubines and resultant offspring, Singha was immediately summoned before the wise man to explain this gross neglect. Unfortunately Singha was unable to convince him that this Tibetan beauty was a demoness in disguise, for the learned sage invited her to live in his own home.

One dark night the Tibetan she-devil summoned her sister demons from Lhasa and they proceeded to devour every person in the household, including the wise man. When he heard this terrible news, Singha took his sword, praying all the while to Karunamaya, and drove the women from the city. Thereafter Singha became the ruling man in Thamal, guiding his people with such justice and wisdom through the years that he was regarded as a king, eventually to be deified by the people, who thereafter called him Chakandeo.

Today his towering scarlet idol stands in a side-porch of Bhagwan Bahal, a monastic shrine in Thamal, and during the Holy Month of Gunla, when Buddhist relics and gods are on display, an immense painted scroll is exhibited on the courtyard wall, vividly depicting the story of Chakandeo, the flying white horse, and his travelling companions who lost their hearts and lives to the women of Tibet.

According to legend, Chakandeo had two wives and, some believe, many concubines. The first and 'inside' wife was the sister of Keschandra, the boy-ruler of Itum Bahal who befriended the demon Guru Mapa of the Tundikhel, instituting his 'feeding' ceremony during Holi celebration. Chakandeo's 'outside' wife was, they say, a demoness from Lhasa. One day he asked this second wife if she would prefer taking her meal prior to Chakandeo, or later, eating the left-overs from his own plate as all religiously orthodox Nepalese wives should do. It seems this foreign wife asked to take her meal in advance of her husband, and for this affront she was given only *jati*, the rice-cooking water which is poured away when the grain is almost cooked. To this day she is called Jati Ajima, the grandmother goddess whose only food offering is the rice water she receives in her little 'outside' shrine near the entrance to Thamal Bahal.

Now each year on Holi Purnima, the full moon day in March, Chakandeo's image is carried from Thamal Bahal to a side-yard, where in a sunken square is enacted a ritual announcing the commencement of his festival. Before a great crowd of worshipping onlookers Chakandeo's heavy image is carried up and down exactly nine times in a ceremony called *Guhru Nya Ke Gu* in Newari language, which means 'to ring nine times'. On the following day, the first of the waning moon, this ceremony is repeated in full, when a group of men and musicians carry a heavy, clanging ceremonial bell, suspended on a pole, around the city streets, collecting donations from merchants and businessmen in Chakandeo's name. This procession circles about the town eight times throughout the day, and on the ninth and final round, usually a few hours after sundown, Chakandeo himself joins the parade for his gala annual festival procession.

The parade is led by men whirling tall ceremonial poles high above the heads of the circling crowd. Music-makers, crashing cymbals and thumping drums, precede a heavy ceremonial covered litter in which rests an ancient, gold-lettered manuscript – the story of Chakandeo. Next the great red-faced idol of Chakandeo is carried in the arms of several men, his head towering impassively above the jubilant crowds, while the clanging 'donation' bell brings up the rear.

At a certain point on the way into the city the noise and music stops without warning while Chakandeo is quietly and mysteriously carried down a narrow dark lane to a garbage-dump area where the neighbouring people present him with offerings, flowers and red *tika* powder. Story has it that once, long ago, Chakandeo, against all caste rules, accepted offerings from a lowly woman garbage collector, an act which brought down upon his head the condemnation of wrathful priests.

Now market gossip maintains it was more than offerings which the garbage women gave to Chakandeo, and that this 'secret' visit to the garbage dump during his festival affirms that she was of such lowly caste that their meetings were always conducted in the dark of night.

When Chakandeo emerges from the lane to rejoin his procession, the music and noise blare forth once more. As the lively parade passes the land owned by the Chakandeo *guthi* (the Newari caste organization whose landholdings maintain Chakandeo, his shrine and festival) the crowd sings an old song of the plough-man who has come to bring Chakandeo's share of harvest with the tenant-farmer's timeless excuse that because the land is poor and unproductive, and the rainfall unusually sparse, the crops and landlord's share are meagre.

In the centre of old Kathmandu, when Chakandeo approaches Itum Bahal area, the music is again silenced and the band members remain at Kilagal Tole while the idol is carried on. For they say that on this night Keschandra, ruler of Itum Bahal, is holding his annual Dewali feast to worship the deities of his ancestral clans-men, just as do all Newari people during a certain period of the year. It seems that should Keschandra hear Chakandeo's music, he would insist that Chakandeo should join his party. Now refusal is both difficult and highly improper, so Chakandeo passes in utter silence through Itum Bahal, lest he be distracted from his own *jatra* procession by Keschandra's invitation. On his return to Kila-gal Tole he is joined by his musicians to proceed gaily and noisily about the city.

When at last Chakendeo returns to his 'home' in Thamal Bahal, the shrine glows with lights and festoons. Crowds pack into the courtyard to leave gifts and offerings, and to watch an eerie per-formance of the *Gubaju* priest re-enacting the chastisement which Chakandeo merits. Holding hands and feet in exotic religious poses, his voice rising and falling in chanted cadence, periodically ringing a hand bell as if to emphasize, the gowned priest for one solid hour soundly castigates the mighty Chakandeo for accepting offerings from a low-caste garbage woman or, as some maintain, for having clandestinely visited the woman in her home near the village dump.

34 PISACH CHATURDASI, PAHACHARE AND GHORA JATRA
Devils, Guests and Racing Horses

In Nepal there are many *ajima* or 'grandmother' goddesses, all underlings of the exalted and terrifying Goddess Kali who controls witchcraft, the black arts of Tantric magic and the casting of spells. In general these *ajima* goddesses are barely distinguishable from the hordes of *pisachs*, the devils and witches who roam the land; and *bhuts* or evil spirits who control each vicinity from their cross-road abodes; or the multitude of wandering *prets*, unhappy, sometimes malignant souls of persons who have died from accident, violence and suicide, such as the many victims of the destructive 1934 earthquake. For the grandmother goddesses and haunting spirits alike possess strange, often evil powers. Both can prevent, cause or cure disease, and both can allay or bring disaster to communities over which they preside.

As the 'scientific' world believes that fear, worry and guilt are causative factors in both physical and mental illness which may be treated by psychiatrists, so many Nepalese believe that angry goddesses, evil spirits and the vengeful spirits of the dead who cause disease and misfortune can be pacified by magic incantations, fire ceremonies, prayer, blood sacrifices, a goodly supply of food offerings and occasionally a lively festival to pay them honour.

On the eighth day of the waning moon of March or early April, a small image of Lord Shiva, who in his destructive aspect is depicted as husband of Goddess Kali, is taken from Pashupatinath temple and carried on a roofed ceremonial palanquin through the streets of Kathmandu with a loud fanfare of music and shouted announcements that Pisach Chaturdasi is only eight days away.

263

Chaturdasi is the fourteenth day of any fortnight, but this one comes when *Pisach*, the Evil Planet, falls under the 'evil eye', a time most auspicious for devils and malignant spirits. It happens to fall when typhoid, dysentery, cholera and smallpox flourish with the advent of hot weather, prior to cleansing monsoon rains. It is a time of uneasiness, especially for those unacquainted with or wary of modern medicines.

On Pisach Chaturdasi, Lord Shiva himself becomes a *pisach* or evil spirit, known and worshipped as Luku Mahadev, the Hiding Shiva, depicted in the usual form of a small lingam which is, curiously, kept hidden in filthy, 'unclean' places such as the neighbourhood garbage dump. Luku Mahadev is maintained and worshipped by Hindu and Buddhist alike, including those who are not normally adherents of Shiva. This is the day when these insanitary disposal places must be cleaned and Luku Mahadev is removed from his stone-covered hole to be washed, anointed, and worshipped with offerings of flowers, smoking incense and foods which include meat, garlic and alcoholic drink, otherwise abhorred by Shiva. A votive oil wick lamp is kept flickering all through the night at Luku Mahadev's hiding place and the lampblack collected therefrom is especially effective, when painted around the eyes of women and children, in curing eye disease and improving eyesight.

Mythology says that Goddess Parbati once questioned her divine consort Shiva regarding his refusal to take meat, garlic and alcoholic drink, inviting him to join her. The Great Lord, allegedly to please Parbati, took her to a lonely field where they could hide among the radish and mustard plants while he gorged on these forbidden foods. Now on Pisach Chaturdasi people offer the Hiding Shiva yellow mustard flowers to symbolize gold, and white radish blossoms to represent silver in memory of this occasion. And on this day only, Luku Mahadev must be offered 'unclean' foods to satisfy and pacify the *pisach* or evil spirit which possesses him, that he may remain tranquil and protect the area from diseases and misfortune.

Old people also tell the story of the demon Bhasmasur who, in

order to gain power over his enemies, fasted, meditated and attended all Lord Shiva's festivals for many years, thereby qualifying
himself for any boon he desired. When Bhasmasur asked that all
persons whose head he touched should turn to ashes, the indebted
Lord Shiva was forced to comply. It so happened that the wary
Bhasmasur doubted the efficacy of his newly-acquired power and
attempted to touch the head of Lord Shiva himself. Now this
Great Lord, to save his own life, escaped and hid himself in a hole
amongst garbage and filth.

It seems that Lord Vishnu, always near by when Shiva involved
himself, came disguised as a lovely dancing girl and spoke to
Bhasmasur. 'Why are you searching in this despicable place?
Come away and dance with me.' Now the demon, vulnerable as
any man, followed the maiden, who gave him drinks to befuddle
his mind. When Bhasmasur admitted his inability to dance, she
scoffed at his reticence, advising him simply to watch and imitate
her every move. As the clumsy demon mimicked the dance, suddenly the girl said, 'Now do this', and placed her hand atop her
head. This gesture cost the demon his life, for he turned into ashes
at the touch of his own hand.

This fourteenth day is also called Pahachare, *paha* meaning
guests while *chare* is a celebration. It is also known as Pasachare,
pasa meaning friends. Traditionally on this day homes and courtyards are thoroughly cleaned and decorated to welcome relatives
and acquaintances in the hope that such a display of goodwill,
generosity and mutual love will dispel evil thoughts and harmful
spirits. Especially is it important to invite married daughters back
to paternal homes for family feasts, that sisters may meet in good
fellowship. Many take their friends and kinsmen to ceremonies
and processions about the town and to temples of the honoured
goddesses, particularly the powerful and popular 'sister' goddesses
who control disease and epidemics.

One deity who figures prominently during Pahachare, though
not one of the famous 'sisters', is Neta Madhu Ajima, the grandmother goddess who reigns over Neta area of Kathmandu, where
she is also called Nar Devi. In former times human sacrifices were

essential to satisfy this influential goddess and, though now she receives only the blood of animals, she still requires the dried human flesh allegedly preserved by priests from cremations and offered to Neta Ajima during her *pujas* and festival. Now each year on the fourteenth night during Pahachare men masked and costumed to represent twelve different divinities, dominated by Neta Ajima herself, come to Nar Devi Tole near Neta's temple. They perform ceremonial dances all through the night and into the following morning. Animals, essentially buffaloes and lambs, are sacrificed to all these dancing deities, and when the blood is drunk by the performers they dance in fiendish glee, possessed thereby with the spirit of the god or goddess they represent. If a dancer vomits this blood, unable to digest it, they say the goddess has refused to enter that unfortunate person's body.

The following day, Aunsi, the fifteenth or last day of the dark lunar fortnight, is called Ghora Jatra, the Festival of Horses, which in actuality is now an official sports day, having lost most of its traditional significance. These events are held on the Tundikhel, a great open field now divided by a wide boulevard leading to Bhadra Kali's temple. It once bordered the eastern edge of old Kathmandu, but now is the central point of the city, reputed to have been in former days the largest parade ground in Asia. On Ghora Jatra day it was the custom of former Kathmandu kings to attend the temple of Bhadra Kali for worship, riding in a courtly cavalcade. The King was preceded by a horse bearing the Living Goddess Kumari to sanctify the royal visit. It is possible that with passing time this visit developed into a parade of horses, and ultimately the horse racing and athletic contest it is today, organized by the military and presided over by the King of Nepal.

Legend has it that the horse festival was originally held to celebrate a victory over a demon named Tundi whose abode has long been this large *khel* or meadow. Tundi was a terror to the populace, and when he met his death the people ran in triumph over his gigantic chest with a herd of horses. Many believe the thundering horses' hooves on Ghora Jatra keeps Tundi's spirit underground, for he still threatens to emerge and demolish the city. They say the faster the horses run, the quicker Tundi's ghost will be dispelled. Rumours persist that a young boy mysteriously disappears each year during the Festival of Horses, indicating that the demon of the Tundikhel is very much with us today.

Many believe that if the horses run very swiftly on this day, this is an omen, foretelling that the people of Nepal will be successful in overcoming their enemies, and that disease and misery will be dispelled.

Horse Racing Day, an event at one time considered exclusively for people of Kathmandu, now brings together Nepalese from all over the valley and beyond. Ghora Jatra is considered the auspicious time for eating an uncommonly large amount of garlic and meat, 'unclean' foods responsible for the term 'Garlic Festival', as it is commonly known. And some still consider it the one day when citizens in the streets may become gloriously inebriated.

The story is repeated that the first Rana prime minister, Jung Bahadur, who titled himself Maharaja and wielded authority accordingly, rode through the streets one Ghora Jatra day on a fine mare and was accosted by a tipsy Newar man who caught the reins and demanded to know the purchase price of the mighty ruler's horse. Now Jung Bahadur, seeing the man's condition, parleyed him with instructions to appear at his palace next day to discuss the matter. In the cold and sober light of morning, when he was brought before the Prime Minister, the candid Newar reminded him that his bargaining spirit and false courage had disappeared with the passing of yesterday's Ghora Jatra festival and went laughing on his way.

On Ghora Jatra in Bal Kumari area in Patan, following the supposedly original custom by which only one horse was raced, great sport is made of feeding a horse intoxicating spirits and when it is drunk putting an equally inebriated rider on its back, dressed in the ancient, traditional, moghul-like costume of the Newars – full white skirt and red turban. People shout to frighten and enrage the animal until it runs wildly to and fro with the bouncing, drunken rider clinging to his perch, much to the delight of his celebrating townsmen. Nobody is entirely certain of the origin of this hair-raising race, but it is thought to have been inaugurated long ago by a Patan king in competition with the grander show at the Tundikhel which, in those days, no one from Patan could attend.

Throughout this day, Pahachare, the meeting of guests, goddesses and friends, is celebrated. Animals are sacrificed at the grandmother goddess temples, especially those of the seven goddesses who were sisters. The most prominent is Bhadra Kali, the term *bhadra* meaning good or well-bred, while Kali is again the goddess who controls black magic. It seems that after a certain king of the solar race established the city of Kantipur – ancient Kathmandu – the Goddess of Wealth appeared to him in a dream, advising that he instal an image of Bhadra Kali on a hillock which borders the eastern edge of the Tundikhel. She became extremely powerful with rulers and peasants alike and in time a Malla king instituted this festival in her honour, by which she and her sister goddesses are fêted for three days during Pahachare.

Newari people worship this Bhadra Kali image under the name of Lumarhi. In ancient times, when her temple site was a cultivated field, a farmer once heard the sound of weeping. When he found a child huddled near by and asked the cause of her grief, her only reply was continued crying. He attempted to pacify the child by placing at her feet a loaf of bread from his lunch, but the girl vanished from his sight. Stooping to retrieve the loaf, the incredulous farmer found it had turned to gold, a miracle which revealed that this was no ordinary child, but a goddess in disguise. From then on she was worshipped as Lumarhi Devi, the Goddess of the Golden Loaf.

Now at midnight on Horse Racing Day a weird ceremony takes place in the Tundikhel. The images of Bhadra Kali and her sister goddess are carried from their respective temples in *khats*, ornate mobile miniature temples, which are hoisted on long poles and carried on the shoulders of a group of men. They are placed in the middle of this dark expanse to await the arrival of the third youngest sister, Goddess Kankeswari, who emerges at last from the narrow streets. She is accompanied by people from her neighbourhood carrying flaming torches to light the way through this darkest night of the month. Just as the people are meeting during Pahachare, so Kankeswari's *khat* is made to circumambulate the *khats* of her waiting sisters in an ancient display of respect, before she 'bows' to them. Then the attendants of each goddess exchange flaming torches on behalf of the sisters, symbolic of the goodwill which exists between them.

Many people fear to attend this eerie midnight meeting of the disease-controlling sister goddesses, for there is always a chance that one may disappear during this time of the Evil Planet. And many remember former days when this was a tumultuous celebration at which the heavy *khats* of the goddesses were made to collide, often resulting in injuries to either the khat-bearers or the celebrating onlookers, a spectacle the King himself often attended.

On Horse Racing Day, usually in the afternoon, around the city where the Hiding Shiva idols are located – the *vihara* or Buddhist monastery shrine in Bharmau Tole in Kathmandu being the most prominent – large groups of children are given food to represent the remnants of Luku Mahadev's rice meal, offered him by devotees. For the *pisach* devil in Luku Mahadev, as well as in the grandmother goddesses, is considered especially helpful in curing the disease of children.

On the day following Ghora Jatra, usually the first day of the bright lunar fortnight, hundreds of people gather at Asantole, where several narrow bazaar streets converge in the most crowded section of Kathmandu. They come to witness and celebrate a most auspicious 'meeting' of the sister goddesses.

It seems that in ancient times there were eight sister goddesses – Bhadra Kali, Kankeswari, Tankeswari, Mhaipi Ajima, Maitadevi, Bachala Maju, Swa or Swet Kali and Indriani, who is also called Luti Ajima. Unlike her sisters, Luti Ajima was a poor widow who struggled to maintain ten hungry children. Once during Pahachare all were invited for a feast at the home of a relative. Seven sisters attended, wearing their richest clothes and most valuable ornaments, and all were treated with great respect. But Indriani and her children, wearing threadbare clothing, were overlooked.

When at last her brood was crying from hunger, the impatient host threw pieces of stale, dry bread at them, one of which struck a child on the forehead with such force that blood flowed from the wound, blood which miraculously turned to gold. Indriani gathered up her children and the gold and left the premises, highly insulted.

After a few days the same host sent invitations to the sisters. This time Indriani and her family arrived as gorgeously arrayed as the others and found themselves grandly treated. When they were given dishes of the finest foods, however, Indriani and her children did not eat. Instead they removed their jewels and ornaments and held them over their plates, which, as Indriani, explained, signified that the host had invited ornaments to dinner, not people.

It was because of this incident that a separate festival is held for Indriani four months earlier, on Bala Chaturdasi, and to this day she does not attend the Pasachare processions of her sisters. Some say that this mistreatment of Indriani brought repercussions, however, for a great fracas arose between the sister goddesses, each blaming the other for this disgraceful family rift. They at last agreed to meet at Asantole to discuss the matter once and for all.

This meeting is re-enacted each year, usually in the afternoon, when Goddess Bhadra Kali and one of her sisters, sometimes called Wotu Kha, are carried in *khats* from their temples with heavy ceremonial umbrellas twirling over their heads. They approach Asantole along different streets, zig-zagging and bouncing through the crowds, borne by men from their own temple neighbourhood who, celebrating in traditional fashion, are in a daring, festive mood. The unwieldy *khats* are tipped precariously this way and that and occasionally one crashes to the ground as the men stagger under its weight. Then it is again hoisted on to the bearers' shoulders, but only after great turmoil, raucous cat-calls, an occasional display of temper and many shouted suggestions.

Each goddess is accompanied by groups of musicians who push their way into the solid mass of humanity, mostly men, to form tight circles around their singing, dancing clansmen. Women and children fill the windows to capacity, the balconies, temple steps and the thresholds of surrounding bazaar stalls. This is notoriously a gay, sometimes turbulent celebration, in which revelling, fun-loving clansmen from various city areas mill about through the mobs and watching policemen, looking for excitement.

At last the approaching *khat* of Goddess Kankeswari is sighted in the narrow lane leading up from her temple near the Vishnumati River. Everyone strains to see over the heads as the Kankeswari delegation pushes through to make this goddess circle the *khats* of her sisters. Flaming torches are exchanged between the goddesses, a ceremony bringing whistles, cheers and hand-clapping. Now the Kankeswari's *khat* is rapidly whisked away, swaying precariously to right and left as she disappears through the mob, returning to her temple. It is said this youngest sister has heard the quarrel discussed, wants no part in the affair, denies all blame, and refuses to remain longer in their company.

35 BALAJU JATRA OR LHUTI PUNHI
Holy Bathing at Balaju at Full Moon

The twelve full moon days throughout the year, called Purnima or
Punhi, are all holy days, but some are holier than others. Such is
the full moon day of Chaitra in April, which falls either just before
or shortly after the New Year Day of the Nepali calendar. It is
considered one of the most auspicious of all days for holy bathing,
while many Buddhists believe this full moon is sacred to Lord
Buddha as well as to the souls of their dead.

Hundreds of brightly dressed hill people make the pilgrimage
into the valley the preceding evening to keep an all-night vigil at
the famous Buddhist shrine atop Swayambhunath hill. Others climb
by the light of the full moon to the side of Nagarjun mountain
where a series of small caves are thought to be holy, having
housed religious ascetics, pilgrims and possibly one of the first
Buddhist settlements in ancient days. As a special penance to gain
religious merit, some pilgrims attempt to thread their bodies
through the narrow mouth of Lahan cave, a feat deemed possible
only for those who are free from sin, for the sinful invariably fail in
the attempt or become wedged in the small opening.

Others ascend to the summit, to the ancient Buddhist shrine
called Jamacho, where it is thought the first human Buddha,
Bipaswi, settled in remotest antiquity, when the valley was still a
lake. It was this Buddha who on the Chaitra full moon sowed the
lotus seed which, when it bloomed on the water's surface, sent
forth the holy flame called Swayambhu, the Self-Existent One.
Now it is to Jamacho that Buddhists bring the frontal skull bone of
their deceased and cremated family members, usually on the first
anniversary of death, to be thrown high into the air. Then a small
Buddhist *chaitya* shrine is built over the spot where the bone lands

and is buried. Thus the long climb to Jamacho is made at Chaitra full moon to pray and leave gifts for the Buddhas and deities enshrined there, and to pay homage to the souls of the dead in the hope that such good deeds will bring them eternal peace.

By far the greatest crowds, however, go to Balaju Park at the foot of Nagarjun Hill, two miles north-west of Kathmandu, to take holy baths at Baisedhara, the long cemented pool into which water flows from twenty-two carved stone dragons' mouths. Many arrive on the eve of the full moon to spend the entire night singing, dancing and lighting lamps for the gods. Long before daylight most of the hill people have finished their baths and have moved on to carry out worship ceremonies, *pujas*, at a near-by square pool in the centre of which a black stone image of Sleeping Vishnu reclines, or Narayan as he is more commonly called. This image is a replica of the large Buddha Nil Katha which lies in a pool four miles north of Kathmandu – the image upon which the rulers of Nepal must never look for fear death may result, or calamity befall the nation. It is thought that the Reclining Vishnu of Balaju was made so that the kings of Nepal might worship Narayan without danger. At the Chaitra full moon throngs of holy bathers worship at Narayan's feet, all but burying his recumbent image with offerings of rice, flowers, coins and red powder.

With the dawn of full moon day the inhabitants of the valley arrive in droves to bathe in the holy waters flowing from the twenty-two dragons after which Baisedhara pond was named, for it is thought that on this day, only once each year, these waters are miraculously connected to the sacred waters of the Trisuli River which flows to the west of the valley.

36 SAPANA TIRTHA MELA
Dreams and Renewed Life for the New Year

There was once an influential man ruling the little village of Tokha, high in the hilly north-western extremity of Kathmandu Valley, who was considered a King by the local inhabitants. One day, when he idly asked his three daughters whom they would choose to marry, the two eldest unhesitatingly asked for wealthy neighbouring princes. Since the youngest daughter remained silent, the King jestingly told her she would no doubt remain poor, possibly marrying the miserable leper who kept to his lonely hut near a stream outside the village. To his amazement the young princess immediately agreed, insisting that since this was the first man named by her father, she would abide by his decision. Despite the King's repeated protestations, the girl never wavered from her vow.

Day after day she visited the unsightly leper, taking food and bathing his disease-ridden body. At last, with sinking heart, the King allowed the marriage, but as time went by and he saw the miserable life of his beautiful daughter, he pleaded with her to return to the palace. This the Princess steadfastly refused so long as her untouchable husband was not invited. As a result the King angrily disowned his daughter and she was ultimately reduced to begging for alms to maintain herself and the leper.

One day, when life seemed at its lowest ebb, the girl had a wonderful dream, which foretold that if she bathed her husband in the stream near their hut on the first day of the year, his leprosy would disappear. She waited anxiously through the days and on the eve of New Year made ready the offerings needed for the sacrament of holy bathing. Long before daylight she carried her husband in her arms to the rivulet, bathing both him and herself.

When they emerged she found her dream come true, for she was lovelier than ever, and he was now a handsome youth, all the disfiguring sores and scars miraculously washed away.

As others tell the story, the ugly but pious leper lived with his wife on the stream outside Tokha village and himself dreamed that a holy bath in its waters would cure his disease and bring him a new life. One New Year Day, as he watched cowherd boys at play, chasing and catching grasshoppers among their cattle, the leper and children alike were dismayed when the wings of a grasshopper were accidently broken and the maimed insect fell into the water. As they watched, to their amazement the grasshopper developed new and shining wings and flew joyfully away. Soon the excited youngsters were breaking the wings and legs of many grasshoppers, which they dropped into the stream to watch them miraculously made whole again. Then, remembering his dream, the leper bathed himself in the stream and stood transformed, his skin spotless and healthy once more.

No matter how the story is told, the field-pond near this stream has since been called Sapana Tirtha, 'the holy place of dreams', whose waters cure ailments of the skin and bring hope for a new and better life to pious bathers. On the eve of the last day of the Nepalese calendar year people pilgrimage in great number, many walking through the night, to bring gifts and offerings to the gods, and to bathe in the healing waters. Many arrive long before dawn of New Year Day to light lamps, sing, dance and make merry, taking holy baths while the stars are still shining, while others arrive through the morning to bathe and pray for renewal of life and health.

Hundreds climb through the night to the northern slope of near-by Shivapuri mountain, where the source of the holy Bagmati River flows from the open mouth of a carved bronze tiger mask. There they take *prasad* from the gods with a sprinkling of the sacred water, and bathe in an adjacent pond. By the light of lamps and flaming torches they gather leaves and flowers from this holy site, tying them in a bouquet at the tip of a long stick. These are *prasad lati*, a pole or stick representing a gift or blessing from the gods, to be carried back over the summit, where they rest and leave offerings at the temple of Shivapuri Bhagwan. Then, playing musical instruments and singing religious songs, they climb the next hill to a cave called Vishnu Nab, Lord Vishnu's Navel, where the worshippers gather to pray and leave offerings at the source of the sacred Vishnumati River. Next they descend to Sapana Tirtha, the pond of dreams, which they circumambulate, pushing their way amongst the gathering crowds of bathers.

Many, unable to accompany the procession further, hand over their flower-festooned sticks to others, who take off singing and laughing across the countryside to Bhadgaon town ten miles away. They arrive in time to place the sacred *prasad* sticks as an offering at the foot of the towering pole of snake banners, before it is pulled crashing to the ground in a riotous Bisket celebration.

Thus the holy bathing and gifts for the gods at Sapana Tirtha bring to a close the festivals of the old year and usher in the new, when, who knows, one's dreams may well come true.

BIBLIOGRAPHY

Bahadur, Pudma J., *Life of Maharaja Sir Jung Bahadur of Nepal*; Pioneer Press, Allahabad.

Bajarajcharya, M. S., *Our Festivals*; Published in Nepali script, Kathmandu.

Bista, Dor B., *People of Nepal*; His Majesty's Government of Nepal.

Coomaraswamy and Nivedita, *Myths of the Hindus and Buddhists*; Dover.

Dubois and Beauchamp, *Hindu Manners, Customs and Ceremonies*; Oxford U. P., London

Durant, Will, *Our Oriental Heritage*; Angus & Robertson, London.

Elliott, J. H., *Guide to Nepal*; Newman, Calcutta.

Hagen, Toni, *Nepal*; Oxford U. P.

Jesuit Scholars, *Religious Hinduism*; St Paul Publications, Allahabad and Bombay.

Karan & Jenkins, *The Himalayan Kingdoms: Bhutan, Sikkim, Nepal*; Van Nostrand, New York.

Mukerji, R. B., *Hindu Fasts and Feasts*; Macmillan.

Nepali, Gopal S., *The Newars*; United Asia Publications, Bombay.

Rajagopalachari, C., *Mahabharata*; B. V. Bhavan, Bombay.

Rajagopalachari, C., *Ramayana*; B. V. Bhavan, Bombay.

Regmi, D. R., *Ancient Nepal*; Mukhopadhyay, Calcutta.

Rubel, Mary, *The Gods of Nepal*; Viswabandhu Press, Kathmandu.

Sekelj, Tibor, *Window of Nepal*; Robert Hale, London.

Shrestha, C. B., Articles published in *Rising Nepal*; Kathmandu.

Shrestha, C. B., *Buddhist Geography of Ancient Nepal*; Fourth World Buddhist Conference, Kathmandu.

Shrestha, Kesar Lal, Articles published in *Rising Nepal*; Kathmandu.

Shrestha, Kesar Lal, *Lore and Legend of Nepal*; Jagat Lall, Kathmandu.

Simpson, Colin, *Kathmandu*; Angus & Robertson, London.

Tucci, Giuseppe, *Tibet*; Oxford U. P.

Wright, Daniel, *History of Nepal* (a translation); Ranjan Gupta, Calcutta.

INDEX

For Product Safety Concerns and Information please contact our EU
representative GPSR@taylorandfrancis.com
Taylor & Francis Verlag GmbH, Kaufingerstraße 24, 80331 München, Germany

www.ingramcontent.com/pod-product-compliance
Lightning Source LLC
Chambersburg PA
CBHW071353290326
41932CB00045B/1678